The Builder's Joke Book

First published in Great Britain in 1993 by Fivecrown Ltd, PO Box 209, Beckenham, Kent, BR3 1WS.

Printed in Great Britain by HarperCollins Manufacturing, Glasgow.
A catalogue record for this book is available from the British Library.
Cartoons by Urne.

ACKNOWLEDGEMENTS

I would like to thank everyone who made a contribution, but those deserving a special mention are as follows:-
Terry R., John, Simon B. (provider of the world's funniest joke!), Yoda, Simon's workmates, the boys from the football team, especially Dave W. and Tim D., the boys from the two tennis clubs, especially Mike T., Allan, Nigel, Mick(you sicko!), Bobby M., Martin G., Tony M. the brickie, Sandra H., Terry T., Torsky, and many, many others...

Contents

"To be honest Brian, me and the Missus haven't been hitting it off recently."

Chapter 1

Jokes you can tell Auntie Agnes

What's invisible and smells of dogfood?
A pensioner's fart.

What do you get if you cross a Pit Bull Terrier with Lassie?
A dog that'll rip both your arms off and then run off to go and get help!

What do you call an Aardvark who keeps getting beaten up?
A Vark.

GRANDAD'S WARTIME HEROICS

The teacher asks her class of eight year olds if there is anyone in the class who can tell a story with a moral in it and little Peter's hand goes up and the teacher nods to him.
"Well Miss, my dad was in the kitchen and he put some salt in the stew Miss, but my mum had already put some salt in the stew Miss and the stew had too much salt Miss," said Peter.
"And what is the moral of the story Peter?" asked the teacher.
"Too many cooks spoil the broth," replied Peter.
"Very good Peter. Anyone else?" asked the teacher.
Little Johnny's hand went up and the teacher nodded.
"Well Miss, it's about my grandad in world war two Miss. My grandad was in this trench right, and he drank half a bottle of whisky and he climbed out of the trench and dodged a whole lot of gunfire before jumping into a German trench, and he shot three Germans dead and ran back to his trench laughing about it. Then Miss, he drank another half bottle of whisky

and climbed out of his trench a second time and dodged a whole lot of gunfire before jumping into a German trench and shooting another four Germans dead. He managed to make it back to his own trench Miss, and he was having a good laugh about it Miss. Then he drank another half bottle of whisky and ran over to another German trench and jumped into it but his gun jammed Miss and this German shot him twice before he could get near enough to strangle the German with his bare hands, but he did manage to strangle him and then stagger back to his trench Miss. Although he had blood pouring from two bad wounds Miss he was laughing his head off Miss. That's all Miss," said Johnny.
"Err..what's the moral to the story Johnny?" said the teacher.
"You don't f*** about with my grandad after he's had a few drinks," said Johnny.

What's the definition of an Italian virgin?
A girl who can run faster than all of her brothers.

What do you call a short-sighted dinosaur?
Doyouthinkhesawus.

Why do the Irish call their Pound the Punt?
Because it rhymes with bank manager.

An Irishman goes into a pet shop and asks to buy a pet wasp.
"I'm sorry sir, we don't sell wasps," said the shop assistant.
"Well you've got one in the shop window," replied Paddy.

Did you hear about the Old English Sheepdog found hanging by the neck from a tree in America's deep south?
The Dulux Clan did it.

THE PANDA AND THE TART

A Panda begs his keeper one night to leave his cage open so that he can get out and have sex. The keeper agrees and that night the Panda slips out and heads off towards Soho. He approaches a tart and she agrees to have sex with him so they go back to her flat.

The first thing the Panda does is open the fridge and eat everything in it. The prostitute thinks to herself, "I'll charge him extra for that." Anyway, they get down to it and after a few hours the Panda gets up, adjusts his fur and heads for the door.
The tart says, "Hang on, haven't you forgotten something?"
The Panda looks perplexed. The prostitute says, "I'm a prostitute."
The Panda says, "Yeah, so what. I'm a Panda."
The prostitute says, "Here's a dictionary, look it up."
The Panda sighs and looks up prostitute. He reads, "Prostitute: Demands money for sexual favours."
The Panda shrugs his shoulders and says, as he tosses the dictionary back to the tart, "Now you look up Panda."
So she does and it reads, "Panda: Eats shoots and leaves."
And the Panda left.

MAKE ME IRISH

This guy is madly in love with this Irish girl and they plan to marry and go and live in Ireland with her parents. He decides that the best way to get accepted is to have an operation to make him just like an Irishman so he goes to see a top surgeon and says, "Can you transform me into an Irishman?"
"Well, it is possible," says the surgeon, "but it'll cost because we'll have to re-line the walls of your stomach to withstand ten pints of Guinness every night and we'll have to remove half of your brain."
The man decides to have the operation...
The operation is completed and the man still hasn't regained consciousness after three days. The worried surgeon is leaning over the man and he says, "Can you hear me? Can you hear me Mr Dawes? The operation didn't go entirely to plan..The anaesthetist gave you double the recommended level of anaesthetic by mistake..... and one of the nurses accidentally stood on your oxygen supply pipe for over four minutes before she realised..and..and..I..I got a bit carried away myself and took away three-quarters of your brain instead of just half."
The body suddenly sprang up and said, "No worries sport!"

What do you say to a mate who's having his hand sewn back on in a Saudi hospital?
I see you've won your appeal then!

What do you call the costume of a one legged ballerina?
A one-one.

A sweet little old nun is teaching theology at a convent school when little Sarah asks, "Who came first, Adam or Eve?"
The nun replied, "Adam ... but then men always do come first!"

Why don't blind people ski jump?
Because it scares the sh** out of the guide dogs.

Why do seagulls have wings?
So they can beat new-age travellers to the rubbish tips.

Why is Lieutenant Uhura black?
Because William Shatner.

DRINK THAT SPITOON!

Two old Cowboys, Jake and Chuck, are getting sloshed in the saloon when Jake says to Chuck, "I bet you wouldn't drink the contents of the spitoon for a hundred dollars?"
"You're right there," said Chuck.
"How about if I bet you two hundred dollars that you won't drink the contents of the spitoon?" persisted Jake.
"No way partner, the bowl is almost full," replied Chuck.
"What about four hundred dollars?" asked Jake.
"No way," said Chuck.
"Alright, my final offer. How about a bet of one thousand dollars?" said Jake.
Chuck is unable to resist the thought of winning such a large amount of money and he accepts and he lifts the spitoon up to his lips and starts to drink...and drink....and drink.
Watching all this is making Jake feel extremely queasy and he quickly cries out, "Stop..stop..you win the bet," but the bowl remains at Chucks lips for some while further as Chuck forces himself to make a few further swallows and finish the contents completely.
"Here's your money," said Jake, "How come you kept drinking even after I told you that you could stop and that you'd won the bet?"
"It was all in one piece," gasped Chuck.

What's the best way to start a small business in Britain these days?
Buy a big business and wait.

When was Mad Cow Disease finally eradicated in the UK?
In 1990, when John Major got her job.

A LETTER TO GOD

A little old lady writes a letter to God, care of the local post office, asking for divine help in paying her £98 electricity bill.
A post office sorter opens the letter and shows it to his work-mates and they all feel a bit sorry for her and they have a whip round and manage to come up with £90 for her and they send it to her.
A few days later the same sorter sees another letter addressed to God and he again opens it, and in it the same old girl has written, "Dear God, can you please send me another eight pounds so that I can pay my electricity bill. I got £90 from you recently but those theiving gits at the post office must have nicked the rest."

What do you call a terrible fear of crap jewellery?
Aratnerphobia.

How can you tell the head nurse?
She's the one with the dirty knees.

VICAR MEETS 3 GIRLS

A vicar is walking down the road and he meets a little girl and he asks her, "And what's your name little girl?"
"Daisy," replied the girl shyly.
"And why did your mummy call you Daisy?" asked the vicar.
"Because when I was being born a daisy dropped onto my mummy's tummy," replied the little girl.
The vicar walks on and sees another girl and he asks her, "And what's your name little girl?"
"Rose," replied the girl shyly.
"And why did your mummy call you Rose?" asked the vicar.

"Because when I was being born a rose petal dropped onto my mummy's tummy," replied the little girl.
The vicar walks on and sees another girl who is not as pretty as the other two girls, in fact she's damn ugly, and he asks her, "What's your name little girl?"
"Breeze block," came the reply.

Why is life like a dogshit sandwich?
The more bread you've got the better it is.

What's the difference between a bucket of sand and a bucket of pigs afterbirth?
You can't gargle with a bucket of sand.

THE ANNOYING BOOZER

A man goes into a pub and asks the barman if they serve lager. The barman replies, "Of course," so the man asks for two pints and drinks both of them.
He then asks the barman if they serve cider and the barman replies, "Of course we serve cider, it's a pub isn't it?"
The man orders two pints of cider and drinks them both. He then asks the barman if they serve bitter and the barman says, "Of course we serve bitter, it's a pub isn't it? What a stupid question."
The man orders two pints of bitter and drinks them both. He then asks the barman if they serve light ale and the barman angrily replies, "Of course we serve light ale, it's a pub isn't it? Listen mate you're starting to get right up my nose by persistently asking if we do this and that when the answers obvious. Understand?"
The man orders two pints of light ale and drinks them both and then says to the barman, "Do you do any shorts?"
The barman replies angrily, "Of course we do shorts. We do all the shorts under the sun, you twat!"
"Good," said the man, "I'll have a pair of light cotton yellow ones as I've just peed myself."

Isn't it a pity that all the people who really know how to run the country are either driving taxis or cutting hair.

Did you hear about the Irish Muslim?
He went out and shot Willie Rushton.

Muffin the Mule is a criminal offence.
So is Dobbin the Carthorse.

What is one of the advantages of havir CENSORED ₃ disease?
You can hide your own Easter eg

VG

QUEEN VISITS AMPUTEES

The Queen is visiting a hospital and she goes up to a man who only has one leg. He's lying in the first bed in the new ward and she asks him, "How are you?"
The man is obviously in a lot of pain but he replies bravely, "Not so bad your Highness, there's always someone worse off than yourself."
"And you are being well looked after?" asked the Queen.
"I'm being very well looked after, your Highness," replied the man.
The Queen then moves on to the next bed where a man with no legs and only one arm is lying and she asks, "How are you?"
"Oh, bearing up, I'm being well looked after," came the reply.
The Queen then moves on to the next bed where there is a man with no arms or legs and she asks, "How are you?"
"Oh, not too bad, your Highness. I'm learning to paint with my teeth at the moment and really enjoy it," said the man bravely.
"I do so admire your courage," said the Queen.

"There's always someone else worse off than yourself," said the man as he nodded towards the next bed. The Queen then goes over to the next bed and sees that all there is is just a man's head lying on a pillow being kept alive by a mass of tubes attached to the neck.
"How are you?" asked the Queen.
"P*ss off will you," snapped the head.
Visibly upset the Queen goes over to the ward sister and says, "He told me to p*ss off."
"Oh, don't worry about him," replied the nurse, "He's having all his teeth out tomorrow!"

Did you hear about the Irish fox that caught it's paw in a trap? It gnawed off three of it's feet before it freed itself.

What's seven inches long and begins with a "P"?
A sh*t.

HUSBAND EATS DOG FOOD!

A wife always makes her husband some ham sandwiches to eat at work. One day she runs out of ham so she puts Kattomeat in the sandwiches instead. When the husband returns home that night he comments on how nice the sandwiches were so the woman decides to carry on giving him Kattomeat and save some money at the same time. The husband has Kattomeat in

his sandwiches for the next six months before the wife gets a phone call that her husband has been taken to hospital and is, sadly, dead. The woman rushes to hospital and speaks to the doctor in charge, and she says, "Doctor, I have a confession to make. For the last six months I have been putting Kattomeat in my husbands sandwiches. Could this have had something to do with his death?"
The doctor replied, "Err..I shouldn't th–."
"How did he die?" interrupted the woman.
"According to the fireman who was trying to get him down from the tree, he broke his neck trying to lick his backside," replied the doctor.

What's the difference between a sperm and a lawyer?
A sperm has a one in thirty million chance of becoming a human being.

Why are scientists now using Estate Agents rather than rats for laboratory experiments?
There are more of them, they breed faster, lab technicians don't get so attached to them and they'll do things even a rat wouldn't do.

Dolphins really are intelligent. After only two weeks in captivity they can teach Americans to stand on the edge of their pools and throw them fish.

Why was the wheelbarrow invented?
To teach the Irish to walk upright.

What do you call a blind Jehovah's Witness?
A Jehovah.

THE 3 SURVIVORS

A Hindu, a Jew and an Estate Agent are the only survivors in a plane crash in a remote part of Northern Canada and they walk for days without food or rest before they finally reach a small farm. They knock on the door and a farmer answers and they explain their circumstances to him and he says, "Of course I can put you up for the night but I've only got two spare beds so one of you will have to sleep in the barn."

After a bite to eat the three men retire for the night and the Jew, who got the short straw, heads for the barn.

A short while later there is a knock at the door and the farmer opens it to see the Jew standing there and the Jew says, "I'm sorry to disturb you but there is a pig in the barn and it is against my religion to share a rest place with a pig. To us they are sacred animals, that's why we don't eat pork. Could one of the others sleep in the barn?"

The Hindu offers to sleep in the barn and off he goes. However, a short while later there's a knock at the door and the farmer opens it to see the Hindu standing there. The Hindu says, "I'm very sorry to mess you around but there's a cow in the barn and it's against my religion to share a restplace with such a sacred animal."

The Estate Agent hears this, and thoroughly fed up with all the too-ing and fro-ing he says, "Right, I'll go and sleep in the barn," and off he goes.

A short while later there's a knock at the door and the farmer flings the door open.....and there stand the pig and the cow.

Did you hear about the Red Indian who drank 50 cups of tea? He was found drowned in his teepee.

When does Saddam Hussein have tea?
When Tariq Aziz.

Who wears yellow checked trousers, yellow checked scarf, yellow checked shirt and dark glasses?
Rupert the Undercover Agent.

THE HAPPY TELEGRAM

An old lady is feeling a bit sad. She's got really bad arthritis, no one bothers with her at all and both her children emigrated to Australia years ago and can't afford to visit her.
The next day is her birthday so she decides to send herself a telegram to cheer herself up.
The next day the postman arrives and she opens the door before he can put anything through the letterbox and he says, "Telegram Maam."

"I know, I've been expecting one," says the old lady excitedly, "Young man, would you mind singing the telegram to me, it's my birthday, I'm 87 you know."
"I ain't got time to do that," grunted the Postie.
"Go one, I'll give you a fiver," pleaded the old girl as she put a fiver in his hand. The postman consented.
"And before you read it would you give me a big birthday kiss?" asked the old girl.
"I ain't got time for that," grunted the postman but he relents

when the old girl puts another fiver into his hand.
"And before you sing the telegram can you do a little tap dance," giggled the old girl as she put another fiver in the postman's hand.
The postman kisses her, then does a little tap dance as the next door neighbours start to applaud and sings, "Kate and the kids are dead!"

A white horse goes into a pub and orders a Teachers whisky and downs it. He then orders a Bells whisky and downs it. He then orders a Glenfiddich whisky and downs it.The barman comes over and says, "Did you know there's a whisky named after you? Why don't you try some of that?"
"What Norman Skegglesworth!" replied the amazed horse.

What do you call a tramp with no legs?
A low down bum.

A day in the life of a Mayfly.
BORN ... EAT ... SH*G .. DIE.

A Martian walks into a pub and says to the barman, "I want to buy everyone in the pub a drink and then you can take me to your leader..."
So the barman serves out ninety three drinks and then says, "That'll be one hundred and eighty one pounds sixty two pence please."
The Martian replied, "What's that in Zogs?"

What was the most violent book Stevie Wonder ever read?
A cheese grater.

What noise does a one-legged horse make?
Clip.

What's the difference between a rabbit doing press-ups and a rabbit with a daffodil in his ear?
One's a fit bunny and the other's a bit funny.

THE STUPID DONKEY

A man goes to town with his donkey but halfway there the donkey collapses with exhaustion so the man says, "I'll give you two carrots if you get up," and the donkey gets up, eats the carrots and carries on walking.
A while later the donkey collapses again and the man says, "I'll give you four carrots if you get up," and the donkey gets up, eats the carrots and carries on.
A while later the donkey collapses again, and this time he's really knackered. The man is desperate to get to town and he says, "Look, I'll give you anything you want if you carry on."
"Look," replied the donkey, "What I really need is a good sh*g. Can you fix it for me?"

"Of course I can, no problem. As soon as we get to town, I'll arrange something there," answered the man whereupon the donkey jumped up and ran all the way to town.
When he arrives in town the man looks for a female donkey but he can't find one anywhere. Eventually, in desperation, he goes to the local circus and starts talking to one of the clowns. The clown listens to what the man has to say and then says, "Tell me, is your donkey a bit stupid?"
"Just about the stupidest mule I ever encountered," replied the man.
"Good," said the clown, "In that case you can put him in the stable with that old zebra over there for a fiver."
"Okay, it's a deal," replied the man and he goes and gets the donkey. He leads the donkey up to the stable door and says to it, "I'll pick you up in the morning then, alright?" and the donkey replies impatiently, "Yeah, yeah, yeah."
In the morning the man returns and walks into the stable to see the donkey walking round and round the zebra in a circle. The man says to the donkey, "Everything alright?"
"You'll have to come back later," snapped the donkey, "I'm still trying to work out how to get her pyjamas off!"

A man phones a mental home and asks, "Can I speak to the man in room 12 please?"
A voice replies, "There isn't anyone in room 12 sir."
"YIPPEE! I'VE ESCAPED!" exclaims the man.

Did you hear about the guy who couldn't keep up with the repayments to his exorcist?
He was repossessed.

What's black and white and hot?
A nun with pierced nipples and tatooed thighs.

THE ART OF ONE-UPMANSHIP

Richard is driving along the road when he stops at the lights and sees his neighbour Eric sitting in his car next to him. He sees Eric is shaving in the car with a plug-in razor, so he goes and has a car phone fitted in his own car.

The next day when Richard pulls up at the same set of lights who should he see but Eric, and Eric is using a fax machine in his car!

"Right, I'll show him," thinks Richard, and off he goes to have a satellite dish and TV installed into his car.

The next day Richard follows Eric in his car and when they both pull up at the same set of lights Richard looks over to Eric's car ready to speak, but Eric's car windows are all steamed up so he knocks on the window and Eric winds down the window.

Richard says, "Hi, Eric, I've got a satellite dish and TV in my car."

Eric exclaims angrily, "You've got me out of the shower just to tell me that!"

Why was the dyslexic musician who played for the London Philharmonic Orchestra arrested?

He kept telling people he was with the PLO!

What's brown and smells of pine?

A turd in a radox bath.

CANINE SEEKS REVENGE

Hopalong Cassidy loses a round of Poker and kicks the puppy lying at his feet in a fit of temper. He then loses the next round as well, and he again gives the puppy a good kicking. The next round of Poker becomes a real nailbiter and Hopalong bets all his money on his hand. Hopalong loses and as he storms out of the saloon he shoots the poor puppy in the foot. The puppy lets out a tremendous yelp and hops out of the saloon.

Two years later Hopalong is again playing Poker when the saloon doors are flung open and there stands a six foot tall dog walking upright on his hind legs! He is wearing leather boots with spurs, a cowboy hat and round his waist hang two ivory handled Smith and Wesson guns. As the piano player stops playing and the room becomes silent the dog scans the room and says, "I've come for the man that shot my paw!"

Motto of the Inland Revenue: "If we can bring a smile to someone, somewhere, at sometime then somebody, somewhere has made a mistake.

DOGFIGHT SETTLES ARGUMENT

A Jew and an Arab are having a long and heated argument in the street over who is in the right on a particular subject. Finally the Jew says to the Arab, "Why don't we let our two dogs fight each other and the one who wins is the one in the right." The Arab looks at his dog, a great big Doberman foaming at the mouth and then looks at the Jew's dog which has short little legs, is stumpy and seems very docile. The Arab, being no fool, accepts that the dogs should fight saying, "Allah will make my dog win and prove that I was right."

The two dogs are unleashed and tear into each other. The Jew's little dog rips the Doberman to shreds within seconds. As the Arab looks down at his dead dog he says, "Who would have thought that, a Doberman whipped by a little ...., what breed of dog is that?"

"It was a baby crocodile before it had a nose job," came the reply.

Six policemen stagger out of a pub. Which one drives?
The one that's too drunk to sing!

What Nazi leader had a hamster concentration camp?
Joseph Gerbils.

What was Brian Keenan's specialist subject on Mastermind?
The Life and Times of John McCarthy 1988–91.

FAMOUS LAST WORDS

"Be careful with that! You'll have someones eye out in a minute."
King Harold, 1066.

"But we always invade Poland!"
Herman Goerring, Nuremburg trials, 1946.

"Where did all those f***ing Indians come from!"
General Custer, Little Big Horn.

"When all this is over Eva, let's go on a long holiday together and get away from it all. Perhaps a tour of Europe?"
Adolf Hitler, the Bunker in Berlin, 1945.

"Are you in a bit of a bad mood dad?"
Marvin Gaye.

"Watch this for a belly flop boys!"
Robert Maxwell.
Or..
"Yes, I know this is my fourth double whisky but don't worry, I'm not going to go overboard!"

Wife: "Don't I look younger without a bra?"
Husband: "Well, it certainly takes the wrinkles out of your face!"

What did the Buddhist yogi say to the hot dog vendor?
Make me one with everything.

What do you get if you cross Jeremy Beadle with the Venus De Milo?
An armless bit of fun.

What's the difference between a Rottweiler and a social worker?
It's easier to get your child back from a Rottweiler.

THE VERY CONFUSED SKIER

A dyslexic man is on the ski slopes and he goes up to a man and asks, "Can you please tell me, I'm a bit confused, should I zig-zag down the slopes or zag-zig?"
The second man replies, "Don't ask me, I'm a tobogganist."
The first man says, "In that case can I have 20 Benson and Hedges."

CAR PARTS FOR NELSON

A man in a delivery truck is driving along in Soweto and he winds down his window and asks, "Where am de Nelson Mandela?"
"It am de house over there," came the reply.
The driver pulls up outside the house and gets out of the truck and knocks on the door and Winnie answers.
"I got here dem 200 car batteries for de Nelson Mandela, yehman," said the driver.
"Nelson no want de 200 car batteries...wot he do wit dem dere 200 car batteries anyways," ranted Winnie.
"Look, it say here on de papers 200 car batteries for de Nelson Mandela so dis is wot I am to leave," said the driver and he leaves 200 car batteries on the front lawn.

The next day Winnie gets a knock on the door and as she opens the door she sees it's the same driver back again and he says, "150 brake linings for de Nelson Mandela, yehman."
"Nelson not here but he no want 150 brake linings....What he do wit 150 brake linings..take dem all away man," demanded Winnie.
"Look lady, it say here on de papers 150 brake linings for de Nelson Mandela so I must..I must," and the driver dumps 150 brake linings on the front lawn and drives off.
The next day Winnie answers the door and it's the same driver back again and he says, "Got dem dere 120 tyres lady for de Nelson Mandela, yerman."
Winnie screeches, "Look Nelson not here right now but he no want 120 tyres..he no want 150 of de brake thingys and he no want de flippin car batteries..you must take dem all away.."
"Look lady..I'm just de driver..you gotta have dem cos it say on this hear dem dere papers," said the driver.
Winnie grabs the papers from him, looks at them and screeches, "It no say Nelson Mandela..it say Nissan Main Dealer!"

1st leper: "How are you?"
2nd leper: "Oh, pus n' crumble."

What is green and takes half an hour to drink?
Your unemployment benefit cheque.

STATUES COME TO LIFE

The Archangel Gabriel was flying about one day when he noticed a statue of two young naked lovers with their bodies entwined and thought how nice it would be if he brought them to life for a while so that they could enjoy for real the obvious, albeit frozen, passion and lust they had for each other.
"You've got twenty minutes of life before I turn you back into stone so make the most of it," said Gabriel as the naked couple ran giggling, hand in hand, into the bushes.

Gabriel hears plenty of rustling in the bushes, plenty of squeals of delight, plenty of moans of satisfaction and the occasional whisper of, "One more time," and ,"Again..again," and, "Hold still a minute."
Their time being up the couple return to their mounting and Gabriel asks them, "I bet you enjoyed that?"
"You bet..after all these years to be able to hold down some pigeons and crap on them was great!" came the reply.

What does "Hezbollah" mean in English?
WOT YOU LOOKING AT!!!!!

Where's the best place to go to get stoned after just one drink?
Iran.

How can you tell an Italian bride?
She's the one with braided armpits.

How many Country and Western singers does it take to change a light bulb?
Five. One to change the light bulb and the other four to sing about how good the old one was.

63 YEAR OLD MAN GETS LUCKY

A man goes into the confession box and says to the Priest, "Father I have sinned."
"How have you sinned my son?" asked the Priest.
"Last night I made love to my Swedish Au Pair. She's a stunning eighteen year old blond haired beauty Father," said the man.
"That is disgraceful. You should be ashamed of yourself. And how old are you?" raged the Priest.
"I'm sixty three Father," replied the man.
"That is disgraceful!!" raged the Priest.

VG

"That's not all Father. The girl's twin sister was visiting on holiday from Sweden at the time and she saw us doing it, and she joined in Father. I made love to her in the bedroom, and in the bathroom, and on the dining room table. We even made love on the garden lawn Father," continued the man.
"That is the most disgraceful thing I have ever heard in all my years at St.Mary's, and you call yourself a good Catholic!!" raged the Priest.
"Oh, I'm not Catholic Father, I'm Jewish," said the man.
"So what in heavens name are you doing at a Catholic confession then?" exclaimed the Priest.
"I just had to tell someone Father," came the reply.

LATE NEWS FLASH ... Archduke Ferdinand found alive!
First World War a mistake!

Why is a tour of Beirut like a vindaloo curry?
With both you inevitably end up with the shi-ites.

WE ALL LOVE XMAS

Three kids, Sean, a Catholic, Charles, a Protestant, and Hymie, a Jew, return back to school after the Xmas holidays. Sean was asked how his Xmas was, and he replied, "It was great. I went to midnight mass and prayed for loads of presents and the next day I got loads in my stocking. I got a bike, computer games, a robot, an action man, some toy soldiers. It was great. Then I had loads to eat and drink and then we pulled loads of crackers. I love Xmas!"
Charles was then asked the same question and he replied, "Wow, Xmas was great. We had a great big tree, there were balloons and decorations everywhere. We sang carols and went to church. Then we came home and I opened my presents. I got a flying helicopter, a board game, a pogo stick, a football, and a racing bike. I love Xmas."
"What did you do for Xmas?" asked Charles to Hymie.
Hymie replied, "I'm Jewish, we don't celebrate Xmas at all."

"Well you must have done something at Xmas," said Charles. "Well," replied Hymie, "We normally go down to my father's toy factory on Xmas Day and look at all the empty shelves and then sing three verses of, 'What a friend we have in Jesus,' and then we all f*** off to the Bahamas for three weeks!"

Why did the Miami Dolphins hire two nuns and a tart for the new season?
Because they needed two tight ends and a wide receiver.

Why don't scousers make good doctors?
You try writing prescriptions with a spray can.

A DIFFICULT DECISION

A manager of a small hotel is looking for a new chambermaid and three girls turn up for the interview and the manager decides to ask the three of them the same question. He turns to the first one and asks her, "If you found a £50 note in one of the bedrooms what would you do?"
The first girl replies, "Finders Keepers."
The second girl is asked the same question and she replies, "I'd hand the money into reception sir, and if the money wasn't claimed after three months it would be mine sir."
The third girl, on having been asked the same question replied, "I'd hand the money into reception and if no one claimed the money after three months it would be mine. With the money I'd then buy everyone who worked in the hotel a free drink and then if there was anything left over I'd give it to one of the local charities."
MORAL...Which girl got the job?
The one with the big tits.

What CENSORED as yo ... n
drivi
How to go round ... the steering

Why should you bury traffic wardens thirty feet below ground level?
Because deep down they're nice people.

THE UNLUCKY PIRATE

VG

Two pirates, Cyril and Ron, who are old friends run into each other and after the initial greetings Ron says, "Cyril, what's happened to you matey?"
"I suppose you mean the peg leg," said Cyril.
"Of course I do," replied Ron.
"Well the other day I was up the rigging and I fell off and into the sea. Before they could haul me back on board a shark bit my left leg off and the rest is history," said Cyril.
"But what about your hand?" asked Ron.
"Oh, you mean the hook," said Cyril, "Well, I had an argument with this young swashbuckler over a woman and we had a duel. We swashed, and then we buckled, and I'm not as fast as I used to be, and he took my hand off, and here I am with a hook."
"But what about your eye?" asked Ron as he looked at Cyril's patch.

"I was up in the crow's nest and a pigeon pooped right in it, so I ended up with this patch" replied Cyril sadly.
Ron continued, "Cyril, I can understand you losing your leg to a shark, and your hand in a duel, but I can't for the life of me see how a pigeon's dropping can cause you to lose the sight in one of your eyes!"
"It was my first day with the new hook," muttered Cyril bitterly.

Why was Dennis Thatcher arrested in bed?
For having an offensive person about his weapon.

What do you say to a constipated cat?
Have a break, have a shit cat!

A little boy arrived home with a settee on his head and an armchair under each arm. His Father smacked him round the head and hollered, "What have I told you about taking suites from strangers?"

What did the husband say to his next door neighbour after discovering that his depressed wife had hung herself on the washing line?
If it starts to rain, can you bring her in?

What's black, made of plastic and sails around the world having fantastic adventures?
Binbag the sailor.

THE GREAT FAITH HEALER

VG

"ALLELUIA, ALLELUIA."

A faith healer was doing his stuff in front of a large audience when he asked for two people with disabilites to come up on stage. Up hobbled Bob, on crutches and in obvious pain, closely followed by a perfectly healthy looking man called Peter whose disability was a terrible speech impediment.
The healer told the two men to go and stand behind the screen on the stage and prepare to be healed by faith alone!
The healer chanted, the audience chanted, the tambourines rattled and the healer bellowed, "Bob, throw your right crutch over the top of the screen," and the crutch did indeed come flying over the top of the screen.
"Bob, throw your left crutch over the top of the screen," bellowed the healer, and over the screen flew the left crutch.
"Now, Peter, say something to me!" bellowed the healer.
Peter replied, "B.B.B.B.Bob's f.f.f.fallen over!"

Wh CENSORED een Britis CENSORED y?
Bri CENSORED people.

Who was born in a stable and has millions of followers?
Desert Orchid.

ZULU MASSACRE

The Welsh guards are fighting the Zulus and they are hopelessly outnumbered by at least a hundred to one. As wave after wave of frenzied Zulus close in and start spearing and decapitating them, Dai, defiant to the end, starts singing Land of our Fathers as loudly as he can.The Zulus keep surging forward until only a few of the Welsh are standing and someone shouts out, "For God's sake Dai, sing something they know!!"

Why is a fifty pence piece shaped like it is?
So you can get it out of a Scotsman's fist with a spanner.

PADDY COMPLETES JIGSAW

Paddy rings the Guinness Book of Records all excited and says, "Oive just completed a ten tousand piece jigsaw in tree weeks."
"So what?" came the reply.
"I thought you might like to put that in your book, it must be some sort of record surely," exclaimed Paddy.
"What makes you think that?" yawned the voice on the other end of the line.
"It's a bloody marvellous achievement, so it is. It says on de box between two and five years!" said Paddy.

Why did the one-legged New Zealander decide to settle down and marry?
You try catching a sheep with only one leg!

THE HOOD MEETS THE WOLF

Little Red Riding Hood, laden with a basket full of goodies for her sick Grandma, is happily skipping through the forest when she stops at a nearby tree and says, "Come out, Mr Wolf, I know you're behind the tree."
The Wolf replies grumpily, "Ow did you know I was behind the tree?"

"Because I could see your big sticking out ears and your big bushy tail," replied Hood.
"Bloody hell," cursed the Wolf as he ran off.
Little Red Riding Hood skips onwards and a short while later she stops at a bush and says, "Come out Mr Wolf, I know you're behind the bush."
"Ow did you know I was behind the bush?" grumbled the Wolf.
"I could see your big sticking out nose and your big sticking out feet," replied Hood.
"Bloody hell," cursed the Wolf as he ran off.
Little Red Riding Hood skips onwards and a short while later she stops at a rock and says, "Come out Mr Wolf, I know you're behind the rock."
"Ow did you know I was behind the rock?" growled the Wolf grumpily.
"It was your great big bushy tail sticking out again," replied the Hood.
"Now look, who are you?" exclaimed the Wolf.
"I'm little Red Riding Hood," replied the girl.
"And where are you going?" asked the Wolf.
"I'm going to Grandma's house," replied the girl.
"Well f****** well hurry up and get there will you because I'm dying to have a crap!!" screamed the Wolf.

What have a Royal Navy Wren and a tramp got in common?
They've both been through many a hard ship in their time.

What's the difference between the Italian Mafia and the Glaswegian Mafia?
The Italian Mafia will make you an offer you can't refuse and the Glaswegian Mafia will make you an offer you can't understand.

What do you call Postman Pat after he's retired?
Pat.

Chapter 2
Jokes you can tell Auntie Hilda

Have you heard about Bernard the Brown-nosed reindeer? He's second in line to Rudolph. He's just as fast but can't stop as quick.

Sign on wall: "DO NOT FEED THE ANIMALS ...
THEY ARE DEAD."
Smithfield Meat Market.

THIS PIG'S A HERO!

A rambler is walking through a farmyard when he notices a pig with a wooden leg and he goes up to the farmer and says, "I must ask you. That pig over there has only got three normal legs. The fourth one is made of wood. Why is that?"

"That's right so it is. Boy I can tell you a story or two about that pig," said the farmer. He continued, "It saved my wifes life it did. She was digging up some potatoes by the edge of the river when she slipped and fell in. The pig saw what happened

and jumped over two fences and into the river and pulled her out. He saved her life he did... We think the world of that pig."
"Yes, but how did the pig come to get a wooden leg?" asked the rambler.
"I remember another time when I was ploughing a field on a steep bank and the tractor overturned and I was pinned underneath it. I was stuck and would surely have froze to death that night but the pig found me and tugged me out from underneath the tractor. He saved my life. We think the world of that pig," said the farmer.
"But how did it come to have a wooden leg?" the rambler asked again.
"Well, we think so much of that pig that we couldn't bear to eat him all at once!" said the farmer.

What do you call an Asian man who loves Karaoke?
Gerupte Singh.

Why was the eye-patch wearing car salesman arrested for GBH?
He heard a window shopper say, "That's the one I'd get."

THE 80 MPH CHICKEN!

A man is driving along in his Jaguar when a chicken overtakes him. He puts his foot on the accelerator and overtakes the chicken doing 40 m.p.h. A short while later the chicken overtakes him again doing about 50 m.p.h. The Jaguar driver is annoyed at his new Jaguar being overtaken not once but twice by a mere chicken and puts his foot down

again and overtakes the chicken doing about 70 m.p.h. A while later the chicken overtakes him again doing about 80 m.p.h. and the driver decides to follow the chicken to try to find out where it was from. The chicken eventually turns off the motorway and runs down some quiet country lanes before turning into a farmyard. The Jaguar driver jumps out of his car and approaches the nearby farmer asking, "Excuse me, but does this chicken belong to you?"
"Surely does guvnor," said the farmer.
The motorist continues, "Well that is the most amazing chicken I've ever seen. First it overtook me doing 40 m.p.h., then 50 m.p.h., and then 70 m.p.h. How come it's so fast?"
"Arh... that'll be on account of the fact that it's got three legs. We breed them specially here so that they've all got three legs," said the farmer.
"But what is the reason for deliberately breeding them with three legs?" enquired the motorist.
"Well you see, I like a leg... my wife likes a leg... and our boy likes a leg," said the farmer.
"And what do they taste like?" asked the motorist.
"Don't know... I haven't managed to catch one yet!" said the farmer.

Did you hear about the Englishman who was told his wife was having an affair with his best friend?
He shot his dog.

What do you call a lamppost in Cardiff?
A leisure centre.

I hear Salmon Rushdie's brought out a new book.
It's called, "*******, you fat ********"

What's the difference betwe
One listens to your confess..  .em for you.

THE 3 DOORS TO HELL!

This guy goes to hell and the devil says to him, "You see before you three doors which lead to three separate rooms. You must choose to go through just one of these doors and when inside you will spend the rest of eternity in that room."
Worried that he will choose the wrong door the guy eventually persuades the devil to allow him to have a little peep behind each door before making his final choice. Behind the first door he sees everyone standing on their heads on a wooden floor and thinks to himself, "Oh no... I don't fancy spending the rest of eternity doing that." Behind the second door it's even worse as in this room everyone is standing on their heads on a stone floor!
Behind the third door he sees everyone standing about in a room with manure up to their ankles and they are drinking cups of coffee. The guy thinks to himself that he doesn't go much on the manure but at least if he chose the third door he wouldn't be upside down for the rest of eternity. He tells the devil of his decision and he is ushered inside... and just as the door slams shut the devil shouts out, "Okay folks, coffee break's over, get back on your heads!"

VG

Did you hear about the wife who turned into a three-piece suite?
The doctor said she was comfortable.

I knew there was going to be trouble in the gulf. Just before the war broke out I walked past an open window and heard Vera Lynn gargling!

What's the difference between an estate agent and a bucket of sh*t?
The bucket.

SAW-MILL BLADES LOP OFF MAN'S FINGERS

Lucky Arthur was the local odd job man in the village who was sarcastically nicknamed "Lucky" because he was always having accidents and injuring himself. One day he approached the local timber merchant to see if he would give him any work. The merchant replied that the only work he could offer was in the saw mill.

Arthur pleaded to be given the job saying that he was much more alert and careful these days and hadn't been involved in any accidents for quite some while. Reluctantly the boss agreed and Arthur started right away feeding timber into the giant saw blades. Poor Arthur hadn't been on his own for longer than a couple of minutes when he stumbled forward and the giant blades cut off all his fingers and thumbs on both hands. In a state of shock poor Lucky run back and forth around the mill like a headless chicken before running overland to the local hospital. When he arrived there he promptly fainted.

Coming round a few hours later Lucky looked up and there was Mr. Foster the hospital surgeon leaning over him shaking his head and saying, "Oh Lucky... not again... poor Lucky... not again... You know if you had brought your cut off fingers with you we could have sewn them back on while they were still fresh."

"I would have brought them with me," cried Lucky, " but... but I couldn't pick them up!"

What is a clunt?

A man who runs out of the Chinese take-away without paying.

Two flies are sitting on someone's bum. Which fly is the drug addict?

The one that's on the crack.

DONALD DUCK WANTS A JOB!

Donald Duck goes into the local job centre looking for work. "What have you got?" he says to the girl behind the counter. The startled girl says, "Well it may not be easy to find you a job... There's a recession on and... and... well, to be honest, we've never had a duck in here before looking for a job... but... but I'll go through all the job cards and make a few phone calls and see what I can come up with. Take a seat this may take some time."
The girl disappears from the room and is gone for over four hours before returning. Looking very pleased with herself she says excitedly, "Donald this could be your lucky day. I rang Billy Smarts circus and told them all about you and they want you to go for an interview right away. They want you to appear with the clowns."
"P*ss off, I'm a Plumber!" replied Donald indignantly.

How do you know you're being mooned by Ronald McDonald? He's the one with the sesame seed buns.

THE VERY GENEROUS TRAMP

A tramp walks into a pub one night and goes up to the bar and says to the landlord, "Good evening, my good man. I'll have a whisky and one for yourself."
The landlord gives him the once over and decides to give him the benefit of the doubt saying, "Thankyou... and that'll be £4.20 please."
"Oh... there's plenty of time for that... It's been a lucky day for me today and I think I'll have another... and... and have another yourself... and one for your good wife... and yes, why not one for all the good people in here tonight," said the tramp and before the landlord could do anything about it everyone was

pushing forward for their free drink.
"That'll be £73.51," said the landlord eventually.
"Oh, yes... but here, I'll have another... I like it in here," said the tramp.
"But I really must ask you to..." said the landlord before being interrupted by the tramp, who said, "And have another one yourself kind landlord... and one for your good wife over there... and one for your kind barmaid... and one for each and every one of you good people in here tonight..." and all the people clamber forward for another free drink.
Eventually the landlord, having served everyone again comes over to the tramp and looking highly stressed he says, "That'll be one hundred and sixty one pounds and two pence sir."
"Oh I haven't got any money," replied the tramp without batting an eyelid.
The landlord flew into a rage and beat up the tramp violently before throwing him into the gutter.
Anyway, who should walk in the next night but the very same tramp. Walking straight up to the bar he says to the landlord, "I'll have a whisky... and... and yes, why not,... and one for your good wife over there... and one for your good barmaid over there... In fact I want all these good people in here tonight to join me for a drink... but you're not having one, you get a bit nasty when you've had a few drinks!!"

"Of course it's your mind I'm interested in, honest."

Did you hear the one about the dyslexic theology student?
He spent four years contemplating the existence of dog!

What's the definition of a University Lecturer?
Someone who talks in your sleep.

1st Snake... "What sort of snakes are we?"
2nd Snake... "How do you mean?"
1st Snake... "Well... How do we kill our prey?... Do we wrap our long muscular torsos around our prey and slowly squeeze the life out of them... or do we kill them with just one a bite of our deadly venemous poison?"
2nd Snake... "We're the deadly poisonous type... Why do you ask?"
1st Snake... "I've just bit my lip!"

Why shouldn't you wear Russian underpants?
Because Cher-nob-ll fallout!

ARGHH!!! . . . . . MY BABY'S INCOMPLETE!

A couple have been trying for over twenty years for a child so they are naturally delighted when the wife finally becomes pregnant and gives birth. The wife becomes anxious because the doctor won't let her see her baby. Then the doctor comes into the room to break the news to the worried couple.
"I'm sorry to have to tell you Mr and Mrs Evans that your baby is incomplete... It hasn't got any legs!" said the doctor.
The wife breaks down and starts to cry as the husband replies bravely, "We'll still love it just the same... We've waited so long for this baby."
The doctor continues, "It hasn't got any arms either... In fact it hasn't even got a torso... It's just a head I'm afraid. But a perfectly normal, healthy head."
"We'll love it just like a normal baby," vowed the wife.
And true enough the brave couple do love, cherish and spoil their new addition.
Seven years later the couple go on a cruise as a much needed break from the demands of looking after their head. Whilst on deck they start to chat to a top surgeon who tells them that it is now possible to attach a whole body, arms and legs to just a head. The surgeon also agrees to undertake the operation.
Beside themselves with joy the couple cut short their holiday and return home to their child.
The husband and wife arrive home and pop their heads round the childs bedroom door and say, "Darling, we've got a truly wonderful surprise for you!"
The head rolls it's eyes towards the ceiling and exclaims, "Oh no, not another bloody hat!"

What do you call a Judge with no fingers?
Justice Thumbs.

What do you say to a scouser in a suit?
Will the defendant please rise.

THE WORLD'S WORST ACTOR

The actor Henry Mortimer Garrick came from a long line of famous actors but, alas, he seemed not to have inherited any of his ancestors' talent and try as he may he hadn't had a part in a play for many, many years until one day his agent rang with the great news...

Agent... "So you'll take it then... It's not a big part you know... Only two words."

Henry (desperately)... "I'll take it... I'll take it."

And for months Henry practised his two words over and over again as the opening night drew closer because though it was only two words they were the two most important words in the play... pivotal one might say. Late into the night neighbours could hear Henry practicing his line in a variety of different expressions as he tried to maximise the dramatic effect...

Henry (sadly)... "It is"

Henry (weeping)... "It is"

Henry (bravely)... "It... Is"

Henry (angrily)... "IT IS!!"

Henry (raging)... "IT IS!!!!"

The opening night came and all was going well... The audience were spellbound... The tension was near breaking point...The atmosphere electric and Henry got his cue to enter the fray and utter the immortal words which would completely change the direction of the play...

Henry strode manfully onto centre stage thinking to himself, "It is, it is, it is." He unfurled his cape, looked upto the stars, held his hands to his heaving chest and said... "IS IT?"...

As he was bundled off stage the director sacked him on the spot to which Henry retorted, "You can't sack me, I've practised so hard... I... I know the part backwards!"

Why do elephants have springs on their feet?

So they can bounce up into the trees and seduce the squirrels.

What do you call a three legged horse?

A reliant dobbin.

MAN CAN'T STOP FARTING

A young man is invited to meet his future mother and father-in- law and is very anxious to create a good first impression. Anyway, things start off well... He's got his best suit on... He hasn't said anything out of place... The parents seem to like him and even Prince, the pet collie, has nestled himself affectionately at the young mans feet as they all sit round the dining room table getting stuck into the Sunday roast. Then the young man starts to feel a small fart collecting in his lower regions and try as hard as he could it escapes with a, "Ppprrhh.. pptt." The girl's mother says, "Prince," in a slightly aggrieved manner. "Thank God they think it's the dog," thinks the relieved young man.

Ten minutes later he feels another fart coming... no small one either but a ripper. He struggles to keep it in... he feels his cheeks burning, sweat on his brow, his conversation drying up... Then the fart escapes with a deafening, "Pppprrrhh... ptt. pt." Again the mother shouts out, "Prince!!"

"Thank God for the dog. They think it's him... Just stay there at my feet, good doggie, gooood doggie," thinks the lad.

After a short while the lad is just starting to congratulate the mother on a fine meal when he lets rip with the mother of all farts, "PPPPPRRRRHHHHH... PRTTT... PRTTT."

The mother shouts, "PRINCE!!... GET OUT FROM UNDER HIS FEET BEFORE HE BLOWS YOUR BLOODY HEAD OFF!!!"

What's the definition of a considerate New Zealander?
One who takes his sheep to the pictures first.

What's blue and can't turn round in corridors?
A girl guide with a spear through her neck.

What's the definition of daring?
Playing leap-frog with a Unicorn.

FATHER AND SON REUNITED AT LAST

Up in heaven Jesus comes across a very sad looking old man sitting on a cloud and he asks, "Why are you so sad old man?"
The old man replies, "I can't find my son. I thought we'd be reunited when I came up here but I can't find him anywhere."
"I know how you feel," replied Jesus, "I also can't find someone very close to me."
The old man continues, "Back on earth I was a carpenter. My son was different from the rest... they didn't understand... he was taken away from me at an early age..."
The significance of the old man's words slowly start to dawn on Jesus and tears start to stream down his face as he steps forward, arms outstretched and cries, "Father! I've found you at last!"
The old man looks up at Jesus and says, "Pinocchio?"

THE VERY DEAF OLD LADY

A young man with a tin knocks on a front door and it's answered by an elderly lady...
"Excuse me madam but I'm collecting for the Accrington Stanley Brass Band... Could you make a small donation?" said the man rattling the tin.
"I'm sorry, I'm a bit deaf. Could you say that a bit louder young man?" said the old lady.
"I'm collecting for the Accrington Stanley Brass Band," said the man much louder this time.
"I'm sorry, I'm a bit deaf... What did you say?" said the old lady.
"I'M COLLECTING FOR THE ACCRINGTON STANLEY BRASS BAND. WOULD YOU LIKE TO MAKE A DONATION?" bellowed the man in her ear.
"What was it you said, dear?" said the old lady.
The rather annoyed man decides to give up and he walks rather stroppily up the front garden path which leads back to the pavement.
"Oh young man... you won't forget to close the garden gate

behind you, will you?" shouts out the old lady.
"Stuff the garden gate," muttered the man under his breath.
"Yes and stuff the Accrington Stanley Brass Band as well!" shouted out the old girl defiantly.

How do you know when you've passed an Elephant?
You can't close the toilet lid.

How many Punk Rockers does it take to change a light bulb?
Two. One to change the bulb and the other to kick the chair from under him.

NIV US A NONG! NIV US A NONG!

Buck and Tilley, the world famous jugglers, are doing a charity performance in an asylum when one of the residents shouts out, "Niv us a nong."
"I'm sorry sir, we don't sing songs... We are Buck and Tilley the world famous jugglers," replied Mr Tilley.
The show continues for a while but then the same man shouts out again, "Niv us a nong... niv us a nong."
"I'm sorry sir, but we are Buck and Tilley the world famous jugglers and we don't sing songs," replied Mr Tilley.
The show continues but the man is quite determined and soon he is shouting out again, "Niv us a nong... Niv us a nong... Niv us a nong."
"We are Buck and Tilley the famous juggling duo and we don't do songs," repeated an irate Mr Tilley.
The show continues but soon the familiar cry can be heard... "Niv us a nong... Niv us a nong... Niv us a nong."
"WE ARE BUCK AND TILLEY"
"YETH, AND I'M BUCKIN THILLEY THOO... NOW NIV US A NONG... NIV US A NONG!!!"

What's the biggest crustacean in London?
King's crustacean.

Why didn't the hedgehog wash his hair?
Because he'd left his head and shoulders on the motorway.

What's pink and hairy and hangs out of a babies pram?
A Rottweiler's ar**.

NUTCASE ESCAPES!

A man walks into a bar and orders a pint of lager. As the barmaid is pulling the pint she recognises him as the escaped nutter on the loose from the local lunatic asylum, as reported on the TV, and she decides to act normally and says, "There's your pint sir... That'll be two pounds please." The man brings out a load of bottle tops from his pocket and gives her two. The barmaid takes the bottle tops and puts them in the till. She then goes into a back room and rings the asylum.
The head of the asylum warns her that the man shouldn't be upset and that she should continue to serve him. He says, "I'll settle the bill when I get there."
Seven pints of lager and fourteen bottle tops later the nutter departs.
A short while later the head of the asylum arrives and asks, "Where is he?"
The barmaid replied, "Sorry, you've just missed him. I did try to keep him here for as long as I could."
"I'll soon catch up with him, he can't be far away," said the asylum chief, "Let me settle up first. What's the damage?"
"Fourteen pounds please," said the barmaid.
The asylum chief rummaged about in his black dustbin liner as he asked, "Have you got change of a hubcap?"

If Tarzan and Jane were Irish what would Cheetah be?
Their child prodigy.

THE FAITHFUL SERVANT

A country squire has a faithful servant called Biddle. He need only say, "What about a drink, Biddle?" and Biddle would get him a drink, or, "What about a book Biddle?" and a book would appear.

One day he asked, "What about a bath Biddle?" and true to form Biddle dashed off to run the bath.

And then the squire asked, "What about a hair wash Biddle?" and Biddle washed his hair.

Whilst still in the bath the squire lets out an enormous fart. At this point Biddle leaves and returns with a hot water bottle.

"What are you playing at Biddle? I never asked for one of them," said the squire.

"I beg your pardon, sir, but I distinctly heard you say, 'Wot-a-bout-a-water-bottle-Biddle!'" said Biddle.

What's the nearest thing to silver?
The Lone Ranger's balls.

Why do Italian men wear moustaches?
So they can look just like moma.

OLD AGE IS SO SAD

Three old men were sitting around discussing who had the worst health problems. The seventy-five year old said, "Have I got a problem? Every morning I get up at 7. 30 and have to take a piss, but I have to stand at the toilet for ages because my pee barely trickles out."

"Hmm, that's nothing," said the eighty year old, "Every morning at 8. 30 I have to take a sh*t, but I have to sit on the can for hours because of my constipation. It's terrible."

The ninety year old said, "Cor, you two think you've got problems! Every morning at 7. 30 I piss like a racehorse and at 8.30 I sh*t like a pig. The trouble is... I don't wake up till 10."

What's the best secretary to have in the whole world?
One that never misses a period.

Did you hear about the Irishman who was asked to be a Jehovah's Witness?
He refused because he didn't see the accident.

BLIND RABBIT COLLIDES WITH BLIND FROG

A blind rabbit and a blind frog are running across a field when they collide...

Rabbit... "Why don't you look where you are going?"

Frog... "I'm sorry... I'm blind... I couldn't see you."

Rabbit... "I'm blind too... Hey, what sort of animal are you anyway?"

Frog... "I'm not sure... I've always been blind and no one's ever told me what I am... What are you?"

Rabbit... "I don't really know what I am either... Hey I've got an idea, why don't we run our hands over each others faces and see if we can work out what we are?"

The frog agrees and he runs his webbed hands over the rabbit...

Frog... "Well, you've got two furry ears coming out the top of your head... a furry face... a furry body... and a furry bobtail... I know what you are... you're a rabbit."

Rabbit... "Oh that's good news, I've always sort of hoped I might be a rabbit... Now let me see if I can tell you what you are. You've got a great big mouth that stretches from one side of your face to the other... You've got big bulbous eyes... and you are all slimy... I know what you are... you're a scouser!"

What's green and jumps all over Australia?
Skippy the Cooking Apple.

What do you call a Mexican with a vasectomy?
A dry Martinez.

THE AMAZING INDIAN MEMORY MAN

A man goes on a working holiday for three months to an Indian reservation in Texas and everyday day he has breakfast sitting opposite Chief Running Bull who is famous as one of the world's best memory men. On the very last day of his holiday, as he is having breakfast opposite the great memory man for the last time, he plucks up enough courage to speak to him to test him out to see just how good he is.

"Chief Running Bull, I hope you don't mind me asking, but what did I have for breakfast on the very first day of my holiday three months ago?" asked the man.

Without batting an eyelid the chief replied, "Eggs," and on hearing this the man was satisfied and he returned home to England that night.

Six years went by and the man had dined out many a time on the strength of his Indian chief memory man story but people were always telling him that he should have asked a more difficult question and this started to annoy him. So the man saved up for a couple of years determined to visit the chief again before the great man died.

Two years later, and now eight since having last spoken to the chief he again visited the reservation and having learnt some Indian etiquette by then he entered the chiefs teepee and said, "How."

"Scrambled," replied the chief.

VG

How many pessimists does it take to change a light bulb?
Oh, what's the point! It'll blow anyway.

How do patients in a burns unit pick their noses?
From a catalogue.

Where do female aircraft pilots sit?
In the c**tpit.

HEDGEHOG MOTORWAY SURVIVAL

Daddy hedgehog had brought his two boys onto the hard shoulder of the M1 motorway to teach them all he knew about

motorway survival.

"Right boys, always remember that a car is much faster than you. So if you ever find yourself stuck in the middle of the road when you see an oncoming vehicle approaching fast always position yourself directly halfway between the approaching car headlights and everything will be okay... Here I'll show you."

Out crawled daddy hedgehog into the centre of the first lane as the car headlights got nearer and nearer.

"Are you watching boys?" said daddy hedgehog, "Are you watching, are you watchSPPPPPLATTTTTTTTT!!"

One of the baby hedgehogs turned to the other and said, "I was going to ask him about Robin Reliants!"

What goes down trees, but doesn't go up them?
Parachutists.

What comes out of your nose at 100mph?
A Lamborgreenie

CHAT-UP LINES AND INSULTS

You've had ten pints of lager and you see a gorgeous bird on her own so you stagger over and give her the.....

Chat-up lines..

Choose one of the following which never ever fail.....

"Lay down I think I love you."

"Bye the way, what would you like for breakfast?"

"Let's go outside and play Mummies and Daddies."

"How would you like to see the souls of your feet in my wing mirrors?"

Or if she's got big charlies...
"Excuse me, but is there much money to be made out of smuggling melons into the country."
Or
"If you're going to drown those two puppies can I have the one with the pink nose."

If those lines don't do the trick then give up being charming and resort to insults to make you feel better!.....

Insults....

"I bet you've been a cover girl for farmers weekly."

"I bet when you went to see that film, The Elephant Man, you spent two hours afterwards signing autographs!"

"The last time I saw a mouth like that it had a hook in it!"

"I bet your legs have spent so much time apart they've decided to become penpals."

"I bet your nickname is Martini....Anytime, anyplace, anywhere!"

"Ghee! You don't sweat much for a fat chick!"

"I bet the only people who have ever asked you to bed have been your parents."

"If a fish were to come out of your mouth I'd have to say, 'What's a nice plaice like you doing in a girl like that?'"

"You know what the difference between you and Jimmy Hill is? He eventually got round to shaving his chin."

"You know the difference between you and Lassie?
One's got bad breath and makes love on all fours and the other appears in films with Elizabeth Taylor."

Or..(if there are two blonde bimbo's who look alike)
"Are you two sisters?..............I'm looking for Cinderella."

She then responds with her own insults which you undoubtedly deserve......

The female put downs.......

"I bet your nickname is bedspread.....you're always getting turned down."

"I bet when you climax you call out your own name!"

"You've got an electric personality....you could light up a room just by leaving it!"

"I bet you and your last girlfriend made a fastidious couple..... She was fast.....and you were hidious."

"You're certainly not two-faced....if you were you definitely wouldn't be wearing the one you've got on at the moment."

"Who cut your hair?..... The Council?"

"I never forget a face...... but in your case I'll make an exception."

"Huh! Ten million sperm and it had to be your one that made it!"

"When you were circumcised they threw away the wrong piece!"

"Why don't you spill some of your lager over your wrist.....that way you'll be able to get your date drunk."

"A night out with you would be about as meaningful as giving Stevie Wonder a ticket to see Marcel Marceau."

Having been rejected yet again you then return to your mates and put on a brave face by using further put-down lines.....

Put down comments to mates....

"She was a bit thick......I asked her if she'd seen Jurassic Park and she said, 'That's just off the M25 init, mate.'"

"She was a bit thick......I asked her if she fancied something from the Karma Sutra and she said, 'Nah mate. Indian food makes me fart like a trooper.'"

"She had no class......I asked her what she thought of Harry Connick Junior and she said, 'I didn't go to school round 'ere mate.'"

THE SILLY HEADMASTER

A school headmaster was stopped on the motorway by a police car and was ordered to get out of his car. The policeman then chalked a circle on the ground and told the headmaster to stand in the circle and on no account move out of the circle while he gave the car a thorough search.
The policeman then proceeded to tear up the carpets, empty the ashtrays, slash open the spare tyre, rip open all the upholstery and pull out the car radio... leaving the car in a terrible mess. When he turned round the headmaster was laughing hysterically.
"What's so funny?" asked the policeman.
"Well," giggled the headmaster, "all the time you were searching my car I've been jumping in and out of the circle, herrr!"

What is a creche?
A car crash in Kensington.

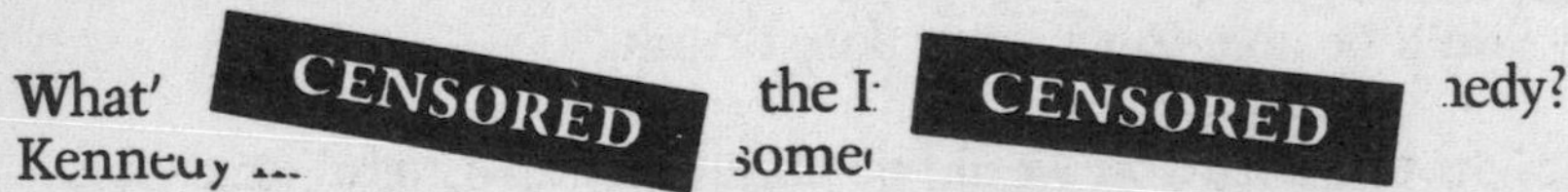

What do you get if you cross a hedgehog with a giraffe?
A Nobel prize for genetic engineering.

Why do traffic wardens have a yellow stripe round their hats?
To stop people parking on their heads.

TRAMP EATS DEAD DOG

Two old tramps were walking along the railway tracks, starving because they hadn't eaten for four days.
Suddenly they both notice a dead and mangled dog by the side of the line. "Oh boy, lunch," says the first tramp and he starts to dig in, stopping only to ask his mate if he wanted some.
"No thanks, I think I'll give it a miss," replied the other tramp, so the first tramp continued to devour the dog.
They continue to walk on when the first tramp starts to complain that he's feeling decidely unwell. He turns green and throws up the dog's remains. All excited his companion says, "That's just what I've been waiting for... hot lunch!!"

Where would you go to find a missing vicar?
The Missing Parsons Bureau.

What do you give to the girl who has everything?
Penicillin.

Emma Thompson calls out, "Kenneth, where are you?"
Kenneth replies, "I'm in the Kitchen."
Emma pleads, "Oh, can I be in it?"

Alex Haley spent six years tracing his family ancestry back many generations to the black slave called Kunte Kinte and then wrote the worldwide best seller "Roots." Sadly Alex Haley recently committed suicide... He discovered he'd been adopted!

What worse than getting raped by Jack the Ripper?
Getting touched-up by Captain Hook.

Some builders are renovating an old building when one of the workers falls through the rotten floor into a previously undiscovered cellar. As the dust settles the man sees to his horror a skeleton lying in the corner. The skeleton is wearing an orange sash with the words written on it, "ALL IRELAND HIDE AND SEEK CHAMPION 1948."

A man's plane crashes in the middle of the desert and just he and his beloved dog Raffles are left to try to make it back to civilisation. The man has plenty of water but as the days go by he soon comes to realise that he is not going to survive unless he eats his beloved dog Raffles. So he kills the dog and eats every bit of flesh on the dog so that all that remains of the dog is a small pile of bones. He is sitting there with a full belly at last and feeling really great when he looks down at the bones and says aloud, "Oh, Raffles would have really loved those bones!"

Why were the Mexicans so determined to storm the Alamo? Because they'd heard that there were four clean walls to spray graffiti on.

A little boy misses school one day so the next day his teacher sternly asks, "Where were you yesterday?"
"My dad got burnt," came the reply.
"Oh I'm sorry to hear that. Was he badly burnt?" asked the teacher.
"Oh yes," came the reply, "They don't mess about at the crematorium, Miss."

What's the difference between a willy and a poo?
Have you ever tried sucking poo!

What's the similarity between a rooster and a lawyer?
A rooster clucks defiance and a ...

THE ATTENTIVE HUSBAND

Husband to wife: "Hello darling."
Wife: "Hello Darling... Err... darling... err notice anything different about me?"
Husband: "New dress?"
Wife: "No."
Husband: "New hair do?"
Wife: "No."
Husband: "New shoes?"
Wife: "No."
Husband: "New earrings?"
Wife: "I'M WEARING A GAS MASK!!!!"

THE REALLY SICK SURGEON

A man with three daughters is told that they've been seriously injured in a car crash so he rushs over to the hospital and waits anxiously outside the operating theatre and as soon as the surgeon comes out he begs him for news of his three beautiful daughters.

"Well," says the surgeon, "your first daughter who wanted to be a ballet dancer?" the man nods, "I'm afraid we had to amputate her legs."

The man breaks down before regaining his calm and asking about his second daughter.

"Ah," says the surgeon, "the one who had just become a professional tennis player? I'm afraid we had to amputate both arms."

The poor man collapses to the floor and two nurses rush over to administer tranquilisers. He mutters, "Wh... what about my third daughter?"

"The one who wanted to be a concert pianist? Her arms and legs are okay... but I'm afraid she won't be able to use them as she's paralysed from the neck down," said the surgeon.

"Tell me it's not true... Tell me it's not true..." wailed the man.

"Oh alright then," says the surgeon, "It's not true... I was only joking... They're all dead really!"

DODGY MAN FOLLOWS BOY

A young schoolkid is walking home from school one evening when a dodgy looking character pulls up in a car and rolls down the car window.
"Hello," he whispers, "do you fancy getting in the car?"
"No, go away!" shouts the boy who then runs off down the road.
The man follows in his car and says, "Look son, I'll give you a bag of sweets if you get into my car."
"No, push off," screamed the boy and he sprinted off up the road.
The man continued to follow him and said, "Okay son, I'll give you a bag of sweets and £10 if you get into the car."
"Listen, I've told you before, I'm not getting into your car," said the kid and off he ran again.
But the man still didn't give up and he continued to follow him and said, "Right, a bag of sweets, £20 and... AND... I'll let you drive if you get into the car."
"Look," hollered the boy, "You bought the Lada dad, you drive the f****** thing!"

What sort of meat does the Pope eat?
Nun.

What's black and white and tells the Pope to get stuffed?
A nun with eight score draws.

Three fathers were having a drink in the pub together when the topic of conversation came round to their sons' names. The first man says, "Me and the wife were going to call our son Eric but he was born on St. George's day so we thought why not... and we called him George."
The second man says, "Funny you should mention that because we actually called our son Andrew because he was born on St. Andrew's day."
"Bey Jeysus!" said the Irish father, "The same thing happened with my boy Pancake."

Man to waiter: "How long have you worked here?"
Waiter: "About six months, Monsieur."
Man: "OH! SO IT WASN'T YOU WHO TOOK OUR ORDER THEN!"

Have you heard that the new united Germany is thinking of relocating it's capital?
To Paris.

AUSTRALIANS LOVE US

An Englishman is on his holiday in Australia and he is driving along when he sees a bull in a field charging towards a little girl. Quick as a flash he dashes into the field and throws himself on top of the little girl and is badly gored in the process. With blood pouring from a gaping hole in his side he still summons up enough strength to grab the bull in an arm lock and kill the beast by stabbing the beast through the eye with his fountain pen. As he lays there in a pool of blood he sees a man gaping at him from over the hedge in disbelief. "My good God... that's the bravest bloody thing I've ever seen," exclaimed the onlooker, "Makes me proud to be Australian. I'm a journalist from the Sydney Herald and I'm going to write a story about you and tell the fine people of this great nation about your courage. You're going to be a national hero. Now let me gct some details. Where d'ya come from... ?"
The next day, when the Englishman comes round in hospital he asks the nurse if he can have a look at the Sydney Herald... and on receiving the paper he sees splashed across the front page the headline, "POMMIE B*****D MURDERS CHILD'S PET."

What do you call a woman who is playing snooker whilst balancing a pint of beer on her head?
Beatrix Potter.

The Lone Ranger and Tonto are suddenly surrounded by 500 screaming Sioux . . .
Lone says, "Well old buddy, it looks like the end for both of us."
Tonto replies, "Die, paleface!"

What's the difference between a seagull and a baby?
One flits across the shore and the other shits across the floor.

MAN GETS TOTALLY RAT-ARSED

Ted goes into a club on his own for a quiet drink and asks this man if he can sit next to him as it's the only spare seat in the place. They soon start chatting and get rounds of beer aplenty brought over by the drinks waitress until both of them are merry to say the least. As the landlord starts to chuck out, the man who gave Ted the seat stands up and says he'll give Ted a lift home but he takes two paces and falls over and busts his nose. Despite Ted's advice the man still insists on driving his new friend home and the man takes two steps outside the club and falls over again, this time knocking out a tooth. The man gets up, takes another two paces and falls over again, ripping his jacket and cutting his knee in the process.

As he's helped to his feet he still insists on driving Ted home and he stumbles to the car. Having then given Ted a lift home he parks the car outside his own home and gets out of the car and takes two paces and falls over, cutting his ear in the process. He manages to put the key in his front door and get inside whereupon he takes two paces and falls over, hits the coffee table, cuts his head and passes out!
The next morning his wife wakes him and says, "You must have had too much to drink last night."
The man with the bloody head, busted nose, cut ear and ripped jacket replied bravely, "Darling, whatever makes you think that?"
"You came home without your wheelchair," came the reply.

Why is a University Lecturer like a lighthouse in a desert?
They are both brilliant but totally useless.

"**I**'ve heard that Englishmen are the fourth best lovers in the world after Cowboys, the Germans and the Jews," cooed the gorgeous blonde actress to a male admirer, "What's your name anyway?"
"Err... Hopalong von Goldstein," replied the man.

I once had an audition with the Chippendales.
They said they'd put me on their short list.

PADDY'S STRANGE REQUEST

A Scotsman, a Frenchman and an Irishman are out in the wild west when they are captured by Apaches. The Apaches' chief goes up to the Scotsman and says, "You got real thick skin. You make real good canoe. You got one last wish before we skin you."
The Scotsman requests as much whisky as he can drink and then proceeds to drink himself senseless so he won't know what's going on. When he's drunk himself into a coma the Apaches kill him, skin him and make a canoe out of him.
The Apaches' chief then goes up to the Frenchman and says,

"You got real thick skin. You make real good canoe. You got one last wish before we skin you."
The Frenchman decides to go out with a bang and asks for as many women as he can manage and the Indians oblige by putting him in a wig wam with ten young squaws. The Frenchman s**gs himself senseless and he's too tired to really care what happens to him when the Indians eventually carry him out, kill him, skin him and make a canoe out of him.
The Apaches' chief then goes up to the Irishman and says "You got real thick skin, you make real good canoe, you got one last wish."
Paddy asks for a fork. The Apaches are a bit puzzled by this but they give him a fork anyway. Paddy grabs the fork and starts stabbing himself saying, "You f****** b******* aren't making a canoe out of me!"

Why do elephants all have grey trunks?
Because they all belong to the same swimming club.

What's blue and stands in a field?
A cow in a shell suit.

CELESTIAL TRANSPORT

Fred dies and finds himself outside the gates of heaven and St. Peter comes out to ask a few questions.
"Were you a good man when you were alive?" asks St. Peter.
Fred says, "Yes I was. I never drank, never smoked, never lied and never did anyone a wrong turn. I was never unfaithful, I never even so much as looked at another woman. I thought the world of my wife, Sadie and she thought the world about me."
"By crikey!" said St. Peter, "You have been a good man. You've been such a good man that I'm going to reward you by giving you a brand new Rolls-Royce to drive around in up here in heaven."
A few days later Harry, a neighbour of Fred's, dies and finds himself outside the gates to heaven being interviewed by St.

Peter who asks, "Were you a good man when you were alive Harry?"
"I've got to be honest," says Harry reluctantly," I was a right git when I was alive. I drank like a fish, smoked like a chimney, beat up the wife regularly and was unfaithful to her all the time. I even slept with my step daughter!"
"My good God," said St. Peter, "you have been a right git... a really horrible git so I'm going to give you this really old rusty bike to go about on up here as punishment."
A few days later Harry is riding along in his bike when who should he see at the celestial crossroads but Fred in his gleaming new Rolls-Royce. Fred rolls down his window and says rather sadly, "Oh hallo Harry... I... I didn't know you were up here."
"Yeah, I died in my sleep. Nice to go out peacefully, I suppose," says Harry.
Harry can't help noticing how sad Fred seems and says, "Cheer up Fred, things aren't too bad up here. Why, look at you driving around in a Roller while all I've got is this rusty old bike."
"It's okay up here it's... It's just that my wife's up here now," says Fred.
"That's no reason to be sad matey. Look, you're together again for the rest of eternity now, aren't you?" says Harry.
"It's... It's just that when I saw her," said Fred sadly, "she was going around on a pair of Roller skates!"

Did you hear about the sexually inexperienced Irishman who went into a bookshop and bought, "How to Hug."
Later on he realised it was Volume 7 of the Encyclopedia Britannica.

How can you tell when someone has a glass eye?
When it comes out in conversation.

What do you get if you cross a politican with a pig?
Nothing. There are some things even a pig won't do.

Two Irish guys are standing at the bar when they see this guy walk in, go straight up to the bar and order 25 pints of Guinness. The guy then drinks all 25 pints straight down, one after the other, without hardly pausing to draw his breath and then walks out of the pub. Paddy then turns to Murphy and says, "I bet he drinks Carling Black Label."

What is black, twisted, hard as nails, and sits around sobbing? Overwrought iron.

MAN PIDDLES IN PUB

A man goes into a pub and orders a pint of beer and he's no sooner drunk the beer when he pees himself all down his leg leaving a pool of urine on the landlords new carpet.
"What's your problem pal?" says the irate Landlord on seeing the puddle on the floor.
The man goes bright red and stutters, "Oh, I'm sorry, I'm really sorry, it's my nerves, I'll clean it up."
"Just get the hell out of my pub," shouted the landlord.
"Please keep your voice down," said the shaking man, "everyone's looking at me."
"Just get out of my pub," growled the Landlord.
"It won't happen again... let me stay for another pint... It won't happen again... I promise," pleaded the man and he eventually persuades the landlord to let him stay in the pub and he orders another pint.
The man had no sooner downed the pint when he peed himself again leaving another pool of urine on the landlords new carpet.
The young man goes red in the face and whispers, "Look I'm really sorry... please don't shout at me... people will look at me," but the landlord's had enough and he throws the man out of the pub saying, "You're banned, don't come back."
A couple of weeks later who should go up to the bar but the same man and he tries to order a pint but the landlord sees him and says, "Oy you, out!"
"It's okay now, trust me," beamed the man.

"How do you mean?" grunted the landlord.
"That nervous problem I had last time... I got it sorted out... I went to see a specialist... It's not a problem for me anymore," beamed the now confident man.
The landlord, noticing the man's confident manner, decides to give him a pint.
The man thanks him for the pint and downs it in one and with a sheepish half-smile then immediately releases a bladder full onto the carpet. The landlord sees this and flips his lid. He jumps over the bar and grabs the man round the throat saying "You c***, I thought you said you'd got your problem sorted out."
"I did get it sorted out," beamed the man, "I went to see a psychiatrist and he cured me... I'm no longer embarrassed about it when it happens... I feel proud."

What do you say to a University graduate with a job?
Big Mac and large fries please.

How can you tell that ET is a young Conservative?
Because he looks like one.

Why do elephant's paint their balls red?
So they can hide in cherry trees.

200 MILES FROM THE NEAREST WOMAN

A man joins the foreign legion and after a few days in the remote desert outpost he hears one of the lookouts shouting from the top of his lookout tower, "They're coming, they're coming."
The soldiers all around him start shouting excitedly amongst themselves, "They're coming, they're coming," and they leave their duties and leave the confines of the outpost and start running up the sand dunes towards the brow of a nearby hill.
The man can now hear the thunder of approaching hooves and see a cloud of dust rising from above the brow of the hill and he

asks the soldier next to him, "What's going on?"
"Never mind what's going on, let's get going otherwise we'll miss out," came the reply.
The man is confused but then he sees a herd of camels coming over the brow of the hill and they are being shooed towards the outpost by some men on horseback.
"What are all the camels for?" asks the new recruit.
"Listen son, if you'd been out here for six months in a place where the nearest woman was 200 miles away you wouldn't be asking such a question," said the man next to him.
"By why's everyone running so fast? There seems enough to go round," asked the newcomer.
"No one wants to get lumbered with an ugly one," came the reply.

How can you tell if you've walked into a gay church?
Only half the congregation are kneeling.

Japanese tourist at foreign exchange counter: "I got more Pounds for my Yens yesterday!"
Counter clerk: "Fluctuations."
Japanese tourist: "Yeah, and fluck you British too!"

What is Waldheim's Syndrome?
When you get old and half kurt you forget you were a Nazi.

BABY CAMEL WONDERS

A baby camel asks it's Mother, "Why have we got long eye-lashes?"
"That's because if we are ever caught in a sand storm in the desert we can keep the sand out of our eyes," answers Mum.
"And why have we got big wide feet?" asks the baby camel.
"That's so that we won't sink in the sand when we are trekking through the sand dunes," answers Mum.
"And why have we got such a really thick hide on us?" asks the

baby camel.
"That's so that we won't dehydrate in the hundred and ten degree heat of the desert," answers Mum.
"So what the f*** are we doing in Dudley Zoo?" asks the baby camel.

What would you have if you had a moth ball in one hand and a moth ball in the other hand?
A bloody big moth.

What you do call a drunk dinosaur?
Staggersaurus.

LITTLE RED ROSENBURG

Little red Rosenburg goes off to see her grandmother and says...
"My Grandma, what big ears you've got."
"All the better for hearing you with," came the reply.
"My Grandma, what big eyes you've got."
"All the better for seeing you with," came the reply.
"My Grandma, what a big nose you've got."
"All the better for LOOK WHO'S F****** TALKING!!" came the reply.

Did you hear about the Irish Jellyfish?
It set.

What do you call a Russian tart?
Nikess Onandov.

SQUASHED HARE LIVES

A farmer is walking along a country lane when a car comes round the corner and hits a hare as it's running across the road. The driver gets out and bends over the hare. It looks to be in a real bad way, it's covered in blood and hardly breathing and apart from the odd twitch it seems dead.
The farmer comes over and says, "Poor thing's a goner, I'll put it out of it's misery," and he loads his shotgun.
"Hold on a minute, I've got something in my car," says the driver and he gets a spray can from the boot of his car and proceeds to spray the mangled remains of the hare with the can's contents.
"There ain't nothing in the world that could save that hare, it's a goner believe me," said the farmer. At that moment the hare started to move, then it got up and ran a few steps and turned to the car driver and lifted one of it's little paws and appeared to wave to the man. The hare then ran a few further steps and turned and waved again, and then ran a few more steps and then stopped turned around and waved again.
"Good heavens, I don't believe my eyes! What exactly was it you sprayed the hare with?" said the farmer.
"Hair restorer and permanent wave," came the reply.

Chapter 3
Jokes you can tell the Vicar

What do you call a Russian boxer?
Nokya Bolokov.

What do you call a child raised in a house of ill-repute?
A brothel sprout.

What's the difference between a Skoda and a sheep?
It's more embarrassing being seen getting out of the back of a Skoda.

THE WALLS OF JERICHO

A new teacher asks his class, "Who knocked down the walls of Jericho?"
Hemmings responds by saying, "It wasn't me sir."
Appalled by the general level of ignorance displayed by his pupils the teacher goes to see the headmaster and says, "I asked 'Who knocked down the walls of Jericho?' and Hemmings said that he didn't do it."
The head replies, "I know the boy's parents very well and if the boy says that he didn't do it, then he didn't do it."
The teacher can't believe what he's hearing and he goes to see the schools board of governors and says, "I asked my class, 'Who knocked down the walls of Jericho?' and Hemmings said it wasn't him so I went to the head and told him that when I'd asked my class, 'Who knocked down the walls of Jericho?'

Hemmings had said that it wasn't him and when the head heard this he said he knew Hemmings parents well and that if Hemmings said he didn't do it, then he didn't do it. Now what do you think of that?"
The board of governors talk amongst themselves for a while before the chairman says to the teacher, "We'll make arrangements for a couple of bricklayers to come round tomorrow."

What's the Greek Army motto?
Never leave your buddy's behind.

What is the connection between Hugh Hefner, Paul Raymond, Cynthia Payne, Lindy St. Clair and Myra Hindley?
None of them are characters in an Enid Blyton story.

VG

MAN BECOMES FAKE GORILLA

A guy applies for a job in the local zoo and he gets it. He's only been there two days when the head zoo keeper asks if he'd do him a favour.
"What sort of favour?" asks the man.
"One of our main attractions, Guy the Gorilla, isn't very well and there's a big crowd of expectant kids out there who will go home very disappointed if they don't get to see Guy. Would you mind putting on this gorilla costume and going on show out there and just ambling about gorilla style and eating a banana or two?" asks the keeper.
"You must be joking. I didn't join the zoo to ponce about in a gorilla costume. Anyway, they'll never fall for it," says the man.
However, the head zoo keeper is a very persuasive man and threatened with the sack the man agrees to help out.
A short while later the man is out in Guy the Gorilla's cage ambling about gorilla style.

The days go by and turn into weeks and still Guy is very poorly so the man continues in his new role as Guy the Gorilla and as each day goes by the man becomes more competent and confident. He starts to swing from tree to tree, wave to the kids, juggle oranges and even spin round on his backside for a banana or two. The man becomes one of the zoo's biggest attractions.

One day, however, the man tries to leap from one tree to another and it's too far and he falls down into the lion's cage and finds himself surrounded by snarling lions. The man screams out, "Help, help, I've fallen into the lion's cage. GET ME OUT OF HERE!!" whereupon a lion says to him, "Shh, keep your voice down or we'll all be out of a job."

What do you get if you cross an elephant with a swallow?
A lot of broken telegraph wires.

VIRGIN BECOMES PREGNANT!!

VG

Doctor... "Well, Mrs Baker, I have some good news for you. Go home and tell your husband to prepare for a baby."
Girl (embarrassed)... "It's Miss Baker actually. I don't have a husband."
Doctor... "Well, in that case, Miss Baker, go home and tell your boyfriend to prepare for a baby."
Girl (embarrassed)... "I don't have a boyfriend."
Doctor... "Well, in that case you'd better go home and ring your last date and tell him to prepare for a baby."
Girl (very embarrassed)... "I've never had a date."
Doctor... "Well, in that case you'd better go home and tell your mother to prepare for the second coming of Christ!"
The girl starts to cry.
The doctor then dashed over to the window, opened it, leant out and looked up to the sky.
Girl (weeping) ... "What are you doing?"
Doctor ... "The last time something like this happened there was a shooting star from the East, and I don't want to miss it this time."
The girl breaks into a flood of tears.
Doctor... "Look! Would you mind staying here until the three wise men turn up with all the pressies!"

What wears yellow-checked trousers and only gets halfway across a railway level crossing?
Rupert the Benetton advert.

The Lone Ranger was riding across the desert and found Tonto lying on the sand with his ear pressed to the ground.
"What's up Tonto?" asked the Lone Ranger.
"Stage coach pass here one hour ago," said Tonto.
"How do you know that Tonto?" asked Lone.
"It ran me over," moaned Tonto.

PRIEST GETS SLOSHED

The new priest at his first mass was so scared he could hardly speak. After the service he asked the Monsignor how he had done.
"Fine," said the Monsignor, "but next time it might help if you put a little gin or vodka into your tea to relax you."
The next week the new priest put vodka in his tea and really kicked up a storm. After the mass he asked the Monsignor how he had done this time.
"Fine," he replied, "but there are a few things you should get straight:
1) There are ten commandments not twelve.
2) There are twelve disciples not ten.
3) David slew Goliath, he did not kick the sh*t out of him.
4) We do not refer to Jesus Christ as the late J. C.
5) The Father, the Son and the Holy Ghost are not Big Daddy, Junior and the Spook.
6) We do not refer to Judas as "El Finko."
7) The Pope is consecrated not castrated, and we do not refer to him as the Godfather."

Why is it that when we talk to God it's called praying ... but when God talks to us it's called paranoid schizophrenia?

THE SYMPATHETIC SERGEANT

A Captain in the army gets the news that Private Williams's mother is dead and he tells the Sergeant Major to break the bad news to the lad. The Sergeant Major goes out onto the parade ground and screams out, "PRIVATE WILLIAMS, YOUR MOTHER IS DEAD!"
The poor lad is overcome with shock and stops marching, vommits over his boots and collapses and has to be carried back to his barracks.
Three months later the Captain receives the news that Private Williams's father has just died and he again tells the Sergeant Major to tell Private Williams the bad news, only this time to be more subtle.
The Sergeant Major goes onto the parade ground and shouts, "ALL THOSE WITH A FATHER TAKE ONE STEP FORWARD... (SCREAMING) PRIVATE WILLIAMS WHERE DO YOU THINK YOU ARE GOING!"

Girl to man at disco: "Your place or mine?"
Man: "Look, if it's going to be a hassle, forget it!"

A man without a woman is like a fish without a bicycle.

THE SALES REP AND POPE

A very ambitious sales rep travelled all the way to Rome and somehow managed to wrangle a private audience with the Pope himself. As soon as they were alone together the rep leaned forward and said, "Your Holiness, I come on behalf of the Brewers Federation and I have their authority to offer The Vatican a million pounds if you can change the wording of the Lords prayer to, 'Give us this day our daily beer.'"
"Absolutely not," replied the shocked Pontiff.
"Okay, okay... I know it's a lot to ask... but if we were to make it two million just think how much restoration work could be done with that," continued the rep.
The Pontiff shook his head.
"Okay... okay... my employers have given me the authority to go up to a maximum of three million pounds," continued the determined rep.
Asking him to leave the room the Pope called in the Cardinal and whispered, "When does our contract with Mothers Pride expire?"

How do you stop an elephant from charging?
Take away his credit cards.

What's the definition of macho?
Jogging home from your vasectomy.

Suicide is the sincerest form of self criticism.

When the troubles in Northern Ireland first began, Ian Paisley made enquiries about a plot in the local cemetery. The clerk told him, "The price is £200. That may sound a lot but you won't be disturbed for 150 years at least."
Paisley gave the matter some thought and then said, "Here, would you take a fiver? After all I'll only be wanting it for three days."

What do you call an abortion in Prague?
A cancelled cheque.

1st Cannibal... "That's no way to bring up your son."
2nd Cannibal... "What do you expect after 12 pints."

Did you hear about the two relatives from Ireland who went to England to appear on The Generation Game.
They won the final and came away with two prizes... a pair of sliding doors and a conveyor belt.

How do you know when an Irishman has been using your word processor?
There's tippex all over the screen.

MAN ABOUT TO BE SIZZLED

A man is sitting in the Electric chair waiting for the end.
"Quick! Get out of the chair!" yells an officer.
"It's a reprieve, thank you oh Lord!!" screams the man joyfully.
"Err... no, we just forgot to spray the non-stick stuff on the chair," said the officer.

Why do mountaineers rope themselves together?
To stop the sensible ones from going home.

THE TWO FISHERMEN

Two fishermen were angling by a bridge. As they were sitting there a funeral cortege drove slowly past. As it did so one of the men removed his hat and placed it over his heart. Touched by his friend's actions the other man remarked, "Ed, that's a nice gesture, showing respect for the dead like that."
"Well it's the least I could do. After all we would have been married for twenty-five years next month," replied Ed.

1st Cannibal: "Your wife makes lovely soup!"
2nd Cannibal: "Yeah, I know . . . but I'm going to miss her."

YOU INSENSITIVE JERK!

A bloke returns from a long trip to the States having left his beloved cat in his brothers care. The minute he's cleared customs he phones his brother and enquires after his pet.
"Your cat's dead," replied the brother bluntly.
The bloke is absolutely devastated as he thought the world of the cat, and then he turned on the brother, saying, "You know how much that cat meant to me. You could have thought of a nicer and gentler way of breaking the news to me. You could have said something like the cat got out of the house one day and climbed up onto the roof... and the fire brigade couldn't get her down... and she finally fell off the roof doing what she loved to do best, chasing the pigeons, or something like that... Would that have been to much trouble? HUH! Why are you always such an insensitive jerk?"
"Look, I'm sorry, I'll try to do better next time," said his brother.
"Okay, let's just put it behind us. How are you anyway? And how are mum and dad?" said the bloke.
His brother is silent for a moment. He then said, "Err, mum's fine... dad's on the roof and..."

Did you hear about the queer Mexican?
He wouldn't let a day go by.

What's the difference between New Zealand and a bowl of yoghurt?
The bowl of yoghurt contains a live culture.

OLD ROOSTER CAN'T GET IT UP

An egg farmer was very concerned because his hens seemed to be laying fewer and fewer eggs each week and he finally reached the conclusion that his ageing rooster was the problem, as he clearly wasn't fulfilling his henhouse responsibilities. So the farmer went out and bought a new rooster. Eyeing the newcomer, the old rooster said, "Listen, let's make a deal... I'll just take four hens and move over to that far corner over there and leave the rest to you."
"Not a chance," said the arrogant young rooster, "This is my henhouse now and all the hens are mine."
"Very well," said the poor old rooster humbly, "but perhaps you'd do me one small favour to save my pride. Let's have a race and the winner gets the henhouse. That way it won't look as if I'm being dumped because I can't perform any more."
Sizing up the stiff and rickety old rooster the young cock agrees and he even decides to give the old bird a half a lap start.
Off the two birds start flying round the course and it soon becomes obvious that the old birds head start won't last long.
The young bird is just coming up on the old bird's inside ready to overtake, when the chicken shed door's burst open and the farmer shoots the young cock from the air.
"Goddamit that's the third gay rooster I've bought this month," cursed the farmer.

What's the definition of jumping to a conclusion?
Forgetting your parachute.

What's blue and sings alone?
Dan Aykroyd.

THE SEX-MAD ROOSTER

A farmer was having trouble getting his chickens to lay eggs so he brought in a rooster who had a reputation as a ledgendary cocksman. The rooster got to work right away and soon there were eggs all over the place. His job done, the rooster went after the ducks and the sheep. The farmer started to worry about the bird for fear that he would burn himself out or even pop his clogs. He said to the bird, "Calm down, calm down," and cut down on his feed. This was all to no avail and the rooster continued his randy ways and started after the pigs and calves as well. One morning the farmer found the cock lying on the flat of it's back, stiff as a board, with it's legs in the air, with it's eyes shut... apparently dead of exhaustion. When the farmer started to scold the corpse the rooster opened one eye and said, "Sshh! You see those buzzards up there?"

Mummy, mummy, what's atomic mutation mean?
Stop sucking your ear and I'll tell you.

Why does your washing machine think it's funny?
It keeps taking the piss out of your underpants.

SHAKY SCALPEL COULD SPELL DISASTER

There was a seventy-five year old "MOHEL" (that's the person who performs ritual circumcisions at Jewish ceremonies) who found to his horror that his hands were starting to shake quite badly. Obviously, in his line of work, that was a serious liability and he dashed off to see if he could get some sort of insurance policy.
A couple of weeks later his broker rang him and said, "Listen, I've got some good news and some bad news."
"Give it to me," said the Mohel.
"Well, the good news is that I can get you cover against being sued for up to two million pounds for a premium of only two hundred pounds a year," said the broker.
Wiping his forehead with relief the Mohel asked, "So what's the bad news?"
"There's a two-inch excess," said the broker.

How can you tell an Italian plane?
It's the one with hair underneath it's wings.

What do you get if you cross a lemming with a rhino?
Empty beaches.

What do you give a holiday rep when you start dating her?
A full medical.

What do you call the Russian snooker champion?
Inoff the Red.

PADDY AIN'T STUPID

The site foreman decides to test Paddy's building knowledge and asks him, "What's the difference between girder and joist?" Paddy replies, "Arr!... that's a tricky one sir... I have often pondered on that one, as have many of the great literary critics of the twentieth century... My own personal compulsion is to rate the gentle humour and empathy of Joyce's Ulysses above the dour yet compelling realism of Goethe's Faust... err... Would you be wanting any more bags of dust sir?"

I was in a gang in school called the Secret Seven.
Boy, we were good!
I never did find out who the other six were!

SIX-FOOT RABBIT PIGS-OUT

A six-foot tall rabbit goes into his local pub and says, "I'll have my usual please, a pint of bitter and a hot cheese toastie," and the rabbit proceeds to down both drink and food with gusto.
"I'll have another bitter and a hot cheese toastie," said the rabbit again.
"I'm sorry sir," said the landlord, "but we're right out of cheese now... How about a ham and pickle toastie instead?"
"I normally only eat the cheese ones... errr... oh alright then," replied the rabbit hesitantly.
The rabbit soon gulped down the beer and the food and being a very gluttonous rabbit he soon found himself saying, "Another bitter and a hot ham and pickle toastie please, landlord."
"I'm sorry sir, I'm right out of ham... I can do you a lovely hot curried lamb toastie?" said the landlord.
"Err... I ... hmm... oh go on then," said the rabbit.
The rabbit continued to pig out for the rest of the evening.
A few days later the landlord was walking along the road when he came across the rabbit who was looking none too well. The rabbit had pus oozing from both ears, big clumps of fur had

fallen out of his coat, he was shivering all over and had gone completely blind.
"Good heavens, what's wrong with you?" asked the landlord.
The rabbit moaned, "Ooohhh... I think I've mixedupmetoasties."

What is it that sparrows can do with difficulty, ostriches with ease, and everyone wishes British Telecom would do?
Take their bills and stuff them up their ars**.

How did ʻ s ear?
Answerinʻ

DON'T SHOOT! DON'T SHOOT!

A man is walking along the streets of Belfast when a man comes up to him and puts a gun to his head and asks him what religion he is. The threatened man thinks, "If I tell him I'm a Catholic he could be Protestant... if I tell him I'm a Protestant he could be Catholic," so he blurts out, "I'm Jewish, I'm Jewish."
The man with the gun exclaims, "A Jew in the middle of Belfast... I must be the luckiest Shi-ite in the whole of the world!!"

"To do is to be" ... Jean-Paul Sartre.
"To be is to do" ... Socrates.
"Be do be do be do" ... Cleo Laine (or Frank Sinatra).

TWO IMAGINARY FRIENDS

A man goes into a pub and although he's on his own he orders three pints of beer and then downs them one after the other. Again he orders three pints of beer and proceeds to drink them all on his own. This continues for a third time, when curiosity gets the better of the landlord and he asks the man why he always orders three pints when he's on his own.
The man replies, "Well, I used to have two really good mates

and we always went drinking together... the three of us were inseparable. Anyway, one moved up north and the other moved down south but I still always order a pint for each of them for sentimental reasons."
The man becomes a regular at the pub and always orders the beers three at a time when one day he walks up to the bar and orders only two pints of beer. The landlord looks confused and says, "Only two beers?... I hope there's nothing wrong with one of your two mates?"
"No they're both fine. I'm not having one for myself because I've gone on the wagon," the man replied.

What do video games and Penthouse have in common?
They both improve hand-to-eye coordination.

Why can't you be a Morris Dancer if you've been circumcised?
Because you have to be a complete pr**k to be a Morris Dancer.

BRUTUS GOES OFF HIS TROLLEY

Brutus returns home from yet another successful crusade killing Christians, and the Roman parliament decides to increase his personal tally of war medals from 35 to 40. On awarding Brutus the five medals Caesar explains that the medals have had to be made of chocolate as all the gold mines in the area are now exhausted.
"I will cherish them as much as the 35 that are made of solid gold," said Brutus as he knelt before his emperor.
Brutus worshipped his medals and every day he took them out to count them and polish them. That year there was a great famine and even then he could not bring himself to eat the five chocolate medals.
One day Brutus was counting his medals, "31... 32... 33... 34... 35..." and he ran to his wife and shook her violently,

screaming, "Did you eat my five chocolate medals? They're missing."
The wife denies it, but says she had seen Caesar sneaking out of the house earlier in the day. Brutus jumped into his chariot and flew across Rome to the senate whereupon he stormed in and on seeing Caesar drew his knife and stabbed him. With his dying breath Caesar uttered the now immortal words, "Et tu, Brutus."
To which Brutus screamed, "You bloody liar! You ate five!"

Did you hear about the Eskimo girl who spent the night with her boyfriend and woke up the next morning to find she was six months pregnant.

What do Estate Agents use for birth control?
Their personalities.

"Any more moaning about radiation levels and you'll be out on all four of your ears."

UNFAIR TREATMENT

A class full of children were telling their teacher about their holidays. Jane said, "I went to the seaside and played in the sand."
"Can you spell sand, Jane?" asked the teacher.
"S-A-N-D," came the reply.
Peter said, "I swam in the sea."
"Can you spell sea?" asked the teacher again.
"S-E-A," said Peter.
"Very good Peter, and what did you do Winston?" asked the teacher.
"I got beaten up by a group of white guys, Miss," said Winston.
"Oh Winston... I am sorry... that's awful... that's what you call racial prejudice. Can you spell prejudice, Winston?" asked the teacher.

MONKEY GOES TO MOON

Ireland's finest scientist is sent on a NASA trip to the moon, accompanied by a monkey. Both man and beast were given brown envelopes containing instructions of what to do after having landed on the moon. After touchdown the monkey opened his envelope and it read, "Gather rock samples at one metre intervals up to a maximum depth of five metres, take seismographic readings every two hours and test hourly for atmospheric pressure and wind speeds."
The eminent Irish scientist opened his envelope and it read, "Feed the monkey."

How many blind people does it take to change a light bulb?
It depends whether the switch is on or off.

What did the drunk say to the priest at Confession?
Got any paper your side.

"She must be a feminist."

Where does Kylie go for a Kebab?
Jason's Donervan.

QUEENIE FORGIVES FARTERS

A Yank is attending a Royal banquet one night and he's seated within earshot of the Queen herself. During the course of the evening he hears the Queen let rip with a vicious fart and notices that the guy to the right of her immediately stands up and says, "Excuse me."

The Yank asks the man sitting next to him why the man to the Queen's right had stood up.

"It was to protect her Royal Highness from any embarrassment," came the reply.

A while later the Queen lets rip with another belter and the man to the Queen's left gets up, coughs, and mutters, "Excuse me," and the Queen nods and he sits down.

A short while later the Queen lets rip with another belter and the man behind her immediately jumps up. Red faced, he coughs and mutters, "Please excuse me." The Queen nods at him and he sits down.

A short while later Her Royal Highness lets rip with yet another one and the Yank jumps up and shouts out, "You guys stay in your chairs, have this one on me!"

A man walks into the doctor's room. The doctor looks up and notices a frog growing out of the front of the man's forehead and shouts out in amazement, "My good God what is that?" The frog replies, "Don't ask me, it started off as a boil on my bum this morning."

What do you do if a bird shits on your windscreen?
Never take her out again.

GENIE GRANTS ONE WISH

An Englishman, Scotsman and Irishman have been marooned on a desert island for twenty long years when one day a genie pops out from a bottle washed up on the beach and he grants them one wish each. The Englishman says, "Please transport me back to the green fields of England, to pretty English girls and English beer," ... and poof... and he was gone.
The Scotsman says, "Please take me back to the bonnie mountains of Scotland so I can hear the bagpipes again and taste great whisky,"... and poof... he disappeared.
The Irishman thought for a while before saying... "It's going to be awful lonely here on my own... Could I have my two mates back?"

What do you call a woodpecker with no beak?
A headbanger.

Why do males who work for the DHSS have thin willies?
Because they are tight-fisted w**kers.

Two men are passing each other in the street in the Bronx, New York.
1st man: "Yo! Motherf***er! What's happening?"
2nd man: "Morning Reverend."

PADDY GETS ENGLISH ACCENT

Paddy had been digging up the roads of England for almost twenty years but his accent was still as heavy as ever and he hated having the mickey taken out of it by his English work-mates so he decides to visit a speech therapist...

"Be Jeysus I'm bloody well fed up wit them eejits toiking de mickey out of me," said Paddy to the therapist.

The therapist replied, "I'm sorry to have to tell you that if you really want to get rid of your accent and sound like the perfect English gentleman it's going to take an awful lot of time and money."

Paddy doesn't hesitate before giving his response... "Oy've been digging up de roads for de last twenty years and saved ten towsand tounds, so I have... So here, be Jeysus, take de whole bloody lot just make me soind loik de English gentry foik."

After three long years the therapist says, "Go now... I never thought I'd ever say it but your accent is perfect now."

Paddy can't wait to try out his new accent and he runs straight out of the therapist's office and into the shop next door where he says to the man behind the counter, "My good man, would you be so kind as to pass me a copy of Country Life and the Horse and Hounds."

The man behind the counter looks at him with a knowing half-smile and says, "You're Irish aren't you?"

Clearly upset but trying not to show it Paddy says, "My good man what on earth could make you think that?"

"Because this is a fish and chip shop!" came the reply.

Did you hear about the Iranian whose wife went missing? He was unable to give the police a full description.

Paddy is standing in a rape identity parade lineout when into the room walks a tearful woman with two police officers. Paddy immediately steps forward and says, "Be Jeysus! Dat's her, I swear it!"

PADDY'S ENTRANCE EXAM

Paddy calls in on a building site looking for work and as it happens the foreman needs a labourer. The foreman, noticing that the applicant is Irish, decides to give Paddy a simple test and he says, "Paddy I'm looking for someone who can add a bit. If I gave you one rabbit then I gave you another rabbit how many rabbits would you have?"
"Err... three?" replied Paddy.
"No, no, no... look if I gave you two rabbits and then later on gave you another two rabbits how many rabbits would you have?" asked the foreman.
"Err... err... oyd have foive??" replied Paddy.
"No no... are you stupid?... Look, I give you three rabbits then I give you another two rabbits so how many have you got now?" continued the foreman impatiently.
"Hmm... err... err... six rabbits sir," said Paddy.
"I'm sorry I can't give you the job, good day," said the highly irritated foreman. Paddy then starts to plead with him causing the foreman to continue, "Look, if I gave you one rabbit and then another rabbit you'd then have two bloody rabbits wouldn't you!!"
Paddy replied, "But I already have one rabbit at home sir."

Paddy is involved in the local pub quiz and is asked, "Can you complete the title of this well known song... Old McDonald had a ... ?"
Paddy's eyes light up, "Be Jeysus it's... is it FARM sir?
"Correct," said the questionmaster, "and can you spell FARM?"
"Be Jeysus any cod would know dat!" triumphed Paddy, "E I E I O!"

What's the difference between an Irish wedding and an Irish wake?
One less drunk!

Did you hear about the Irish gynaecologist who used two fingers?
He wanted a second opinion!

Why did eighteen Irishmen get together to go to the same movie?
Because they had seen the notice UNDER EIGHTEEN NOT ADMITTED!

What do you call a stork who brings Irish babies?
A dope peddler!

Paddy and Seamus are coming in to land in their new private light aircraft. The landing is very rough with the plane screeching to a halt in the shortest possible distance after touching down. Paddy says to Seamus, "Be Jeysus... me heart was in me mowt... dat was a bloody short runway so it was."
"But look how bloody wide it is!" added Seamus.

Why did the Irish give up trying to climb Everest?
They ran out of scaffolding.

ONLY ONE LUXURY FOR 10 YEARS

An Englishman, an Irishman and a Scotsman are about to be incarcerated in the dungeons of the Tower of London for a ten year period during which time they must not have any contact with the world outside their cell. The gaolkeeper feels a bit sorry for them and says they can take one luxury or pleasure with them into their cell, in large supply, for the duration of their sentence.
The Scotsman chooses whisky, whisky and more whisky.
The Englishman chooses women, women and more women.
The Irishman chooses cigarettes, cigarettes and more cigarettes.
The three men are then sent to their respective cells and locked up.
Ten years later to the day the men are released. The Scotsman's cell door is opened first and out he staggers, blind drunk, singing and smelling of urine. There are empties everywhere. The Englishman's cell door is opened next and out he comes

looking tired but happy with an array of women and young children in tow.
The Irishman's cell door is opened and Paddy sticks his head round the door and asks, "Anybody got a light?"

How can you tell the bride at a scouse wedding?
She's the one wearing the white shell suit.

Why did Satellite TV not catch on in Athens?
They kept breaking the dishes.

THE MYSTERIOUS VOICE

A man by the name of Mark is trying to fall asleep late one night when he hears this voice saying, "Mark... mark... mark," so he gets up and looks out of the window but he can't see anyone so this really frightens him and he has trouble falling asleep. The next night he hears the voice saying, "Mark... mark... mark," again and he gets up to look out of the window but again can see no one out there.
The third night he again hears this voice saying, "Mark... mark... mark," so he dashes downstairs and out of the front door and sees a collie with a harelip going, "Mark, mark... mark."

What have Jeffrey Archer and William Shakespeare got in common?
Neither has written a decent book in the last 300 years.

How many policemen does it take to break an egg?
None. The egg fell down the stairs on it's own.

What's the definition of a kept woman?
One who wears a mink all day and fox all night.

QUEEN VISITS NUT-HOUSE

VG

The Queen is attending a large mental hospital to officially open a new wing when she somehow gets separated from the rest of her party and finds herself lost in a maze of endless corridors. She goes up to this man in a white coat and asks, "Excuse me, I'm the Queen, and I appear to have got myself lost. Could you tell me how I get back to the main reception area where the plaque is to be unveiled?"

"Certainly your Highness. Go down the end of this corridor and take the second right. Then go up the short flight of stairs signposted for the canteen. At the top of the stairs turn left and take the second on the right. Don't take the first on the right otherwise you'll end up in one of the top security wings where some of our more, err, shall we say unstable, patients reside. After taking the second right keep walking and you'll see a pair of large double doors in front of you. Go through them and you'll find a large gathering of dignatories waiting for you," replied the man helpfully.

"Thankyou for being so helpful doctor," said the Queen.

"Oh, I'm not one of the doctors here Madam, I'm one of the patients," said the man to a surprised Queen.

"Are you young man? Well you seem a perfectly normal young man to me," said the Queen.

"I am perfectly normal your Highness. I should never have been put in here in the first place. It was a case of mistaken identity," said the man.

The Queen and the man then have quite a long conversation and before parting the Queen says, "Goodbye Mr Skinner, nice meeting you. I don't think you should be in here either and I'll be having a word with the Home Secretary tomorrow about your case."

"Thankyou your Highness," said the man, and the Queen starts to walk down the corridor. A few seconds later a brick flies through the air and hits the Queen on the back of the head and the man shouts out, "You won't forget now, will you?"

"Father O'Riley, can I have a word?"

Did you hear about the dyslexic devil worshipper?
He sold his soul to Santa.

What's an Irish seven course meal?
A potato and a six pack.

Why do women parachutists always wear trousers?
Because they don't want to whistle on the way down.

TEN HELLS ANGELS

Ten Hells Angels go into this pub and their leader orders eleven pints of lager and the barman replies, "What do you want eleven pints for? There's only ten of you."
The leader leans over the bar and grabs the barman and hauls him over the bar and head butts him in the face and says, "If I say I want eleven pints of lager then I want eleven pints of lager, RIGHT!"
As blood pours down the barman's face he says, "Eleven pints coming right up sir. I'm sorry, I didn't mean to cause offence."
The bikers all get a lager each and their leader gives the spare pint to an old man sitting in the corner of the pub.
"Well, that's a very nice gesture," said the old man all pleased.
"That's okay," said the leader, "I don't mind doing things like that for a cripple."
"Oh, I'm not a cripple," said the old man.
"You will be if you don't get the next round in," said the leader.

A father bursts into his teenage sons bedroom and says, "If you carry on doing that to yourself you'll go blind!"
The lad replied, "Can't I at least carry on until I need glasses!"

What do you call two Tokyo sewer workers who have worked in the same sewer for twenty years yet never met?
Two nips passing in the shyte.

Chapter 4

Right Rude Jokes

I'VE JUST HAD MY WHATSIT'S LOPPED OFF!

A mongrel and an alsatian are sitting side by side in the vet's waiting room when the rather distraught mongrel turns to the alsatian and says, with tears in his eyes, "I've just had my whatsits cut off!"

"Cor, that's a bit tough," sympathized the alsatian, "Why did your owner decide to get you seen to?"

The mongrel replied, "Well, I was feeling randy and the cat lifted it's tail into the air and I ... I ... I couldn't help myself. I gave it a good seeing to! How about you? What are you in here for?"
"Well, my mistress came out of the bathroom with just a towel around her. I was feeling randy. She dropped the towel and as she bent over to pick it up I just couldn't help myself," mumbled the embarrassed alsation.
The mongrel perks up a bit as he says, "So you're here to have the same treatment as me then?"
"No, I'm here to get my nails clipped!" replied the alsatian.

Man to Chinese girlfriend: "Fancy a 69?"
Girl: "I'm not cooking at this time of the night."

THE TART AND THE WEIRDO

A customer asks a prostitute back to his flat for a session but when she gets there he has some unusual requests ...
"Would you please put on this anorak?" asked the man.

"Yeah, whatever you like, you're paying," replied the girl.
"And would you put on this pair of wellies for me and climb

under the shower and turn on the water," asked the man. The girl thinks to herself, "Bloody hell, I sure do pick em," but she decides to play along with him as he seems harmless enough.
"While you are in the shower could you reach out with one hand and keep switching the bathroom light on and off so as to simulate lightning?" asked the man.
"Okay," replied the girl.
"And with your other free hand can you keep banging this box so as to simulate the sound of thunder?" asked the man.
While the girl is doing all this the man just stands there watching her but not touching her.
After a while the girl starts to tire and she says, "Well come on then ... aren't you going to do anything?"
"What, in weather like this, YOU MUST BE JOKING!!!!!" exclaimed the man.

What do you give a Cannibal who is late for dinner?
The cold shoulder.

A poof goes into the butcher's and asks for a roll of salami. The butcher starts to cut the salami into small slices whereupon the poof exclaims, "Stop that ... what do you think my ar** is, a moneybox?"

VG

TAKE AWAY THE SLACK PLEASE!

The ageing film starlet who had slept with just about everyone who was anyone, was in her sixties when she turned up at her plastic surgeon's clinic and announced, "I want to be as tight between the legs as an eighteen year old virgin."
The surgeon asked the actress to strip off and lie back on the couch with her legs apart. He then bent down for a torchlight

inspection and exclaimed, "Oh my, it is big ... Oh my, it is big."
"I do wish you'd stop saying that," the actress shouted.
"But the second time was an echo! ... But the second time was an echo!" said the surgeon.
Anyway, the surgeon decides an operation is possible and it goes ahead ... As the ageing film star comes round from the anaesthetic she feels down below. She is well pleased. Also by the side of the bed is a large bunch of flowers and a card which reads, "Here's wishing you a speedy recovery ... and many thanks for the new pair of ears, regards Nicki Lauda."

What's the definition of balance?
A pregnant hunchback.

Why did the pervert cross the road?
Because his k**b was stuck in the chicken.

JC SAVES WOMAN OF THE NIGHT

A wh*** is being stoned on the main street in Jerusalem when Jesus steps out in front of the crowd of angry women and holds up his arms and says, "If there be any woman amongst you who is totally without sin then let her cast the first stone." The crowd falls silent. The women look down at the ground ashamed of themselves. The crowd has just started to disperse when all of a sudden a massive great boulder is thrown from the back of the crowd and it hits the wh*** right between the eyes and kills her stone dead!
Jesus turns round and says, "You know sometimes mother you really p*ss me off!"

What's pink and fluffy and has never moved?
The Mother Superior's clit****!

What have fat girls and mopeds got in common?
Both fun to ride until a friend sees you.

MAN SEDUCES GORILLA

A plane crashes onto a remote uninhabited tropical island and Bob and Ted are the only survivors.
After a short walk Bob cries out, "What are we going to do now? We're in the middle of nowhere!"
"Don't worry, I've been on a survival course," said Ted.
And sure enough Ted shows Bob how to make a home out of bamboo shoots and banana leaves, how to light a fire, how to trap and eat monkeys and pick and eat the right berries. He even shows him how to make an alcoholic drink from coconuts!

After a few weeks Bob says, "It's great here ... much better than home. We've got good food, loads of alcohol, no mortgages, continual sunshine and peace and quiet. There's just one thing missing ... SEX!!!"
"Don't worry, we covered that on the survival course as well. Apparently the genetalia of the female gorilla is practically identical to that of a woman's," replies Ted.
Next day the two men dig a hole and cover it with branches and within no time at all they have caught themselves a female gorilla. They proceed to tie it's arms and legs to stakes in the ground so that the gorilla is stretched out in a five of diamonds type position.
Ted says, "Go on then. You have first go."
Bob takes his clothes off and sidles up to the gorilla but before getting down to it he stops and complains, "Phorrr, it's a bit ugly isn't it? You couldn't put a bag over it's head could you?"
Ted obliges and Bob starts to do the business ...
"You know what?" says Bob, "This really isn't that bad."
In fact Bob is really starting to quite enjoy himself when one of the gorillas arms breaks free from it's tether and wraps itself around the man. Then the other arm breaks free and also wraps itself around the man who is now trapped in a giant bear hug.
Bob starts shouting, "Get it off ... get it off," whereupon Ted starts trying to wrestle with one of the giant arms.
"No, no," gasps Bob, "Get the bag off it's head I want to kiss it!"

What's the definition of gross?
Siamese twins joined at the mouth 

-ing sick.

What do you call three lesbians in a bed together?
A menois-a-twatt.

How do you know when you're getting a really good blow-job?
The bedsheets start to disappear up your backside.

WHY DAD, WHY?

A little Apache boy goes up to his father and asks, "Father, why is my sister called, 'Two white doves?' "
"Well son, at the very moment she was born I stepped out of the wigwam and saw two white doves flying over," replied the father.
"And father, why is my older brother called Running Bear?" asked the boy.
"Well son, at the very moment he was born I stepped out of the wigwam and saw a bear run right past me," replied the father before saying, "Why so many questions, 'Just trod in dog shit?' "

What's the definition of mass confusion?
Father's day on Merseyside.

What do you call natural dental floss?
Pubic hair.

TODGER GETS EXTENSION

A young man with a very small appendage goes to see a plastic surgeon about the problem. The surgeon tells him that there's only one way to increase the size successfully and that is to have a small section of a baby elephants trunk implanted. The young man agrees to the operation and after the operation he decides to celebrate with a romantic meal for two with an old flame. As he starts to explain why things will be better between them second time around his new appendage whips out from his trousers and rises above the table and grabs a roll.
"Wow, that's some party trick ... I'm impressed," says the girl who then asks, "Could you do that again?"
The young man winces before replying, "I'm not sure if my backside could stand another hard roll!"

What's the difference between the Red Arrows and the Italian National Flying Display Team?
Audience participation.

How many local authority councillors does it take to screw in a light bulb ?
44. One to do it and 43 to see how light bulbs are changed in the Bahamas.

LET MY DOG INTO THE PUB

Fred is having a drink in a pub while his dog is outside crying it's eyes out.
"Why can't my dog come inside?" Fred asked the barman.
"I'm sorry, but rules are rules. No dogs allowed," replied the barman.
Just then a blind man walks into the pub with his guide dog and the barman serves the man and passes no comment about his dog.
Fred sees all this and says to the barman, "He's got his dog in here, why can't I have mine?"
"That's different, he's blind," replies the barman.
Fred decides he can't bear to leave his dog yelping outside any longer and he leaves the pub.
When outside Fred puts on a pair of dark glasses and together with his dog he goes into the pub across the road.
As he goes up to the bar he half-stumbles into some chairs and then says to the barman, "A pint of lager please."
"Sorry, but dogs aren't allowed inside the pub," says the barman.
"Surely you'll let my dog stay," exclaims Fred, "I'm blind and Rover's my guide dog."
"He doesn't look much like a guide dog," sneered the barman.
"Why, what did they give me?" asked Fred quickly.
"Your dog's a Jack Russell," said the barman.
"The b*****ds," shouted Fred, "They told me Rover was a labrador."

What part of Popeye never rusts?
The part he always puts in Olive Oyl.

A little girl is wandering through the woods when she comes across a naked man who is standing crouched over with his head in his lap, with his hands on his head.
"Excuse me," says the little girl, "are you a goblin?"
"No, I've got a headache," came the reply.

I come from a place so small that the mayor and the village idiot are the very same person! ... and the local hooker is still a virgin!

PANIC ON BOEING 747

The captain of the Boeing 747 says over the intercom, "Please fasten your seat belts as we will be landing in New York in ten minutes. I hope you enjoyed your flight." He then forgets to switch off the intercom and the following conversation is heard by the whole plane ...
Co-pilot: "What's the first thing you're going to do when you land in New York?"
Captain: "The first thing I'm going to do is have a bloody good crap ... I've been dying to go for ages ... and then I'm going to give that gorgeous new blonde air stewardess a right seeing to!!"
The gorgeous blonde who is serving at the back of the plane goes bright red and starts to run to the cabin to warn the captain. Alas, she trips and falls in the aisle spreading coffee and coffee mugs everywhere.
As she picks herself off the floor a little old lady who is sitting by the aisle says, "There's no need to run dear ... he said he was going to have a crap first!"

Dublin swimming baths have announced that, due to the drought, three lanes of the pool will be closed.

Why do estate agents wear ties?
To stop their foreskins from crawling up their chins.

THE ABUSIVE REGULAR

A bloke runs into a pub one night and shouts out, "W****RS down that end of the pub and C**TS down that end," and then runs out again before anyone can approach him. This happens for three nights running and the regulars are starting to get upset so the landlord decides to be ready for him the next night.

Sure enough the next night the man runs into the pub and shouts out, "W****RS down that end of the pub and C**TS down that end of the pub."

This time the six foot six, seventeen stone, tatooed landlord has the door covered and he approaches the man, snarling, "Hoy mate! ... I'm not a C**T."

The man replies, "Well get down the other end with the W****RS then," before running out of a different door.

What do you call a New Zealander with more than four sheep?
A pimp.

3 WISHES

This coloured guy is walking along the road when he kicks a bottle in the road and the cork pops off and out comes a genie who grants him three wishes ... The guy thinks for a while before saying ... "I want to be white, uptight and out of sight, and surrounded by pussy," whereupon he was changed into a tampon!

And the MORAL: You don't get anything in this life for free unless there are strings attached!

What's the good thing about having sex doggy style?
It's a lot easier for the dog.

THE FRUSTRATED MONK

A man decides to become a monk and has been in the monastery for a couple of months when he goes to see the head monk wanting to leave ...

New monk: "I'm sorry Father but I feel I must leave this holy body ... everything is fine but ... I ... I'm finding it very difficult to abstain totally from ... you know what."

Head monk: "Don't worry my son ... others have suffered from the same problem before you and ... well their problems have been relieved by the barrel in the courtyard with the hole in the side of it ... Feel free to use the barrel on Sunday, Mondays, Tuesdays, Thursdays, Fridays and Saturdays."

New monk: "Terrrr.. riff.. icc ... excellent ... err ... what about, well, if Wednesday just happens to feel like the day ... eh, eh?"

Head monk: "My son please understand that if you are able to use the barrel on six days of the week then it is only fair that you should spend one day a week inside the barrel."

What does a New Zealander call a flock of sheep?
A leisure centre.

Why does Rupert the Bear wear yellow checked trousers?
Because he's a c***!

THE RANDY COUPLE

A hot blooded young couple were half-undressed and having a roll in the long grass when they are discovered by the local vicar who says, "Young man, save it until you are married and you will have God's blessing."
"Right you are Reverend," said the randy dim-witted lad as the couple ran off together.
A whole year had passed when the vicar stood in the aisle waiting to marry the very same couple he had caught a year earlier. One of the first to arrive was the groom who was labouring up the aisle with a full bucket in each hand.
"Ere Reverend, what do you want me to do with it now then?" said the groom.

An estate agent, a solicitor and a bank manager jump off a cliff together. Who hits the ground first?
Who cares.

What's blonde, got a 42 inch bust, wears six inch stillettos and lives in Rio-de-Janiero?
Salman Rushdie.

Did you hear the one about the guy who bought an inflatable doll in Beirut? ... He blew it up and it took him hostage.

THE OVERSEXED PATIENT

"Doctor you've got to help me ... every morning I wake up early and make love to the wife for an hour before going to work ... When I get into the office I'm hardly there a moment before I take my secretary into the store room for a session ... and then later it's the same treatment for two of the girls in the typing pool ...
When I get home me and the wife have a bit of a romp before dinner. Later, after the wife has gone to her evening class I'll go into the au pair's room to give her a service before having another session with the wife before lights out," said the worried young man.
"Well, what exactly is the problem?" asks the doctor.
"It hurts when I mast****te," replied the man.

What's the most popular choice of precaution before having sex with a female Russian shot putter?
Strapping a scaffold board across your backside so that you don't fall in!

What wears a yellow checked scarf and goes click, click, click?
Rupert the Geiger Muller Counter.

BROOMS HAVE A FUNNY EFFECT!

Back in Victorian times most kids started work much earlier and one such girl, Lucy, started work at the local broom factory on her twelth birthday.
At first Lucy settled in well to her job and seemed happy and contented with her daily task of putting the broom heads onto the broomsticks, monotonous as it was. However, as time went by Lucy seemed to become quieter and slightly troubled. Then one day she walked into the managers office and announced that she wanted to leave.
"Why do you want to leave Lucy, I thought you were getting on well with the job?" said the manager.
"It's ... it's a bit personal sir," the girl said shyly.
"Come now, you can tell me," he said putting a comforting arm round the girl.
"It's ... it's working with those broom bristles all day long sir ... They're having a funny effect on my body mee thinks ... mee thinks I'd better get away from them once and for all ... before mee whole body's covered in bristles ...," said the girl.
Suddenly realising what she was getting at the manager starts to laugh aloud and says, "Don't be silly girl everybody's got bristles down there," and he whips down his pants to show her whereupon she runs screaming from the building shouting, "Oh my God! ... It gets worse. He's started to grow a broom stick handle as well!"

What comes after 69?
A bloody good mouthwash.

What goes boing, boing, boing, bang!
Skippy the kangaroo in a minefield.

What's the Australian definition of foreplay?
Here sheepie sheepie.

THE MOST EMBARRASSING TV MOMENT EVER!!

Frank Bough, so the story goes, was presenting a programme called Nationwide many years ago and one particular day they had Fanny Craddock on, in the kitchen, showing the cameras how to make perfect doughnuts. After her stint is over Frank Bough, the linkman, looks the camera straight in the eye and says, "Now you too know how to make doughnuts look like Fanny's."

"Dad, what year exactly was it that you worked in Chernobyl?"

MY DAD'S GOT TWO OF THOSE

"My dad's got two of those," said the little boy as he watched his grandfather urinate in the gentlemen's toilets.
"I think you must be mistaken son," said his grandfather.
"Oh yes he has," came the reply, "a small one for weeing with and a great big purple one for cleaning the au-pair's teeth with."

THE JAPANESE STOWAWAY

When visiting London, a beautiful young oriental girl found herself completely out of money just as her visa expired. Unable to pay her passage back to Japan she was in a real fix until an enterprising sailor made her a sporting proposition ...
"My ship is sailing to Tokyo tomorrow, I'll smuggle you aboard, hide you in the hold and provide you with a mattress, blankets and food. All it will cost you is a little love," said the sailor.
The girl consented and early next day the sailor smuggled her on board the vessel. And twice a day thereafter he smuggled her a large tray of food below deck, took his pleasure with the young stowaway and departed.
The days turned into weeks and the weeks turned into months before the Captain noticed the young sailor carrying food below one evening and decided to follow him. After witnessing the unique piece of barter he waited until the sailor had departed and then confronted the girl, demanding an explanation. The poor girl broke down and told him the whole story in a flood of tears.
"Hmmm," thought the Captain, "A clever arrangement. I must say I admire the young man's ingenuity, however Miss, I feel I must tell you that this is the Woolwich ferry."

What's the difference between an old tart and a young tart?
One uses superglue and the other vaseline.

V ; in brownies?
B(

TERRIBLE WIND

A woman goes to her doctors and says, "Doctor, you've got to help me, I just can't stop farting when I walk. Look I'll show you."
The woman walks across the room and sure enough, "Prrh ... prrrhh ... pprrrrhhhupp."
"Hmm," says the doctor, "Try walking again with your buttocks clenched really tight."
The woman walks again but sure enough, "Prrh ... prhhh ... prrhh."
"Right," says the doctor, "Take all your clothes off and bend over and touch your toes." This the woman does.
The doctor reaches for a great big long pole with a hook on the end of it.
"Oh my God, you're not going to put that up my backside are you?" said the ashen faced woman.
"I'm going to open the window. It smells bloody terrible in here," said the doctor.

What do you get if you cross a Piranha fish with a hooker?
Your last blow job.

What do you call a bear without a paw?
Rupert the b*****d.

Why do hippos screw under water?
You try keeping a f***y that big wet!

What's the speed limit for sex?
68. At 69 you have to turn around.

POPE FACES TERRIBLE DILEMMA

VG

The Pope had been suffering from prostrate trouble for quite a while when suddenly the complaint became much more serious. The Vatican's best physician was called in to explain the seriousness of the situation to the Pontiff.
"You see, your Holiness," said the physician, "Your complaint is being caused by a very large build up of seminal fluid in your reproductive organs due to the fact that you have abstained from sex all your life. You must have sex to reduce the pressure or you will certainly die within months."
"But I can't do such a thing," moaned the Pope, "I've taken an oath to be celibate all my life ..."
The physician tells him again that he must take a woman, if only once, or he will surely die and gives him a couple of days to think about it.
For days the Pontiff agonises over what to do, his soul is truly troubled and tormented.
A few days later the physician calls round for an answer and the Pontiff says, "If it's the only way I can be saved then we must do what we have to do ... but only on these conditions. She must be a virgin. She must be catholic. She must be blind so she cannot see who I am and she must be dumb so that she cannot speak of what has happened to her."
The physician nods and heads for the door.
"And get one with bigs tits," added the Pontiff.

Why do gay men have moustaches?
To hide the stretch marks.

Why does the Pope wear underpants in the bath?
He can't bear to look down on the unemployed.

What's the difference between a dead dog and a dead estate agent?
There are skid marks in front of the dog.

What's a female cockerel called?
A c**terel.

Why don't Polish women like using vibrators?
They keep chipping their teeth.

What does an elephant use for a vibrator?
An epileptic pig.

A VERY, VERY BLEAK FUTURE

An egg, a tomato and a willy are sitting around having a moan about life.
"What have I got to look forward to," moaned the egg, "I'm just going to sit here for a few days until someone comes along and cracks my shell open and then pours me into a frying pan full of boiling fat."
"What about me," moaned the tomato, "What have I got to look forward to? Someone's going to come along and slice me up into loads of little bits and then rub salt into my wounds."
"At least it only happens to you guys once," moaned the willy, "Regular as clockwork I get a rubber bag put over my head, get shuvved into a dark damp hole and have my head banged against a wall until I throw up!"

What's the difference between a washing machine and your first girlfriend?
Dump your load in a washing machine and it won't follow you around for a week.

Who wears yellow checked dresses and gets wolf whistles?
Rupert the cross-dresser.

What's pink and hard?
A pig with a flick knife.

COR!!! WHAT A PAINFUL RIDE!!!

The Inter-City 125 is belting through Stevenage at about 120mph when someone pulls the communication cord. The driver screeches the train to a halt and people, suitcases, drinks and food go flying everywhere. The angry driver goes from one end of the train to the other but can't see any broken communication cords. Finally he notices that a toilet has been engaged for a long time and he knocks on the door and says, "Oy, you in there. Was it you who pulled the communication cord?"
"Y ... Yes it was," came the reply.
"Well you better have a bloody good reason, it's a £500 fine otherwise. We've got drinks all over the shop out here you know. Why did you pull it?" said the driver.
"It's my piles ... they're killing me," came the reply.
"Well I've got piles but I don't bloody well pull the communication cord just because they're annoying me a bit," said the driver indignantly.
"Yours weren't wrapped around one of the train's axles," came the reply.

What do you call a New Zealander with a sheep under each arm?
A bigamist.

"Stop exaggerating and wash it down the plug-hole dear."

Why do tampons have strings?
So you can floss after you eat.

What's the difference between a Skoda and a Jehovah's Witness?
You can shut the door on a Jehovah's Witness.

What do you call a Spanish wh*** who specialises in blow jobs?
A Senorita.

Why is Halley's comet so frustrated?
He only comes once every 75 years.

THREE ORIFICES

A woman goes to her doctor's and says, "Doctor you've got to help me, I've ... this is so embarrassing ... I've got more than one opening between my legs."
"Good heavens, that is unusual," says the doctor, "I'd better have a look. Can you take your clothes off and lie down on the couch please," and this the woman does to reveal three orifices all in a line.
"Hmm," says the doctor, "I'd better put a dressing on the left one and a dressing on the right one."
"Will that help doctor?" asks the girl.
"Well," replies the doctor, "It'll certainly stop you being f***** left, right and centre."

What's the definition of a Knightsbridge girl?
A girl who thinks cooking and f**king are two cities in China.

Maggie Thatcher once said of William Whitelaw, "Every Prime Minister should have a Willie."

RUDE JOHNNY STRIKES AGAIN

The teacher asks her class of six year olds if anyone can give her a word beginning with "A."
Rude Johnny shouts out "Ar** Miss ... AR**."
"Be quiet Johnny," says the teacher, "I didn't ask you."
Little Lucy's hand goes up and the teacher says, "Yes Lucy," and the girl answers, "Aeroplane."
"Very good Lucy. Now can anyone give me a word beginning with 'B?'" asks the teacher.
Rude Johnny shouts out, "B*****d Miss ... B*****D."
The flustered teacher tries to ignore the boy and asks Freddie who's put his hand up. The boy says, "Bicycle Miss."
"Very good Freddie. Now can anyone give me a word beginning with 'C?'" asked the teacher.
Rude Johnny shouts out, "C**t Miss ... C**T."
"Johnny, you mustn't say anything unless you put your hand up and I point to you," scolds the teacher and she points to Jane.

"Car Miss," answers Jane.
"Now can anyone give me a word beginning with 'D?'" asks the teacher, but no one's hand goes up apart from rude Johnny's. The teacher thinks to herself that there are no swear words beginning with "D" so she decides to point to Johnny.
The teacher was relieved to hear the answer, "Dwarf Miss" and she says, "Well done Johnny, well done!"
"Yeh," says Johnny, "A dwarf with a massive p***k and a hairy ar**."

What is a woman's belly button for?
Somewhere to leave your chewing gum in on the way down.

What is the similarity between the KGB and soixante neuf?
One slip of the tongue and you're in the sh*t.

What's the hardest part of a sex change operation?
Stuffing all the anchovies in.

Why do men like big tits and tight pussys?
Because they have big mouths and little willies.

THE PSYCHIATRIST

A prison psychiatrist is assessing a sex offender and he draws a circle and asks the man what it is.
"It's a naked woman," came the reply.
The psychiatrist then draws a triangle and asks the man what it is.
"It's a naked women sitting down," came the reply.
The psychiatrist then draws a square and asks the man what it is.
"It's a naked woman taking a shower," came the reply.
"Hmm," says the psychiatrist, "It's pretty obvious to me that you're obsessed with sex."
"It's you who keeps drawing the dirty pictures," came the reply.

Why was David Kennedy, son of Robert Kennedy, buried at sea? So Uncle Ted could drive to the funeral.

When does a blind parachutist know when to bend his knees? When his dog lead goes slack.

THE WORLD'S WORST PRISON CELLMATE!

A guy starts his prison sentence and the guards take an instant dislike to him so they decide to put him in the same cell as McTavver, a particularly fierce and fiery Scot. The man not only bats for both sides but is also one brick short of a full load. At over seventeen stone in weight and six foot eight inches in height he instilled abject terror, without exception, in all of the prison's other inmates. His last two cellmates had had to be transferred to the medical wing of the prison for major internal repairs.

For the first two days with his new cellmate McTavver teased the man with little half smiles and knowing looks and then on the third day the big beast asked the question that his cellmate had been dreading.

"Let's play a game. Do you want to play Doctors and Nurses or Mummies and Daddies?" asked McTavver.
As perspiration ran down the man's forehead he decides that it would be safer to opt for Mummies and Daddies and he says so.
"And do you want to be Mummy or Daddy?" asked McTavver.
The man, frozen with fear, decides that it would be safer to opt to be Daddy and he says so.
"Well come over here and suck Mummy's c**k then," growled McTavver.

Why don't scousers like blow jobs?
They're worried that it might interfere with their DHSS payments.

What's the difference between Lady Di and a two year old?
One sometimes chucks a Farley ...

COFFIN DODGER MARRIES 17-YEAR OLD

A seventy year old guy is going to marry a gorgeous seventeen year old virgin the next day when he is hit between the legs by a 90mph bouncer whilst playing cricket. The ball does serious damage to the man's wedding tackle just when he needs it most.

As he lays on the doctor's couch he moans, "Can you do anything to repair it so that I can use it tomorrow night?"

The doctor replies, "Your penis has suffered serious bruising and though you might be able to use it tomorrow night it mustn't get bent so I'm going to put a small wooden splint on either side of it and then bandage it up," and this he does.

After the wedding reception the next day the newly weds retire to their bedroom and start to disrobe.

The seventeen year old girl takes her bra off and says, "See these breasts, these are virgin breasts. No man has ever touched them before."

The girl takes her skirt off and rubs her backside and says, "See this backside, it's a virgin backside. No man has ever touched it before."

The girl takes her pants off and says, "See my f***y, it's a virgin f***y. No man has ever got to make use of it up till now."

The man then pulls down his pants and says, "This must be pretty new as well ... look, it's still in it's crate!"

Lawyer: "You're both ninety. Why did you wait so long before deciding to divorce?"
Husband: "We decided to wait until the kids were dead!"

What's the smelliest thing in the whole world?
An anchovies f***y.

THE FLAMINGO AND THE CAT

A man goes into a pub with a flamingo on his shoulder and a cat under his arm and orders a pint of Guinness for himself, a gin and tonic for the flamingo and a whisky for the cat. When the barman asks for the money he hears the cat say to the man, "Your round matey," so the man pays.

Another round of drinks are ordered a short while later and when he asks for the money the barman hears the cat say, "Your shout flamingo," so the flamingo pays.

Another round of drinks are soon ordered and when the barman asks for the money he hears the cat say, "I'm a bit brassic at the moment, if you pay for this one I'll owe you one and make it up to you later," so the man pays.

Anyway, the visit to the pub turns into a real heavy drinking session and the number of rounds ordered is soon in double figures but the cat still hasn't paid for a round having come out with excuses such as, "I'll see you alright later on," to, "I can't afford a round," to, "I've forgotten my wallet."

The landlord has watched the proceedings all night with great amusement, and curiosity gets the better of him and he enquires as to how the man came to get the flamingo and the cat. The man informs him that he had been visited by his fairy godmother the night before and that she had granted him one wish and that he'd asked for a bird with long legs and a tight pussy and that this was what he'd got!

Funeral director: "Would you like your mother-in-law buried, embalmed or cremated?"
Man: "All three please!"

What do elephants use for tampons?
Sheep.

SKINHEAD SPOUTS POETRY

A teacher asks her classroom full of kids to try to make up a rhyme which incorporates the word, "Timbuctoo," and she gives the kids thirty minutes to do it in.

"Right children, your thirty minutes are up, who's got a rhyme for me?" says the teacher.

The skinhead at the back puts his hand up but the teacher ignores the foul mouthed yob and asks Jenny and Jenny recites:

"As I was walking down the strand,
I saw three ships not far from land,
The hull was red, the deck was blue,
And they were sailing to Timbuctoo."

"Very good Jenny," enthused the teacher, "Now can someone else tell me their rhyme."

Only the skinhead at the back puts his hand up and the teacher decides, somewhat reluctantly, to let him have a go and he recites:

"Me and Tim went down to Kent,
We saw three girls in a tent,
We had nothing else to do,
So I f****d one and Tim f****d two."

What do you call a dinosaur who loves meat vindaloos?
Megasoreass.

I could tell my parents hated me.
My bath toys were a toaster and a radio.

What's the worst thing about sh**ging a cow?
Every time you want to kiss her you've got to get off the bucket and walk round the front.

What's the definition of indefinitely?
When your balls are bouncing off her ar** that's when you're in-definitely!

PRIEST IS HUNG LIKE A DONKEY!

A priest decides that he must get laid just once to see what it is that he's missing out on so he goes to Soho and pops into a brothel. A price is agreed and the priest is told to take all his clothes off and this he does whereupon the girl sees that he's hung like a donkey and she says, "No way mister. I'm sorry but with a weapon like that you could inflict some serious damage, I've got my career to think of," and the priest is shown the door.

Determined to get his end away he goes into the brothel next door and a price is agreed and he's told to take his clothes off and this he does whereupon the girl sees his mammoth python and says, "I'm sorry but there's no way that thing is coming anywhere near me, you could do me some serious damage," and again the priest is shown the door.

By now the priest is getting a bit fed up with being turned away so when he goes into a third brothel and agrees a price he asks if he can have the lights turned off before he takes his clothes off because, being a man of the cloth, he's a bit embarrassed. The girl agrees and lies back naked on the bed looking up at the ceiling.

In total darkness the priest disrobes and climbs on top of her ready for action. The girl says, "Come on then don't be shy," and as the priest homes in on the target she continues, "Funny you being here as a punter ... when you came into the room with your dog collar on I thought you wanted to talk to me about JEEEEEEEEEEEEEEEEEEEEEEEEEEEEEEEEEEEEESUS CHRIST!!!!!"

What's the definition of being really drunk?

When you're lying face down on the floor and still have to hold on!

What's the similarity between a woman and a turd?
The older they are the easier it is to pick them up.

SATISFY NYMPHO OR DIE!

The King's only child was a beautiful young woman and a raving nympho to boot and no man seemed able to satisfy her needs so one day the King let it be known throughout his kingdom that all the young men of the kingdom were free to deflower his beautiful daughter and if one could satisfy her he would be allowed to marry her and one day become King. However, if they couldn't satisfy her they would be beheaded. So Robin goes along to try his luck and finds himself at the end of a long queue of young studs waiting outside the Princess's bed chambers. One by one the men go into the bedroom only for all of them to be carried out as bloodied headless corpses. This naturally scares the sh** out of Robin especially as he's very rapidly getting near the front of the queue.

Robin decides to slip out of the queue and shortly returns with something concealed up his jumper.

Robin's moment of truth arrives and he's ushered into the Princess's bedroom where the girl looks fresh and hungry despite just having been deflowered by over 400 young men. Robin explains that he's very shy and asks if it would be okay to have the lights turned off and the girl agrees. As the girl lies on the bed naked stretched out like the five of diamonds Robin brings out his concealed secret weapon ... a large green marrow, and he proceeds to use it on the girls erogoneous zone. The girl starts to moan and appears to be lapping it up. Robin thinks he's got it cracked and he can visualise the crown being placed on his head when the girl says, "Hmm, that's good, that's good ... I like a bit of fingering first!"

What's white and slides across the floor?
Come dancing.

Why were there more black US soldiers killed in Vietnam than white US soldiers?
Because when their corporal shouted at them to get down they all started dancing.

Two girls wake up in the morning after a really wild party and one moans, "Phorr, my mouth tastes like the inside of a birds cage."
"I'm not surprised," says the other girl, "you had a cockortwo in there last night."

"Darling, there's a couple of things that I feel I ought to tell you."

What's brown, got four legs and a c**t half-way up it's back?
A policehorse.

What's got eight legs, three heads and two wings?
A man on a horse holding a chicken.

I hear Archbishop Desmond Tu Tu is dead!
Dead? ..... I didn't even know he'd been arrested.

An innocent sixteen year old girl asks her mother on the eve of her wedding, "Mum, what are those two round things about 18 inches back from the tip of a man's willy called?"
The mother replied, "For your sake, I hope they're called buttocks!"

"Three million unemployed and you picked him!"

Chapter 5

Jokes for Male Chauvinist Pigs

THE SEX-CHANGE

This bloke called Fred from the tennis club had just had a sex change operation and within a day Freda, as Fred was now called, was running about playing tennis.
I said, "I'm amazed to see you running about so soon after the operation, I would have thought your groin area was really sore?"
"No it's okay down there," replied Freda, "but the top of my head is absolutely killing me. That's where I had my brain removed."

What's the difference between PMT and Mad Cow disease?
There isn't any.

Why does it take a woman with PMT over an hour to make the breakfast in the morning?
IT JUST DOES!!!!!!! OKAY!!!!!!!!!!

How do real men know when a woman has climaxed?
Who cares.

What's the difference between a woman with PMT and a Pit Bull Terrier?
Lipstick.

Why did God stop women from swimming in the sea?
He found he couldn't get the smell out of the fish.

Marriage has three rings:-
Engagement ring
Wedding ring
Suffering.

When do you realise that your girlfriend is starting to get fat?
When she sits on your face and you can't hear the stereo.

What do you call the useless piece of skin around the clit****?
A woman.

EXPOSED IN TESCO'S!

VG

Two girlfriends are sitting around bitching about how stingy their husbands are when one says to the other, "I've found a really good way of making my old man give me some more money. The other day we were shopping at Tesco's. I wasn't wearing any knickers and when I bent down to get some Frosties from the bottom shelf my pussy popped out. My husband was furious and wanted to know why I wasn't wearing any knickers. So I said, 'With the money you give me I've barely got enough for the housekeeping let alone buying myself clothes.' He then took out a fifty quid note and told me to get properly dressed."

"Wow, that's a great idea," said the other woman, "I think I'll give it a try."

The next day the friend comes back from the supermarket looking very depressed and she calls round to see her friend.

"What happened?" asked her friend.

"Well, we went out to the supermarket and I didn't wear any knickers, and I bent down to get something from the bottom shelf and my pussy popped out. My husband was furious and he said, 'Why aren't you wearing any knickers?' so I told him. The next thing I know he's putting a fifty pence piece in my hand. When I said to him that I couldn't buy a pair of knickers with that he said I was to buy a comb and tidy myself up!"

What's the difference between PMT and Rabies?
Rest periods.

What's the difference between PMT and the PLO?
With the PLO there is just a faint chance that you might be able to reason intelligently and rationally with them.

ADAM AND EVE PAY DEARLY! VG

Adam and Eve are in the garden of Eden and Eve is approached by the serpent and tempted to take an apple from the tree. She is too frightened to take a bite on her own so she goes over to Adam and tells him to take a bite.

Adam replies, "You know that God has forbidden us to eat any of the fruit from the garden. We've got all this beauty and luxury around us and only one condition to obey so, why don't you leave it be, eh?"

"If you don't take a bite out of this apple then I'll never sleep with you again," said Eve.

After further persuasion Adam takes a bite from the Apple and then so does Eve.

Immediately, God appears in the garden and he's looking seriously pissed off. He says, "I give you all this and in return I imposed only one condition and yet you both broke that condition. You both disgust me and you shall have to be punished. Adam, your punishment is that you are to be exiled from the garden of Eden for a life of hardship and toil. And as for you Eve, your sin was even greater because you were the temptress who made Adam bite the apple. Your punishment is that you must return to me all the blood that runs through your body!"

"You want all my blood?" shreiked a horrified Eve.

"Yes," said God.

"What, all of it? Right now?" shreiked Eve.

"No, you can pay in equal monthly instalments," said God.

What's the definition of eternity?
The time between when you come and when she leaves.

Why do women have periods?
Because they can't always have a headache.

GOOD FATHERLY ADVICE

Luigi is getting married in the morning and his father decides to give him some last minute advice on married life.
"Luigi my boy, when you getta married you gotta learn what to do with your fingers so your wife does what you want," said the father.
"Okay, papa, tell me what to do," said Luigi.
The father said, "Firstly your little finger. You use your hanky and your little finger to clean out your ears so they are clean when she wants to nibble them. The middle finger I'll come to later. You use your first finger when you wanna tell her off. You wag your finger at her and say bad girl, bad girl. You use your thumb when you wanna tell her you're pleased. You go, great dinner, and put your thumb in the air. Now about your middle finger. Say you make love to your wife once and she wants more, so you make love to her again and she still wants more and you make love to her a third time and she still wants more, and you justa can not do it any more ... you takka your middle finger."
"And I try to carry on with that, eh Papa?, eh?" interrupted Luigi.
His father continued, "You takka your middle finger and put it up to your temple and twist it and say, What are you crazy woman? Go to sleep!' "

How many women does it take to change a lightbulb?
Just one you sexist b*****d! . . . AND IT'S NOT FUNNY!!!
OR
Six . . . One to be elected spokeswoman and the other five to coax her into asking the nearest man to do it for them.

How do you stop a woman giving you a blow job?
Marry her.

PADDY ISN'T IMPRESSED

Paddy goes to the local brothel and says to Vera, "I don't mind paying but the girl's got to be tight."
Vera, on seeing the two fifty pound notes that Paddy is holding in his hand immediately says, "I'm the tightest girl in here tonight, come this way," and she leads him to her boudoir.
They both strip off and Paddy starts to do the business. However, after a short while he stops and goes over and opens the french windows. There he then stands, stark naked in front of the windows, with his hands on his hips. He then starts to thrust backwards and forwards.
"What on earth are you doing?" asked a confused Vera.
"Well this is just as tight," said Paddy, "and this way I get some fresh air as well!"

What's the difference between a woman and a jumbo jet?
A jumbo jet stops whining when you reach your holiday destination.

What do you call a newly divorced woman?
A born again c**ksucker.

What's the definition of a lesbian?
Just another damn woman trying to do a man's job.

What's the difference betw CENSORED having
You don't have to h ter you've CENSORED

What does WIFE stand for?
Washing, Ironing, F******, Etc.

Why did the woman cross the road?
Never mind that, what I want to know is why she wasn't in the kitchen!

How many men does it take to cook an Omelette?
None, it's a woman's job.

What do you do when the washing machine breaks down?
Slap her.

When does a husband realise for the first time that he's married a good for nothing, lazy so-and-so?
When he goes to pee in the sink and finds it full of dirty dishes.

A woman's place is in the wrong.

Why do women have legs?
Have you seen the mess snails make....
Or
So they can get from bedroom to kitchen.

Why do Sumo wrestlers shave their legs?
So that people can tell them from feminists.

What's the first thing you do after y 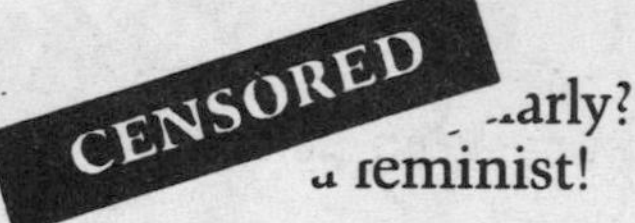

arly?
You give up trying to get a boyfriend ... feminist!

"Go easy on him...
This is his first post-mortem."

"Yes tonight, Reginald Adams, Battle of Britain flying ace, best-selling author, TV celebrity and sheep-sh**ger, This is your life."

Chapter 6

More Right Rude Jokes

Written above a warm-air hand drier at a Tory party conference: "Push button for one minute speech by John Smith."

What's the difference between a wh**e and a b**ch?
A wh**e sleeps with everyone. A b**ch sleeps with everyone except you!!

What do you call a Judge after he's upset a Rottweiler?
Justice Stumps.

Mummy, mummy, is it true that babies come out of the same place that boys put their willies into?
Yes dear.
Well, when I have a baby will it knock my teeth out?

What's the difference between an overtime bonus and a willy?
You can get your wife to blow your bonus.

What's the definition of an orgy?
A party where everyone comes.

Why did the cannibal return from his holiday with a wooden leg?
He went self-catering.

GIRL HAS 72 INCH CHEST

A man is a talent scout for a strip orientated night club. One night the scout rings the nightclub owner breathless with excitement and says, "I've got a great new act for your club. She'll really pull the punters in."
"Oh yeah," yawned the owner who'd heard it all before, "What's so special about her then?"
"Get this. She's got a 72" chest!" said the scout.
"Hmm ... interesting. What does she do? Is she a good singer, or a good dancer perhaps, or a comedian or juggler?"
"Naa, naa," said the scout, "she don't do none of that. She just crawls onto the stage and tries to stand up."

What does Norman Lamont get after five days of self abuse?
A weekend.

Why do women go out with men?
Vibrators can't mow the lawn.

What has 332 teeth and guards a monster?
My trouser fly.

BRIDEGROOM IS PASSIONLESS!

Young newlyweds are on the first night of their honeymoon and the wife is waiting expectantly in bed to be ravaged by her husband for the first time. But he comes out of the bathroom with his vest and pants on and climbs into his side of the bed and promptly falls asleep. The wife's a little bit peeved by this but she doesn't say anything.
The next night the wife is waiting expectantly in bed in her really sexy baby doll nightie and the husband comes out of the bathroom fully clothed. Without taking a stitch off he then climbs into his side of the bed and promptly falls asleep. The wife is more than a little bit peeved by this but she doesn't say anything.
The next night the wife is strutting about in her french lace bra

and suspenders trying to look her most alluring when her husband comes out of the bathroom and he's not only fully clothed but he's wearing fur boots, a woolly hat and a thick overcoat. He climbs into bed and is starting to nod off when his wife exclaims, "Do you know there's a hole between my legs!" The husband replies, "I wondered where that bloody draft was coming from."

Paddy and Sean are in bed together and Sean turns to Paddy and says, "I don't think much of this wife-swapping lark."

Did you hear about the dyslexic who was invited to a toga party?
He went as a goat.

THE PROUD FATHER

A little boy comes home from school one day and asks his father what a penis is, so the father immediately drops his trousers and with great pride says, "That my son is what you call a penis ... yes siree!, mmm ... mmmm. In actual fact that my son is what you would call the perfect penis."
The little boy then runs up the road to one of his little mates and gets out his willy and says, "Do you know what this is?" and when his mate shakes his head he continues, "This is a penis ... and according to my dad if it was a little bit smaller it would be the perfect penis."

Two stoned hippies are walking along a railway track.
1st hippy: "Hey man, this long staircase is freaking me out."
2nd hippy: "It's these low bannisters that get me down man."

What do you call a f***y that answers back?
An answering cervix.

I LOVE EGGS!

Dr Bertholtz, one of the world's leading sex psychologists, was sitting in his surgery waiting for the next problem case to walk through the door when in comes Mr Dennis.

"Take a seat Mr Dennis ... Now according to this letter of referral from your GP you appear to have a fetish for eggs," said the doctor.

"Well don't you like them doc?" said Mr Dennis as he brought an egg out of his pocket. He continued, "Look at the curvature on that ... Just feel the smoothness of that shell ... Just check out the firmness of the structure, no saggy bits there ... What a fantastic bit of fertilisation."

Dr Bertholtz is intrigued by his new patient and asks, "Do you really mean all that?"

"Of course not," whispered the man, "but you've got to say all that if you want the egg to go to bed with you!"

"You promised you wouldn't laugh."

TRENDY COUPLE WIFE-SWAP WITH MARTIANS! VG

A male and female Martian land in someones back garden and decide to explore. The couple whose garden it is are a little bit taken aback at first but eventually decide to invite the Martians inside for a drink. After a few drinks the couples decide to swap partners for the night and the woman and the male Martian go off together. Having made the beast with two backs the woman is extremely disappointed to notice that the Martian has only got two inches, at best. However, the Martian then tells the woman to twist his left ear and as she does she can feel him getting longer inside her. The Martian then tells her to twist his right ear and on doing this she can feel him getting wider inside her. By constantly twisting both his ears the woman has the most fantastic night of passion ever. Consequently, the next morning she literally has to crawl down the stairs and feels totally limp.
The husband asks, "How was your night?"
The wife replies, "It was maaaaaaarvellous! Sorry darling but it was the best sex I've ever had by a long way! And how was your night?"
"Bloody terrible!" cursed the husband, "All she did was lie there all night long like a sack of potatoes twisting my ears hour after hour!"

Doctor: "Your wife has acute angina."
Husband: "Yeah, and her tits aren't bad either!"

What do you call nuts on a wall?
Walnuts.
What do you call nuts on your chest?
Chestnuts.
What do you call nuts on your chin?
A blowjob!

Bill and Ben are the flowerpot men.
Bill says to Ben, "Blobablob-a-flob-a-loba etc etc."
Ben says to Bill, "If you really loved me you would swallow that."

VG

NATIONAL SPERM BANK GET DONATIONS

Three of the top brains in the country agree to a request from the government to make a donation to the national sperm bank for the good of the country and they arrive in the waiting room together. The first bloke goes into a cubicle and the nurse does her job.
As the first man leaves the cubicle the second one asks him, "How was it?" to which he replies, "Not bad."
The second guy went into the cubicle and the nurse did her stuff again. As he came out the first guy asks him, "How was it?" to which he replies, "Oh, alright."
Then it was the turn of the third guy and the other two decide to take a peek at the proceedings for a laugh. As they pull back the screen they can see that the nurse is on her knees with her mouth around the man's appendage. The other two are up in arms about this and push into the cubicle and ask, "How come you used your mouth on him when you only used your hands on us?"
"He's BUPA," replied the nurse.

Did you hear about the Irish prostitutes who picketed the "Do It Yourself" exhibition?

Why shouldn't you suck a twelve inch c**k?
You might get foot in mouth disease.

What's half a mile long and has a c*** at either end?
A police speed trap.

VICAR MEETS A TALKING FROG!

The vicar was taking his Saturday afternoon stroll through the woods when he came across a pond where lots of fish and reptiles were swimming about very contentedly. However, there was one large frog who was looking very sorry for himself and the vicar said out loud to himself, "Oh poor old frog ... What's the matter with you then ... It's a shame you can't talk and then you would be able to tell me what was the matter with you and I might be able to help you."

"But I can talk," said the frog and it continued, "I am very sad because I used to be a choir boy but I upset a wicked witch and she turned me into a frog. The only way I can revoke this curse is if someone takes me home, looks after me and lets me spend the night with them."

So the vicar being a very caring person and a man of the cloth who had dedicated his life to caring for others said he would take the frog home and care for it and let it spend the night in his bed. The very next day it turned out that the frog had indeed turned into a choir boy.

"And that, your Honour, is the case for the defence."

What are a test tube baby's first words?
My dad's a w**ker.

THE APPRENTICE CHEMIST

A young lad starts work in a chemist's as a counter assistant but unfortunately he is always getting very embarrassed about requests for items of a very personal nature. Such was the case when one day a woman came in and asked for a packet of tampons whereupon the man went bright red and dropped the

packet on the floor. Then, sweating profusely and with hands shaking, he made a mess of giving her her change and started stuttering. Consequently, the woman also got flustered and hurriedly left the shop. The shop manager noticed what had happened and said to the lad that in embarrassing situations it was sometimes better to make a joke of the whole thing as this could put people at their ease.
A couple of months later the same woman returns to the shop for the same item but on seeing the same assistant she loses her nerve and asks for some cotton wool instead.
"Ahar!" said the lad very loudly as everyone turned round to stare, "I see you're rolling your own this month then!"

A New Zealander on his driving test is asked if he can make a U-turn.
"Make her turn, I can make her eyes water," he replied.

A man goes to the doctor and says, "Doctor, will you take a look at this?" and he proceeds to undo his flies and pull out a massive weapon.
The doctor examines it very closely and after about ten minutes says, "I'm sorry, but I can't find anything wrong with it."
"I know," says the man, "It's a beaut isn't it?"

THE FEMALE MIDGET

A female midget went to her doctor with the complaint that her crotch was hurting her.
"When does the pain occur?" asked the doctor.
"When it's raining out, oddly enough," came the reply.
The doctor does a thorough examination and says, "Since I don't see anything amiss why don't you come in the next time it hurts?"
The very next rainy day the midget limped into his office and said, "Doctor, my crotch is killing me right now."
The doctor had her lie on a couch with her feet in the stirrups. He then covered her knees with a sheet and reached for some surgical scissors and began to snip away.

"That should do the trick," he said after a short while and the midget stood up.
As she got dressed and walked about a bit the woman exclaimed, "Doctor, the pain seems to have gone completely! How did you manage that?"
The doctor replied modestly, "Oh, I just cut an inch off the top of your wellingtons."

What do you do if a Rottweiler gets frisky and tries to mount your leg?
Fake an orgasm.

What do Pit Bull terriers and two inch willies have in common?
No on wants to f**k with them.

How do you circumcise a whale?
Send down four skin divers.

What is 69 + 69?
Dinner for four.

What do you say to an Anteater who has just won the pools?
So why the long face?

GIRL MARRIES A GREEK

A widowed father was devoted to his only daughter and was naturally very concerned when she decided to not only get married but to marry a Greek. The father decided to have a little heart to heart with his daughter about the birds and the bees and about men, particularly Greek men. However, the girl shooed him away saying she knew all there was to know about those sort of things and that he was not to worry.
"Well remember just one thing," emphasized the father, "If he asks you to turn over, you don't have to."

The young couple were married and very happy until about six months had gone by. Embracing his wife in bed one night the Greek said, "Why don't you roll over dearest?"
"Oh no you don't!!" exclaimed the girl, "My father said if I don't want to roll over I don't have to."
"Whatsamatter! ... don't you want to get pregnant?" exclaimed the Greek.

How do you know when two elephants have made love in your backyard?
Your dustbin liner is missing.

What's the difference between a train and a man?
You can be sure a train won't come too early.

VG

WANTED: APE SH**GER!

In a remote part of the himalayas an incredibly vile looking beast is discovered. Because it has certain human characteristics and behaviour patterns but also seems quite ape-like, a group of scientists believe that they have found the Missing Link on man's evolutionary path from Ape to Human. In order to develop their theory they decide that a human being should mate with the ugly beast to see what characteristics the progeny would inherit. They put an advert in the local paper which reads: "£2,000 to mate with Ape."
The next day Sean rang up in response to the advert and said he'd be willing to take part in the experiment on three conditions and the scientists agree to hear him out.
Sean says, "Firstly, my wife must never find out.
Secondly, the children must be raised as Catholics.
And thirdly, if I can pay in instalments I'd definitely be interested."

Do you know what makes a gentleman in Greece?
He's a man who takes a girl out at least five times before he propositions her younger brother.

You can now buy records and tapes that teach you the art of oral sex . . .
They're made by a company called Cunnilinguaphone.

OPERATION GOES WRONG!

Paddy books into a private hospital for a penis enlargement operation and when he finally comes round from the anaesthetic he asks the doctor if everything went okay, not daring to reach down for a feel.
The doctor replies, "I've ... err ... got some bad news, some good news and err ... some bad news for you."
"By Jeysus, what's the bad news?" said Paddy, ashen faced.
"Well, err ... the surgeon sneezed violently at precisely the wrong moment and your penis ended up on the floor where one of the nurses slipped on it thereby rendering it unrepairable."
"Oh!! Holy Mother of God. .... Ohhh!" cried Paddy with tears in his eyes.
"Hold on," said the doctor, "The good news is that minutes after that unfortunate slip we managed to salvage a penis from a big strapping lad who had sadly just died in a motor bike accident and we performed a penis transplant."
"Oh ... ohhh, praise be to him up dere," rejoiced Paddy.
"Err ... the ... err other bit of bad news is that your hand rejected it!!" muttered the doctor.

Husband: "All my mates do it doggy style. Can we do it doggy style? Please luv."
Wife: "Oh, very well, if you insist, but on one condition ... You choose a street where no-one will recognise us!"

Gynaecologist: "My, it all looks very spic and span down there."
Lesbian woman: "Yeah, I know . . . I have a woman in twice a week!"

WOMAN'S THIGHS GET TATTOED!

Ever since she saw Butch Cassidy and the Sundance Kid for the first time this woman had had an obsession for both Paul Newman and Robert Redford and one day she decided to have the face of one of them tattooed on her right thigh and the face of the other tattooed on her left thigh. The tattooist agrees to do it but says that he's the best there is and it's going to cost. They agree a price and the tattooist goes about his task and after five hours finally sighs, "There ... perfect ... finished at last. Go and have a look in the mirror."
"It's nothing like either of them," roars the woman and she demands her money back.
"But it's the spitting image of both of them ... It's the best thing I've ever done!" says the man, "I'll go out onto the street and get a second opinion."
The tatooist drags a man in from the street who just happens to be a drunk. "Who are they then?" demands the tattooist.
The drunk sways and squints a bit before saying, "Err ... I'm not too sure about the one to the left nor the one on the right but the one in the middle is definitely Billy Connelly."

How c[...] parents punish him when he misbehav[...]

CENSORED

They [...] on all the doors.

Why did the British ships come back from the Falkland Islands full of sheep?
War Brides.

I WANT RESPECT!

A man who had obviously made a good contribution to the well-being of the village was moaning about the seeming lack of respect he was shown from his peers despite his efforts.
"See all those fishing boats down on the river ... I built every single one of them but do they call me Simon the Boatbuilder around here? ... THE HELL THEY DO!"
He continued, "And look at all the horses trotting up and down with perfect fitting horseshoes ... I made all those horse shoes ... but do they call me Simon the Blacksmith around here? ... THE HELL THEY DO!!!"
And he continued, "And look at all those houses built over there by the bridge ... I built all of those lovely houses myself ... but do they call me Simon the Housebuilder? ... THE HELL THEY DO!!! ... But just one, just one bloody sheep ..."

Do you believe in sex before you get married?
As long as it doesn't hold up the ceremony!

What does DNA stand for?
National Dyslexia Association.

SEX WITH SHEEP SURVEY

A team of eminent sociologists decide to investigate the phenomenon of man-sheep relationships in remote parts of the world.
In New Zealand they interview a sheep farmer who says, "There's no women around here. It's a two day ride to the nearest town and a man can get lonely so sometimes I slip the two hind legs of a sheep down my wellies and do the business

from behind, doggy style."

In Australia they interview a sheep farmer who says, "There's nothing but bloody sheep out here for 500 miles. No women and you can't catch the kangaroos so sometimes I trap a sheep up on the cliff edge and do the business doggy style ... With the sheep being on the cliff edge it pushes back real hard!"

In Wales they interview a boyo from the valleys who says, "Plenty of women round here boyo but they want you to buy them nice things see ... and say nice things to them see ... and I can't be bothered with all that nonsense see ... so when I'm feeling a bit frisky I just grab myself a sheep and lay it on it's back and do the business see."

The interviewer is a bit surprised at this and says, "It's very unusual to lay the sheep on it's back and assume the standard missionary position. Why don't you do what appears to be the norm and do it doggy style?"

The boyo looks aghast and says, "What and miss out on all the kissing!!"

Why is sex with a SAS man normally disappointing?
Because they are trained to slip in and out unnoticed.

What do you call a man with syphilis, herpes, AIDS and gonorrhea?
An incurable romantic.

VG

TERRIBLE, TERRIBLE NEWS

A woman goes to her doctor's complaining of feeling generally unwell, tired and dizzy. The doctor orders some tests and tells the woman to come back in a week.
A week later her husband turns up at the surgery and says, "I've come to pick up my wife's results doctor. I'm afraid she's not feeling well enough to come herself. The name is Mary Evans."
The doctor sifts through a pile of envelopes before saying, "I've got results for two different Mary Evans here so I'll open both envelopes." Having opened and read both letters the doctor says, "Your wife has either got Alzheimers disease or VD!"
"Oh God! This is terrible news ... b. but which one?" exclaimed the husband, "What shall I do doctor?"
The doctor replied, "Take your wife on a bus trip, then catch a train, then have a walk and then put her on another bus. If she manages to find her way home on her own then don't f*** her!!"

What's the difference between Cosmopolitan and Woman's Own magazines?
One teaches you how to fake an orgasm and the other teaches you how to knit one.

What's got four legs and an arm?
A Rottweiler coming back from a stroll in the park.

KINKY SEX GAMES

A just married couple were spending their wedding night with the bride's parents and that night the bride's father, a dirty old lecher, decided to have a peek into the newlyweds bedroom to see how things were going. He saw the bride and groom in opposite corners of the room, completely naked, with their legs spread apart. The bride had a pile of hoops beside her and the groom a pile of marbles.

Suddenly the bride picked up a hoop and threw it across the room and it landed over the man's erect penis with deadly accuracy.

"One nil," shouted the bride with glee.

Straight away the groom picked up a marble and rolled it along the floor straight between the legs of his wife.

"One all!" said the man triumphantly.

The bride's father was impressed by the fun they were having.

The next day the mother was preparing the shopping list and she asked the father if there was anything that he wanted to add.

A sly grin crept across his face as he said, "Can you get a bag of spuds and a packet of polo's!"

SWIMMING POOL SHOCKER

Swimming club manager: "I'm afraid I'm going to have to ban you. There have been complaints about you urinating in the water."

Essex girl: "Leave it out mate. Everyone does that!"

Manager: "Not from the top diving board they don't!"

Why do Aussies call Castlemaine XXXX?
Because they can't spell beer.

A LACK OF CLASS

A boy asks a girl if he can go back to her place after a night out. She replies, "Well alright, but be very quiet because my dad's very strict and he doesn't like me bringing boys back late at night."
Later, at her place, they engage in a heavy kissing session on the lounge sofa before the boy says, "Can I use the loo?"
The girl replies, "Use the sink downstairs, if you go upstairs you'll wake my dad and he'll have a fit."
The boy disappears into the kitchen and is gone quite a while.
"What kept you?" the girl enquired on the boys return.
"I had trouble finding some paper!" replied the boy.

Did you hear about the man who changed his dogs name to NIREX?
Because it started burying it's sh*t in other people's gardens.

The Kiwi's have discovered two new uses for sheep.
Eating them and shearing them!

What's worse than your doctor telling you you've got VD?
Your dentist.

Have you heard about the male contraceptive pill?
You take it the morning after and it changes your blood group.

MY MUM'S A STRIPPER!!!

A primary school teacher is teaching a group of six year olds and she is asking the children if their mothers have gone back to work and what is it that they do.
Little Anthony stands up and says proudly, "My mum's a nurse. She makes ill people well again."
Little Johnny stands up and proudly says, "My mum's a vet Miss. She makes people's pets a lot better Miss."

"Now Terry, what does your mother do?" asked the teacher.
"She's a stripper Miss," replied Terry bluntly.
The teacher was shocked and embarrassed by this and quickly changed the subject. Later that night she called round to Terry's house and confronted his mother. Having told her what was said in class she demanded an explanation.
Terry's mother replied rather dejectedly, "Well, actually I'm a politician, but how do you explain a thing like that to a six year old?"

Mummy, mummy, can I keep the goldfish I won at the school fete?
No you can't. And take it out of your knickers before you start to smell like your big sister.

"Don't sit in that chair Edna, it just isn't safe."

What's worse than having a dead cat on your piano?
A rancid pussy on your organ.

What's the difference between a woman and a fridge?
A fridge doesn't fart when you take the meat out.

SHIP-WRECKED MAN COPES

A man has been marooned on a remote island on his own since childhood when one day a beautiful woman is also shipwrecked on the same island. They start talking and after a while the woman asks him, "How do you cope when you're feeling more than a little bit randy?"
"Ah ... see that tree over there," said the man, "There's a hole three feet up the trunk which is just the right size to gratify me. That's how I've managed to cope without women all these years."
At this the woman takes all her clothes off and says, "Well how about some of the real thing?"
The man definitely isn't going to refuse an offer like that and he strips off and runs up to the woman, who is lying on her back in the sand, and kicks her viciously between the legs. The poor woman doubles up in agony and eventually cries out, "What did you do that for?"
"Just checking for squirrels," came the reply.

Mummy, mummy, can I play in my doll's house today?
Don't be silly darling. You know I've let it to six art students.

What's the human bronco?
That's CENSORED apon i CENSORED nd then sa ot AID y in for as long as possible!

DISGUSTING!

What's the definition of disgusting?
You're sitting on grandad's lap and you can feel that he's getting a hard on.

What's even more disgusting?
You kiss him goodbye and he slips you his tongue.

What's even more disgusting still?
You're a boy.

What's even more disgusting still?
You slip your tongue back.

LOTS OF WEIRD DRINKS

A man goes into his local and confides to the barman that he's out celebrating his very first blow job. He orders a Martini and quickly downs it.
"Same again?" enquires the landlord.
"No, this time I'll have a Pernod and blackcurrant," replied the man.
Very shortly afterwards the barman says, "Same again?"
"Err ... no ... I'll have a rum and peppermint this time," came the reply.
"You really are celebrating ... she must be quite a girl," said the landlord.
The customer quickly gets legless downing a whisky and ginger, an Ouzo and lemonade, and a double gin and lime in quick succession.
"You really are celebrating, haa, herrr," said the landlord.
"I must have had every weird drink going tonight and I still can't get the taste out of my mouth," groaned the man.

Did you hear about the man who went to his doctor's with a mole on his willy?
He was reported to the RSPCA.

THE BROTHEL CARETAKER

A man saw an ideal job advertised in his local paper ... "Caretaker wanted for brothel." On application he learned the conditions; Free meals, pay at £200 per week, and his choice of woman every night.

Naturally he was thrilled when he got the job. At the end of the first day he went up to the owner and asked shyly for his woman. The owner recommended room 22, so he went in and found a gorgeous blonde reclining on a fur rug.

"Ready when you are," the man said gleefully, but the woman replied, "No can do, you'll have to satisfy yourself in the corner!"

The next night the man decided to pick room no. 7 as he'd heard that it contained a real goer! He walked in and found a beautiful brunette wearing nothing but a smile. The man undressed as fast as he could and said rather cheekily, "Ready when you are hot lips!!"

"No can do, tichy ... sorreeee! Go into the corner over there and abuse yourself instead," she said dismissively.

The same thing happened on the next two nights and the man was understandably a little bit cheesed off. He approached the owner and told him that the main reason he took the job was because of all the crumpet and that he was going to quit as none of the women would have him.

"Oh, didn't I tell you?" said the owner, "Thing's should be a bit better next week ... Here you have to work the first week in hand!"

Mummy, mummy, do Au Pairs have removable bottoms?
No dear, why?
Well, I've just heard daddy say he sc**wed the ar** off ours!

What's the Do It Yourself Herpes Test?
You tell her you've got Herpes and if she doesn't get up to leave, you do!

AFFAIR CAUSES THREE DEATHS

Three men arrive at the pearly gates of heaven at the same time and St. Peter comes out to register them in his book.
St. Peter asks the first man how he came to be there.
"Well," said the first man, "I got home from work early today and found my wife upstairs in bed. There was a bucket of champagne by the bed, the room smelt of after shave, and a cigar was still smoldering in the ashtray by the bed. I confronted the wife but she wouldn't admit to anything. The window was slightly open and this man was rushing along the pavement outside whilst trying to pull on his coat at the same time. In my rage I picked up the fridge and hurled it out of the window and had a heart attack at that very moment and died."
St. Peter turned to the second man and asked him the same question.
"Well," said the man, "I was rushing out of the house late for work when, believe it or not, a fridge fell out of the sky and killed me stone dead."
St. Peter turned to the third man and also asked him the same question.
"Well ... I was in this fridge ..."

Why do Scotsmen wear kilts?
So the sheep can't hear the zips.

What goes in and out when the doorbell rings?
Salman Rushdie's backside.

If Tarzan and Jane were Italian, what would Cheetah be?
The other woman.

WHO DESIGNED WOMAN?

Three students were in a pub solving the riddles of existence. The conversation turned to who had done the original designs for creating women.

"It must have been an architect," said the first student, "All those sweeping curves."

"It must have been an engineer," said the second student, "Women are extremely functional reproductive machines."

"Rubbish," said the third student, "It must have been a town planner ... Who else would put the recreation area in between the water works and the sewage disposal plant?"

"Nothing personal Mr Harris, but your CV shows that you're not the one for us."

Mummy, mummy, do I look pretty with pig-tails?
No! And don't show Uncle Peter because he works for the RSPCA!

What's the difference between Eddie Kidd and Cindy Crawford?
Eddie's got a cunning stunt ...

DARBY AND JOAN CLUB FLING

An old guy goes to a Darby and Joan club dance and he goes up to this rather rough old girl and says, "I fancy you."
As quick as a flash the old girl replies ,"I fancy you."
The old guy continues, "I'm bored with all this dancing lark so how's about coming back to my place for a bit of how's your father?"
"Oh, I should say so," replies the old girl enthusiastically.
The old pair get back to the old boys flat and he asks, "Well, what do you fancy?... How about a 69?"
"Oh yes please," replies the old girl so they both strip off and start the 69.
"Yeah, it was a shame about the Titanic wasn't it?" said the man.
"Err ... yeah," said the woman.
"They said it was unsinkable when it was launched," continued the old boy.
"Err ... yeah," replied the woman.
"Doesn't bear thinking about does it," continued the man, "3,112 people drowned and 336 were children."
The old couple continue with the 69 and after it is all over they thank each other for the experience and agree to do it again sometime. The old boy shows the old girl to the door and just as she's leaving she enquires, "By the way, why did you start going on about the Titanic while we were doing the 69?"
"I read about the sinking on a bit of newspaper that was stuck to your backside and it brought it all back to me!" came the reply.

Mummy, mummy, I'm too hot with all these clothes on.
Shut up, the store detective might hear you!

What did Judas say to Jesus after the last supper?
Have a nice weekend.

THE GOLFING HIT-MAN

A man is having a round of golf with another man who he doesn't know that well and he enquires as to what his profession is. The man replies, "I'm a professional hitman, I charge £5,000 a bullet."
"No seriously, what do you do?" says the first man.
"I'm not joking, I'm a professional hitman. Look here's my high-powered rifle," says the man as he pulls his rifle out from his golf club bag. He gives the astonished man the rifle and starts to brag about it's capabilities, "With that laser eye sight on it I can see and hit a button on a man's shirt up to a mile away."
"Really? Well in that case I should be able to see the TV in my lounge from here," says the man as he spins down round to zoom in on his own house which is in the far off distance.
"I don't believe it," says the man as he looks at his own house, "My wife's topless in the bedroom and she hasn't even bothered to close the curtains ... and ... and ... THE B**CH!! There's a man in the room ... He's coming over to her ... He's kissing her ... They're both taking all their clothes off ... THE CHEATING B**CH!!! ... I WANT HER SHOT IN THE FACE SO NO MAN WILL EVER LOOK AT HER AGAIN ... AND ... AND ... YOU CAN BLOW HIS TODGER OFF!!"
"Are you sure, it's £5,000 a bullet. That's £10,000 and that's a lot of dosh!" says the hitman.
"I don't care about the money I just want both of them ruined," screamed the man.
"Okay," says the hitman as he put his gun up to his shoulder. He then looks through the sight. He steadies himself to fire the first shot and then pauses for a moment and turns to the man and says, "Do you want me to hold on for a second or two? I might be able to save you the cost of a bullet?"

Why do only women have piles?
When God created man he created the perfect ass****.

A guy says to his girlfriend, "Hey babe, I'd really like a little p***y."
She replies, "So would I, mine's as big as a house!"

What's the difference between a Dachshund dog and a market trader?
One bawls out his wares on the street....

VG

MAGGIE SEEKS MEDICAL HELP

Maggie goes into the doctor's and says, "Doctor are you sure we're not overdoing it with the Hormone Replacement Therapy treatment?"
"Why do you say that Margaret?" replied the doctor.
"Well doctor, I've started to grow hair around the base of my neck," said Maggie.
"Oh, that's nothing to worry about. A lot of women of your age get a bit of hair growing there," replied the doctor.
"But it's not just there doctor. I've got hair growing on my chest as well," said Maggie.
"I've seen chest hair on quite a few women of around your age before so I wouldn't worry too much," comforted the doctor.
"It doesn't stop there doctor. I've got hair on my belly as well," continued Maggie.
"Hmm," thought the doctor becoming more concerned, "How far down does this body hair continue?"
"All the way down to my bol***ks," replied Maggie.

What is 69 in Chinese?
Tu-chan-chew.

What do you do to a girl who says, "Give me twelve inches big boy and hurt me!"
Put it in twice and head butt her!

THE CHEEKY DOCTOR!

A woman goes to her doctor's suffering from a bad back and the doctor says, "Okay Mrs Jones, go over to that window over there and in the bright light let me see you stick your tongue out as far as possible and scrape the white coating of it as best you can." This the woman does.
"Well done," said the doctor, "Now can you please pull down your lower garments and bend over facing towards the centre of the room with your backside in the light of the window and put this thermometer up your rectum." This the woman does.
"Well done Mrs Jones," said the doctor, "You can get dressed now."
Mrs Jones pulls up her togs and then asks, "Well doctor, what's the verdict?"
"You've got a bad back Mrs Jones," replied the doctor.
"I knew that before I came here," said the aggrieved woman, "What was all that business about me bending over and the like?"
"Oh that ... I can't stand the bloody family that live opposite!" replied the doctor.

What's red, white and fluffy and sits in a tree?
A sanitary owl.

Chapter 7

All Time Classics

Why do French girls cut the strings off their tampons?
To stop the crabs from bungy jumping.

Did you hear about the two seater plane that crashed into an Irish graveyard?
Police recovered 512 bodies.

DON'T SIT IN THAT CHAIR!!

A man walks into the saloon and having got himself a drink he goes to sit in the only empty seat in the place whereupon the barman says, "You're new around these parts aren't you partner ... I wouldn't sit in that chair if I were you. That's Pedro Gonzales's chair."
"I don't care whose chair it is," says the man as he sits in the chair.
Immediately the whole saloon becomes silent and the pianist stops playing ... The barman continues, "You have never met Pedro Gonzales hombre ... Any man that had ever met Pedro Gonzales would never be so stupid as to sit in his chair."
"I don't give a damn about Pedro Gonzales ... Shut-up and get me another drink," said the man.
"I beg you meester to get out of the chair of Pedro Gonzales for the sake of your wife and children ... He will be coming here

soon. If you had ever met Pedro Gonzales you would never sit in his chair," warned the barman.
"Well that's where you are wrong," said the man, "I met him only this morning as I rode into town. He ambushed me and took all my money. He then decided to have some fun with me and told me at gunpoint to drop my trousers ... so I dropped my trousers. He then told me to have a sh** there and then or he would kill me ... so I had a sh**. He then told me to eat my sh** or he would kill me, so I had to eat my own sh**. But then, HAA HAA HERRRRRRR, I knocked the gun out of his hand and picked it up and the tables were turned. So I asked him, ever so nicely, to drop his trousers and he dropped his trousers. I then asked him to have a sh** and he had a sh**. Then I asked him to eat his own sh** and after a little persuading he ate his own sh**. So you see you are wrong!! Not only have I met Pedro Gonzales but I have dined out with him as well!"

Did you hear the one about the retired gynaecologist? He did some part-time work to keep his hand in.

"I'm sorry, but we are a very poor country and we cannot afford electrodes for your testicles."

MAN SWALLOWS RAT!

VG

Brian walks into his regular pub closely followed by a newcomer to the area and as they both approach the bar together Brian hails the landlord for a drink.
"What'll it be Brian?" asked the landlord.
"Rat please," replied Brian.
"Half pint or pint?" asked the landlord.
"I'll have a pint please," replied Brian.
"Coming right up," said the landlord and he then put on a large leather gauntlet and reached into a cage below the bar and brought out a large brown struggling rat.
With a mighty swing he then smacked the rat's head down on the edge of the bar thereby concussing it . He placed it into a pint glass. Brian then downed it in one and looking refreshed said, "Bye heck I needed that."
"And what can I get you sir?" the landlord said to the newcomer.
The stranger, by now rather ashen-faced, replied, somewhat half-heartedly, "Err ... I'll have a Rat please."
"Pint or just a half?" asked the landlord.
"Err ... I'll just have a half for starters thanks," the stranger replied weakly.

"Coming right up, I'll get you a small one for that then," smiled the landlord as he reached under the bar and grabbed a small, scrawny, somewhat mangey specimen. With a mighty swing the landlord whacks the rat's head down onto the edge of the bar and pushes it into a half pint glass. However, the rat's back legs are still sticking out of the top of the glass and twitching slightly and push and prod as he does the landlord cannot get the whole of the rat into the glass. He then takes the rat out of the glass and bites it's head off, spitting the head into the slops tray where it floats about in a pool of lager. He then places the torso back in the glass and this time it fits neatly, tail and all. With blood spewing into the glass from the still twitching torso the landlord holds out the glass to the stranger. "I'm not drinking that," says the man looking rather upset, "It hasn't got a head on it!!"

Mummy, mummy, can I pick my nose?
Not yet dear. Wait until the burns have healed properly first, eh?

What do you do if you see an elephant coming down the road?
Swim for it.

GROWN MAN GETS BREAST-FED!!!!

Feeling rather ill a man consulted his doctor.
"I'm afraid to have to tell you Mr Wright that you have a very rare illness and the only known cure for it is plenty of fresh human breast milk," explained the doctor.
"Oh ... terrific," replied the man sarcastically, "Where am I

going to get that from? I'm not even married!"
"Look, I've got a pretty good idea of someone who might be able to help you ... Go to this address and say that I sent you ... There's an unmarried mother there who's just had a baby and who's a bit hard up and for a price she just might help you," said the doctor.
Because the condition is quite serious the chap decides to take the doctor's advice and calls round at the written address. The door is answered by a rather voluptuous young blonde who on being told the reason for his visit is at first shocked but then feels rather sorry for him. She decides to help and invites him in. After some polite conversation the woman pulls off her top and offers him a breast which he starts to suck readily. This in turn makes the young lady feel a bit turned on and she asks the man if there is anything else he would like, to which he replies, "No." After a while the man moves on to the other breast and sucks ... and sucks. This makes the woman feel extremely randy and she again asks if there is anything else he would like but he says, "No," and continues to suck.
By now, the woman is starting to wriggle and pant and pulls the man off her breast by his hair and looks him straight in the eye and says again, in her most alluring voice, "Are you sure there's nothing else you want?"
The man replied rather shyly, "Could I perhaps have a Farleys Rusk?"

Mummy, mummy, do we really have to drown all these lovely kittens?
Yes dear. Now stuff them tightly down your jumper and jump.

Did you year about the local flasher who was going to retire?
He decided to stick it out for another year.

What's the ultimate in trust?
Two gay cannibals having a 69.

POOR MAN ONLY HAS 3 STIFFIES LEFT

A man goes to his doctor complaining that he has been unable to get an erection for the last five years. The doctor tells him that it's a very serious condition and not much can be done apart from the administering of a new, voice activated, hormone secreting drug which, because of it's powerful side effects, can only be adminstered once. The doctor also explains that the pill will only give the man three very powerful erections and that that would be it then for the rest of his life.
"Only three more erections for the rest of my life! BLOODY HELL!" moaned the man. However, he soon thinks that it's better than nothing and agrees to take the pill saying, "I'll take it but what do you mean when you say it's a voice activated pill?"
"Well," explained the doctor, "To get the erection just say, 'BEEP BEEP,' and to loose the erection just say again, 'BEEP BEEP.' Do remember that you can only activate the pill three times and that's it, hasta luego nookie for the rest of your natural!"
The patient then swallows the pill and leaves the surgery. Finding this major advance in modern medicine hard to believe the man decides to test out the pill on the way home and shouts out, "BEEP BEEP," whereupon a rock hard python breaks through the front of his trousers for all of Chiswick High Street to see. Very embarrassed he immediately shouts out, "BEEP BEEP," and his appendage returns to it's resting state. The man starts to run for home where he knows his beautiful but rather frustrated wife is waiting for him. Running across a road he almost gets hit by a taxi which goes, "BEEP BEEP," and once again the massive rock hard crimson crusader breaches it's defences and shocks passers by.
"BEEP BEEP," shouts the man again and his weapon returns to its resting state again. He reaches home without further incident and fully aware that this will be his last session of love making ever he pulls his wife to the floor and tears her clothes off. With tears streaming down his face he cries, "I LOVE YOU, I LOVE, I'VE NEVER STOPPED LOVING YOU, BEEP BEEP."
"What's all this BEEP BEEP business?" his wife asked.

To a New Zealander, "Is that sheep for shearing?"
His reply, "You bloody well get your own!"

What do Bill Wyman and the tortoise have in common?
They both got there before the hare.

"Darling, I think we've caught that mouse at last."

An Irish couple are appearing on the ultra-raunchy satellite TV quiz called "The Newlyweds" and the compere asks, "Where was the weirdiest place you ever made, "WHOOPEE!"
The Irish girl replied confidently, "Got to be up the bum Bob!"

LITTLE BILLY GETS A RIDE

One day, little Billy comes home from kindergarten early. As he can't find his mother in the kitchen, or the lounge, he heads upstairs to check her bedroom.
He pushes open the door and sees his father, stripped naked, on top of his mother, also naked, both heavily into the act of lovemaking.
Not wanting to traumatize the boy, the parents continue as if nothing was wrong.
Billy watches and after a couple of minutes asks, "Daddy, can I climb on and have a horsie ride?"
"Of course son, we're a family," replies the father.
Billy climbs onto his fathers back and wraps his arms round his fathers neck.
The lovemaking continues and becomes more frantic.
Little Billy starts to whip his fathers backside with an imaginary whip and shout, "Faster dad, faster! Giddy up!"
Billy's mother starts to moan and writhe about really wildly.
"Hang on tight dad!" cries Billy as he grabs his fathers long beard tightly, "This is where me and the milkman usually fall off!"

Did you hear about the man caught eating fireworks?
The Judge let him off.

What's the bit of skin between a woman's f***y and ar** called?
A chin rest.

What do call an Anorexic sikh?
A cotton wool bud.

THE LONELY HEARTS CLUB MEETING

A man with one of his eyes made of wood isn't having much luck finding himself a woman so in desperation he decides to write off to the Lonely Heart's Club and about a week later, via the club, he receives a very nice letter and photo from a young lady. On studying the photo he sees that the girl is quite attractive apart from one slight peculiarity, that being that the corners of her lips run from top to bottom rather than from side to side. The man thinks to himself that he's got something wrong with him, ie. an eye made of wood and she's also got something wrong with her, ie. a vertical mouth, so he decides to write back. A week later they meet at Waterloo station, both wearing the mandatory red carnations and seem to get on well.

"Would you like to go for a meal Rose?" asked Malcolm.

"Oh Malcolm, yes please," she cooed.

A little later ...

"Would you like some more wine Rose?"

"Oh Malcolm, yes please," she cooed.

A little later ...

"Would you like a kiss Rose?"

"Oh Malcolm, yes please," she glowed.

A little later ...

"Would you like a cuddle Rose?"

"Oh ... oh Malcolm, yes please," she exuded.

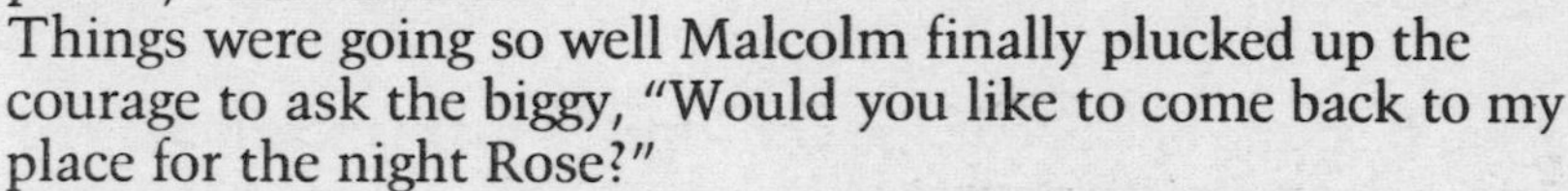

Things were going so well Malcolm finally plucked up the courage to ask the biggy, "Would you like to come back to my place for the night Rose?"

"Oh wouldn't I?" cried Rose.

"Who the bloody hell do you think you are calling me wooden eye .... C**t face!!" shouted Malcolm as he stormed off.

What did the queer rodent say to his mate as they walked past the gay bar?
Do you fancy going in and getting rat-arsed?

Did you hear about the man found drinking battery acid?
The police said they'd charge him in the morning.

PRINCE CAUGHT WITH TROUSERS DOWN!

One day Prince Juan is out for a stroll in the palace gardens when he feels a bit randy and pops into some bushes for some self abuse. A few moments later he hears a rustling in the bushes and out jumps a photographer who starts taking photos of him.
With his trousers round his ankles the Prince chases after him shouting, "I'll buy the camera for £200, please!"
"No way," replied the photographer.
"I'll give you £500 for it then," begged the Prince.
"No chance ... I can sell these photo's all round the world," laughed the photographer.
"I'll give you £5,000 then," pleaded the Prince.
"Sold!!" came the reply.
With monies exchanged the Prince then grabbed the camera and promptly ripped the film out.
The Prince then continues to stroll through the grounds and meets a friend who enquires, "Hey nice camera ... It's got all the extras ... How much did it cost?"
"£5,000," replies the Prince sheepishly.
"£5,000!!!" replies the friend increduously, "He must have seen you coming!!"

Did you hear the one about the constipated maths teacher?
He worked it out with a pencil.

What does Mr Kipling do in his spare time?
Fills tarts with fresh cream.

3 LUCKY WIVES

Three coloured women are sitting on the porch in deepest Louisiana discussing their respective husband's sexual potency.
"Hey, Mary Jo, does your old man have a special nickname?" asked Flo.
"Yep, he sure does," says Mary Jo, "I calls him Big Whoppa cos his tool am damn near on thirteen inches long may the Lord strike me down right now if I lie!"
"Wow," sigh the other two.
"What about you Flo?" asks Mary Jo, "What do you call your old man?"
"I call him Helmut ... cos his tool is like a baby's arm holding an orange, may the Lord strike me down right now if I lie," beamed Flo.
"Wow," sigh the other two.
"What about you Sue Ellen, what do you call your old man?" asked Mary Jo.
"I call him Drambuie," sighed Sue Ellen.
The other two are a bit puzzled at this and are quiet for a moment before Flo says, "Ain't that some sort of fancy liquor?"
"It sure is!! Yes sireee that's my boy!" sighs Sue Ellen.

Did you hear the one about the queer shepherd?
He kept mountain sheep.

What's the definition of a wom
The life support system o
CENSORED

Why was it lights-out in the nunnery at ten?
Because it was candles out at eleven.

YORKSHIREMEN SURE KNOW HOW TO CHARM THE GALS!

A Spaniard, a Frenchman and a Yorkshireman are talking in a bar. The conversation, as often happens, gets around to sex and the best ways of doing it.

"Si Senores," said the Spaniard, "The best way of making love is simple. Take a bottle of best Spanish sherry, pour it over your woman, massage it over her entire body, then make mad passionate love to her for at least an hour. When you finish she will be at least an inch off the bed."

"Aaah Oui Monsieur," responds the Frenchman, "but there is a better way. Get a bottle of finest Champagne, pour it over your woman, slowly lick it off, then make slow tender love to her all night. By the light of dawn she will be two inches off the bed."

"Nay lads," says the Yorkshireman, "if it's levitation yer after, us Yorky's have it licked. Go down your local at eight, down ten pints o'best bitter, then crash in through your front door about one in the morning. Throw up on the doormat, go upstairs, throw up again over yer gal's bed, get down on her for about twenty seconds top whack and then when you've finished wipe yer tool on the curtains and she'll hit the bloody roof!!"

Did you hear the one about the queer milkman?
He never left an empty behind.

Why does an Irishman wear two condoms?
To be sure, to be sure.

THE JAM-PACKED CAR PARK

A salesman couldn't help noticing the abundance of expensive looking cars in the car park of the motel he was booking into. As he was signing the register he asked the owner of the motel, a stunning blonde, who owned all the cars.

"As a matter of fact they all belong to me," she replied.

"You must be extremely rich," remarked the salesman.

"Not at all," replied the woman, "I won them all in bets with men who have stayed here. You see, I bet them that they can't do what my seven year old nephew Ian can do."

"But that's silly," exclaimed the salesman, "Any grown man can do what a kid can do."

"I'll bet my motel against your car that you can't," said the woman.

"Okay, I accept," said the salesman.

The woman called for her nephew.

"Right, Ian kiss me here," said the women to her nephew.

To the man's amazement she took out one of her breasts and the boy kissed it.

"Now it's your turn," she said to the salesman.

The man didn't need to be asked twice as the woman was incredibly gorgeous.

The woman then dropped her silk panties and told her nephew to kiss her erogenous zone. This the boy quickly did followed by a stunned but very keen salesman.

With this deed done the salesman thought he had won the bet saying, "I told you a man could do anything a little boy could do. Have you got the deeds to the motel handy, heh, heh?"

"Not so fast!" said the blonde, "there's one more thing. Ian ... bend your willy in half and ask the gentleman for his car keys."

Did you hear the one about the Irishman who was raking up leaves in his garden?

He fell out of the tree.

Why is dealing with the Inland Revenue like wearing a condom?
Because with both you get the feeling of safety and security while being scr**ed with no sensitivity at all.

EVERYONE'S PLAYING CRIB

A little boy goes into his parents bedroom and finds his parents doing the business! "What are you doing daddy?" enquires the boy.
"Err ... err ... I'm playing crib and mummy's my partner," replied his father, "Go and play downstairs."
The boy goes downstairs and finds his older brother doing the business with his girlfriend and enquires, "What are you doing?"
"I'm ... err ... I'm playing crib and Sally's my partner," replied his brother, "Now go outside and play in the garden will you."
The boy goes outside and wanders into the garden shed where his grandfather is abusing himself. "What are you doing?" enquires the boy.
"I ... er ... I'm playing crib ... ," said the old man.
"Oh yeah," said the boy suspiciously, "Where's your partner then?"
"With a hand like this you don't need a partner, now get lost!" growled the old man.

Mummy, mummy, the Au Pair is in bed with a strange man! ... HA! HA! APRIL FOOL! It's only daddy!

What do you call a real mate?
Someone who will go into town and get two blow jobs and come back and give you one.

Mummy, mummy, what's a werewolf?
Shut up kid! And go and comb your face.

PADDY HAS A 69!

Paddy gets out of prison having been in there all his adult life and decides it's about time he went with a woman so he picks up a prostitute and she takes him back to her place. She then says, "So what do you fancy?"
"I don't rightly know, oive never been wit a woman ... what is there?" asks Paddy.
"How about a sixty-nine?" asks the girl.
"What's dat?" asks Paddy.
"I'll show you," replies the girl.
So they take their clothes off and the girl's just getting down on Paddy's face when she farts.
"Oh, I am sorry," says the girl as she dashes off to the bathroom.
A while later she returns and she is just getting down on yer man when she again farts right in his face. Apologising profusely she again dashes off to the bathroom. When she returns to the room she sees Paddy has got dressed again and she says, "You're not going already are you?"
"I tink oy will," said Paddy, "To be honest wit you oy couldn't stand another 67 of dem."

What's the useless piece of skin attached to the penis called?
A man.

Mummy, mummy, why are we pushing the car over the cliff?
Shut up or you'll wake up daddy.

What do you call a prostitute with a runny nose?
Full.

What do you do if an Irishman throws a pin at you?
Run, he's probably got a grenade in his mouth.

What's a 68?
You go down on me and I'll owe you one.

What's the difference between 69 and a mugging?
At least with one you know the c*** who smacked you in the mouth.

ERIC, THE RUDE SKINHEAD

A teacher's got a classroom full of nine year olds and she wants to test their vocabulary so she says, "Can anyone give me a sentence which uses the word, 'definitely?' "
Four little hands go up and the teacher points to little Lucy.
"There are definitely seven days in a week," says Lucy.
"Well done Lucy," says the teacher, and she points to little Ronald.
"There are definitely twelve months in a year," says Ronald.
"Well done Ronald," says the teacher, and she points to little Louise.
"There are definitely ten years in a decade," says Louise.
"Well done Louise," says the teacher and she scans the classroom hoping to see another hand go up apart from the hand belonging to the rude little skinhead called Eric. Alas, no others do go up.
"Go on then Eric," says the teacher reluctantly.
"Have farts got lumps Miss?" says Eric.
"Err ... wha ... no they haven't," mumbled the teacher.
"Well, in that case Miss I've definitely just shit myself!" said Eric.

Mummy, mummy, how come sis gets to watch TV and I can't?
Shut up or I'll cut your ears off too!

What do bungee jumping and prostitutes have in common?
Both cost £55, both last 35 seconds and if the rubber breaks you're f**ked.

LABOURER DRIVES ROLLER

Wise boy Eddie parks outside a building site in his Rolls Royce and goes onto the site looking for work as a humble labourer. The site foreman asks, "Why the bloody hell do you want a job filling skips all day long when you can afford a car like that?" Eddie explains that he has no other qualifications and that labouring is all he can do and that he can only afford the car because he has proven to be a highly successful and skilful gambler. The foreman was rather envious of this smart ar** and didn't take to him that much but because he was short of labourers he told him to start work the next day.

The next day as Eddie arrives at work the first person he meets is the foreman and Eddie immediately says to him, "I'll bet you a fiver by five o'clock tonight you've had a rupture."

Now the foreman thinks to himself that this is a bet worth taking because he never did any lifting anyway and he was keen to take the smart ar** down a peg or two. So he accepts the bet and sleeps all day in his hut while Eddie goes off about his duties. At five o'clock the foreman rushes out of his hut and shouts gleefully, "Hey Eddie, you big mouthed plonker, you owe me a fiver."

Eddie came over and told the foreman that he would have to prove he hadn't ruptured himself before he paid out. Eddie asked him to drop his trousers and pants and this the smiling foreman did. Eddie then put his trowel under the foreman's testicles and asked him to cough. The foreman coughed and Eddie said, "Fair enough here's your fiver."

The foreman laughed at Eddie and sneered, "I thought you reckoned you made a lot of dosh out of gambling then."

Eddie replied, "You see those twelve men up on the scaffolding there ... Well I bet them all a tenner apiece that I'd have your goolies on the end of my trowel by the end of the day."

Mummy, mummy, why don't I have a big thing like daddy's between my legs?

You will when you're older dear.

What's the difference between a Scouser and Batman?
Batman can go without Robin.

THE COLONEL AND THE CAMEL

The new Colonel has just arrived at a foreign legion outpost in the middle of the desert and he immediately goes on a tour of inspection during which he comes across a camel tied up in a small shed.
"What's this camel kept here for?" asked the Colonel.
"That's for when ... err ... the men's carnal desires get the better of them sir," replied the Lieutenant.
"How disgusting! ... I won't tolerate that sort of thing in my platoon, take the camel outside and shoot it," ordered the Colonel.
After six long months in the hot womanless desert have gone by, the Colonel casually whispers to the Lieutenant one day, "That camel ... did you ever get round to shooting it?"
"Well ... err ... actually it's still in the same shed sir ... sorry sir," came the reply.
"Well, let's go and have another look at it, shall we?" said the Colonel, and they both go to the shed whereupon the Colonel drops his trousers, stands on a bucket and lifts the camels tail and proceeds to give it a vigorous seeing to.
Red-faced, breathless and sweaty the Colonel then turned to the Lieutenant and said, "Well? ... Is that how the men do it?"
"Actually, no sir," said the Lieutenant, "Usually the men ride the camel to the nearest brothel."

Did you hear about the world's leading gynaecologist?
He wallpapered his hallway by putting his hands through the letterbox.

What do you call The Three Degrees with a vibrator?
Wet, Wet, Wet.

DE KLERK SEEKS NELSON MANDELA IN HEAVEN

F.W. De Klerk dies and floats up to heaven where he meets St. Peter outside the pearly gates .....
De Klerk says, "Hello, I'm F.W. De Klerk. Can you tell me where I can find Nelson Mandela?"
St. Peter replies, "If you want Nelson you'll have to go up those stairs up onto a higher plane."

De Klerk goes up the stairs onto a higher plane and sees Mother Theresa and says, "Hello, I'm F.W. De Klerk. Can you tell me where I can find Nelson Mandela?"
Mother Theresa replies, "Oh! .... If you want Nelson you'll have to go up to a higher plane than this. Go up those stairs over there."

De Klerk goes up the stairs and sees Moses and says, "Hello, I'm F.W. De Klerk. Can you tell me where I can find Nelson Mandela?"
Moses replies, "If you want Nelson you'll have to go up those stairs over there, up onto a higher plane."
"Really?" comments De Klerk as he climbs yet another set of stairs. At the next level he sees Jesus and says, "Hello, I'm F.W. De Klerk. Can you tell me where I can find Nelson Mandela?"
Jesus replies, "If you want Nelson you'll have to climb up those stairs and keep going until you reach the very, very top."
"Really?" remarks a stunned De Klerk......
De Klerk finally makes it to the very top level and he goes into a room where he sees God sitting on a sofa, and he says, "Hello, I'm F.W. De Klerk. I want to speak with Nelson Mandela."
God replies, "Would you like to take a seat while you're waiting?"
"Thankyou," says De Klerk nervously.
God asks, "Would you like a cup of tea while you're waiting?"
"Yes please," replies De Klerk nervously.
"Two teas Nelson," bellows God at the top of his voice.

"That wasn't a very good start Mrs Evans."

PUNK ROCKER LUSTS AFTER NUN!

VG

Every morning a punk rocker and a beautiful nun get on the same bus. The punk rocker becomes infatuated with the nun and every journey he tries to chat her up but always gets the same response, "I have given over my mind and body to serving the Lord."

One day the bus driver whispers in the punk rocker's ear, "Look son, I can help you get your wicked way with the nun. Every night she prays in the graveyard of St. Michael's at 11 o'clock. If you were to catch her at a deeply spiritual moment your luck might change."

Later that night in the graveyard the hidden punk rocker sees the nun approach. She begins to pray, "Oh Lord, oh Lord, send me a sign, any message, and I shall obey your every wish."

Seizing his chance the punk rocker throws a sheet over himself and comes out moaning eerily, "I am a messenger from God. He has declared that via my body you shall give your body unto him in physical union."

"Your wish is my command my Lord ... but up the rear passage as it's the wrong time of the month my Lord!" said the nun as she bent over doggy style and lifted her cassock.

The punk rocker proceeds to s**g the nun senseless and when he is finished he triumphantly pulls off his ghostly sheet and, laughing hysterically, shouts, "Ahar! ... Punk Rocker!! ... Punk Rocker!!"

The nun pulls off her cassock and wig and shouts, "Ahar! ... Bus Driver!! ... Bus Driver!!"

Which fast food chain didn't do well in Tel Aviv?

Scud-u-like.

What do you call a New Zealander with a sheep under one arm and a goat under the other?
Bisexual.

LEARNING MONKEY LANGUAGE

A man gets a job at the zoo looking after the monkeys. He soon comes to notice that the monkeys are great imitators. He winks at a monkey and the monkey winks back. He jumps up and down and the monkey jumps up and down. He sticks out his tongue and the monkey sticks out it's tongue. He then scratches under his armpit and the monkey suddenly becomes very aggressive and jumps on the man and starts punching and scratching his face. Eventually the man escapes and goes off to see the head keeper to explain what's happened.
When he's listened to the story the head keeper says, "No wonder the monkey got upset, if you scratch underneath your arm it means F*** OFF in monkey language."
The badly cut and bruised man went home that night determined to get the monkey back.
The next day the man went into the monkey cage with a banana stuffed down the front of his trousers and a pair of scissors in his pocket. Once inside the cage the man went over to the same monkey and winked at it and the monkey winked back. He then jumped up and down and the monkey jumped up and down. He then stuck out his tongue and the monkey stuck out it's tongue. The man then took out his scissors and cut a hair off his chest whereupon the monkey took the scissors from the man and cut a hair off his own chest. The man then unzipped his trousers, exposed the banana and cut the end of it off ... and the monkey scratched under it's arm.

How can you tell if a Procrastinator is sadistic?
He likes to beat around the bush.

Did you hear about the gay smuggler?
He had a false bottom in his suitcase.

THE ONE-EYED LADY OF THE NIGHT

A guy picks up a prostitute and she takes him back to her place and says, "Okay, how do you want it?"
"Well actually," says the man, "I'm a bit perverted, is there anything you can offer me that I haven't done before?"
The girl says, "Well, I've got a glass eye. How about if I take it out of its socket and you can put it in there!"
"Yeah okay then," says the man enthusiastically, "I've never done that before." The man does the business and has a great time.
After it's all over the man says, "That was the best sex I've ever had, can I see you tomorrow?"
"Course you can, luv," said the girl.
"Where will I find you?" asked the man.
"I'll be on the street corner outside the Chinese take-away around eight o'clock," said the girl.
"I'll drive slowly past at about eight in a red Jaguar," said the man.
"I'll keep an eye out for you," said the girl.

Mummy, mummy, why is daddy zig-zagging across the lawn?
Shut up and pull the trigger.

How do you find the f***y on a really fat girl?
Roll her in flour and look for the damp patch.

3 DOUGHNUTS AND CREAM

Bob, Ted and Andy are walking around Soho at a loose end when they see a girl wearing a mini skirt up to her armpits and six inch stillettos so Bob asks, "Are you working?" and when she nods he continues, "Can you do anything for me, I've only got a tenner?"
The girl nods and she takes him down a dark alleyway and he reappears ten minutes later with a big smile on his face.
"What did she do for a tenner?" the other two eagerly enquire.
"She put a ring doughnut over my d**k and ate it off, it was great," beamed Bob.
Ted says, "Cor I fancy some of that," and turning to the girl he says, "What can you do for me, I've got twenty quid on me?"
The girl smiles knowingly and leads him down the dark alleyway and he reappears twenty minutes later with a look of sheer bliss on his face.
"What did she do to you for twenty quid?" the other two eagerly enquire.
"Oh, it was fantastic. She put two ring doughnuts over my d**k and then poured cream all over it and then she ate the doughnuts and licked the cream off. It was magic ... maaaagic!" exclaimed Ted.
Andy thinks to himself that he's got to have some of this and a sly grin comes over his face when he feels into his pocket and realises that he's got forty pounds on him and he says, "What can you do for forty?" The girl winks and leads him down the dark alleyway.
Andy returns after only a couple of minutes looking a bit downcast to say the least.
"You weren't gone very long. What happened?" asked Ted.
"Well," said Andy sadly, "she got it out and put three ring doughnuts over my d**k and then poured cream and raspberry sauce on top. She then sprinkled chopped almonds all over and stuck a cherry on the end of my k**b."
"Wow," said Bob.
"So how come you're back so soon?" said Ted.
"Well," muttered Andy dejectedly, "It looked so good I ate it myself."

What's a Russian woman and an ice hockey goal keeper got in common?
Both change their pads after three periods.

Did you hear the one about the Irishman who tried to iron his curtains?
He fell out of the window.

VG

A FATE WORSE THAN DEATH!!!

An Irishman, a Scotsman and an Englishman are on a jungle expedition in deepest Africa when they are captured by a tribe of savages.
The Chief comes up to the Irishman and says, "You got two choices. Death or Mahkumbha?"
The Irishman thinks nothing's worse than death so he chooses Mahkumbha whereupon he is stripped naked and tied over a fallen down tree trunk. Then all the men and the boys of the village are assembled. They all partake in drinking the milk of the Guava tree and then the wild beats of the bongo drums whip them all into a wild frenzy. Then every man and lad interferes with the Irishman madly.
The Irishman is eventually cut free and he crawls half dead into the jungle.
Then the Chief comes up to the Scotsman and says, "Death or Mahkumbha?"
The Scotsman replies, because he doesn't want to die, "Mahkumbha."
The Scot is stripped naked and tied over a fallen down tree trunk while all the men and lads of the village assemble. They all partake in the milk of the Guava tree and the wild beats of the bongo drums whip them all into a wild frenzy. They all then interfere with the Scot furiously. A while later the Scot is cut free and he crawls into the jungle barely alive.
A while later the Chief comes up to the Englishman and says, "Death or Mahkumbha?"

The Englishman says proudly, "I am Major Blenkington-Smythe of the fifth household cavalry and I am an Englishman. You can take away my life but you can't take away my dignity. I choose death!"
The Chief grunted, "Death by Mahkumbha!"

PUNK OF THE YEAR CONTEST

Adam, a punk rocker, is flicking through his local paper when he reads, "PUNK OF THE YEAR CONTEST, The Hammersmith Palais, Sat, 8pm," and he thinks, "I'll have some of thaaaaaaTT!"
So Adam finds himself on the Saturday in the Palais standing in a long row of punks up on the stage and the compere is going along the row interviewing each contestant in turn....

Brian has a metal stud through each nipple and green hair.
Eric has his hair sprayed orange and it stands 18 inches higher than his scalp and its been laquered with five coats of yacht varnish. He also has a giant safety pin through his nose and a toilet chain attached to each ear lobe.

The compere reaches Adam and says, "What's so special about you?"
Adam drops his trousers to reveal no less than six large safety pins running right through the middle of his willy!(Don't try this at home children!) The crowd gasp and scream and Adam eventually wins the contest to wild applause!
Two days later, almost inevitably, Adam has to go to see his doctor about his willy.
The doctor looks at the penis and asks, "Does it hurt?"
"Nah," replies Adam, "It's just that when I pee it comes out of all the holes and goes all over the shop mate."
The doctor starts to write on a bit of paper and says, "I want you to go and see this man."
"Is he a specialist mate?" asks Adam.
"Err..not exactly," replies the doctor, "He's a professional clarinet player, he'll show you how to hold it properly!"

Did you hear about the two queer Judges?
They tried each other on the bench.

Mummy, mummy, can I wear a bra now I'm fourteen?
No, Johnny.

What do you call a man with a one inch willy?
Justin.

THE SPECIAL HANDBAG

Hymie goes into see his old friend Moyshe who owns a Ladies' clothes and accessories shop and he says, "Moyshe, it's my wife and I's twentieth wedding anniversary tomorrow and I want to get her a nice handbag so show me what you've got."
Moyshe shows Hymie a very nice handbag for £25 but Hymie says, "It's not special enough for her, show me something more exclusive."

Moyshe shows Hymie a lovely crocodile skin handbag for £110. Hymie says, "It's nice but not nice enough. Show me something really special. I want something really exclusive that can't be bought from anywhere else."
Moyshe then takes Hymie to the storeroom out the back and he unlocks the safe and brings out a lovely but slightly wrinkled handbag and says, "Hymie, this is the most exclusive handbag I've ever had in over twenty years. The price is £1800 but to you £1600."
Hymie replies, "Moyshe, £1600 for just a handbag, on my life I ask you."
Moyshe responds, "This is no ordinary handbag Hymie, it's made of human foreskins ... rub it and you've got a suitcase Hymie."

Why is college like a woman?
You work real hard to get in, then nine months later you wish you'd never come.

VILLAGE IDIOT WANTS KIDS

The village idiot and his none too clever bride have been married for a couple of years and they want children but don't know how to go about getting them, so they go and see their doctor ...

The doctor says incredulously, "You've got to have intercourse first if you want to have children."

"Wot be that then?" said the idiot.

"You've got to give her a good seeing to," said the doctor.

"I can see her from here ... . wot you mean doctor," said the idiot.

"You've got to scr** your wife," said the increasingly agitated doctor.

"Scr** her to wot? Anyways I ain't got a screwdriver!" said the idiot.

"You've got to f*** her," exclaimed the doctor.

"How'd you mean?" said the idiot.

The doctor shook his head saying, "I don't believe this ... Look you've got to put your p***s up her v***na."

"What's that then?" said the idiot.

"This is a p***s," said the doctor as he lost his temper and dropped his pants, "and this is a v***na," continued the doctor as he removed the wife's underwear. "And this is intercourse," said the doctor as he mounted the wife and gave her a good seeing to.

After the doctor had finished the idiot asked, "How often does that have to be done to get a child then?"

"Three times a week should be enough," replied the doctor.

The idiot then turned to the wife and said, "I can give you a lift here at weekends but if you want to come during the week you'll have to catch the bus."

Mummy, mummy, why does grandma read the Bible so much?
She's cramming for her finals.

What do you do if a Leper rolls his eyes at you?
Roll 'em back.

COVER ME IN HAIR!

A teacher says to her class of seven year olds, "Now children, I want you to use your imaginations here. If you could have your skin covered with anything what would you chose?"
Little Simon's hand shot up and he said, "I'd like my skin to be covered with gold Miss."
"And why would you like to have your skin covered with gold Simon?" asked the teacher.
"Because if my skin was covered in gold Miss, then I could keep scratching some of it off and collect the gold flakes Miss, and eventually sell the gold I'd collected for a whole load of money and then I could buy a Mercedes car Miss," replied Simon.
"Well done Simon, that's a very imaginative and entrepreneurial answer. Anyone else?" said the teacher.
Little Brian's hand shot up and he said, "I'd like my body to be covered in platinum Miss."
"And why would you like your body to be covered in platinum Brian?" asked the teacher.
"Because platinum is even more valuable than gold Miss, and I could stratch bits of the platinum off my body Miss and collect it, and when I'd got a whole load of platinum Miss I could sell it and get a whole load of money Miss, and with that money I'd buy a Ferrari Miss," said Brian.
"That's a very good answer Brian, well done. Anyone else?" said the teacher.
Little Johnny's hand shot up and he said, "I'd like my body covered in pubic hair, Miss!!"
"Err ... wh ... what Johnny?" muttered the embarrassed teacher, "err ... Why would you want your body covered with p..p..p.. hair?"
"Well," said Johnny, "my big sister's only got a little patch of it on her body Miss, and you should see all the flash cars parked outside our house Miss!!"

Did you hear about the cross-eyed circumciser?
He got the sack.

What did the Leper say to the prostitute?
Keep the tip!

THE THIRSTY CROCODILE

An African walks into a bar with his pet crocodile on a lead and says to the barman, "I'll have a pint of lager for me and a Zulu for my crocodile please."
The barman nods and pours the man a lager and then throws a Zulu over the bar and the crocodile swallows him in one.
After the man has drunk his lager he again says to the barman, "I'll have a pint of lager for myself and a Zulu for my crocodile please," and the barman responds by pouring the man a lager and throwing a Zulu over the bar. The Zulu is again immediately swallowed in one snap of the greedy crocodile's jaws.
A while later the man again orders a lager and a Zulu for the crocodile but the barman replies, "I'm sorry sir, but I'm right out of Zulus."
"The crocodile won't like that," said the man.
"I tell you what sir, why don't I give him a pygmy instead?" the barman said helpfully.
"You don't want to do that," said the man shaking his head, "if he starts on the shorts I'll never get him out of here!"

Did you hear about the Hari-Krishna disciple who refused Novocain at the dentists?
He wanted to transcend dental medication.

Did you hear about the Leper colony against nuclear proliferation?
They have already disarmed.

VICAR IS ACE RABBIT CATCHER

VG

A gamekeeper is walking through the fields when he sees the local vicar bending over a rabbit hole. The vicar then puts his first finger into the hole for a moment and then takes it away. Then a rabbit pokes it's head out of the hole and the vicar hits the rabbit over the head with a hammer and puts it into a sack. The gamekeeper is amazed to see the vicar do exactly the same thing again over a different rabbit hole and he goes over to the vicar and asks him, "How d'you manage to make them rabbits pop their heads out of the hole then vicar?"

"It's easy my son. You just put your finger up between a woman's legs and then put the very same finger down a rabbit's hole. The smell is irresistible to rabbits and they can't stop themselves surfacing to see where the smell is coming from," said the vicar.

"F*** off vicar, you're pulling my leg," sneered the gamekeeper.

"No, I'm telling the truth my son. Why don't you try it yourself and see if it works?" said the vicar.

"I'm not falling for an old wives tale like that vicar," said the gamekeeper and he carried on on his way. However, as soon as the vicar was out of sight he made a dash for home, thinking to himself that he would have to try this theory out as soon as possible. He went into the kitchen of his own home and saw his wife down on all fours scrubbing the floor so he went up behind her and put his finger right up her crack!
His wife just carried on scrubbing the floor before saying casually, "Going rabbit catching again are we vicar?"

"Oh my God, we've had social workers!"

Did you hear about the leper who couldn't speak?
The cat got his tongue.

Woman to man, "Cor, you've got a small organ!"
Man to woman, "I've never played in a cathedral before!"

ATTEMPTED SUICIDE ON BRIGHTON PIER!

A little old lady is wheeling her wheelchair as fast as she can down Brighton pier and as she approaches him it becomes clear to a man fishing off the pier end that she fully intends going over the edge. The man stops her just in time and asks, "What's wrong?"

The toothless old dear has tears in her eyes and says, "I'm 80 years old and I've never been kissed."
The man looks at her crumpled up old face with it's soft white moustache, hollow cheeks and sunken gums and...and shuts his eyes and kisses her...JUST!!..and almost heaves when she slips him her tongue!
The old lady's face lights up and away she wheels as she hums a happy tune.
About an hour later the same man sees the same old lady in her wheelchair storming towards the end of the pier again at full speed, apparently determined to go off the end.
At the very last minute the man stops her and asks, "What's wrong now?"
With tears streaming down her gnarled-up old face she says, "I'm 80 years old and I've never been hugged."
The man manages to hug her....JUST!!!

The old lady's face positively beams as she wheels away humming a happy tune.
About an hour later the man catches a biggy..a real biggy. He is wrestling to wind in the reel when he sees the old girl in the wheelchair trundling towards the end of the pier yet again. The momentary distraction causes the man to loose not just the fish but also his rod to the sea. As she approaches the man she slows down and says, with tears streaming down her saggy jowls, "I'm 80 years old and I've never been f***ed!"
The man gently lifts the old girl from her wheelchair and she whispers excitedly, "Lie me down on the sand beneath the pier, it's almost dark and there's no one around."
The man nods and lifts up two loose planks from the pier's decking. He then drops the old girl onto the soft sand below.
"I've never been f***ed before," giggled the old girl as she twitched and wriggled excitedly in the sand.
"Well you are now," said the man, "The tide'll be in in fifteen minutes!" and he walked away.

Did you hear about the gay astronaut?
He went in search of Uranus.

Mummy, mummy, what makes children delinquent?
Shut up, pour yourself another drink and deal.

FANTASTIC NEW PUB IN CAMDEN!

Two Irish mates, Sean and Patrick, are having a few pints together when Sean says, "Hey Pat, have you heard about this great new pub in Camden? You buy one drink for yourself then they buy all your drinks for you for the rest of the night. Then when the pub closes they take you out into the beer garden and

provide you with sex all night long."
"Dat sounds loik a terrific noyt oyt," replies Pat, "but it sounds a bit too good to be true. Who's been telling you about dis place?"
"It's true enough," said Sean, "the whole thing happened to my sister just the other night."

A father bursts into his teenage son's bedroom and says, "If you carry on doing that you'll go blind!"
A voice from behind him replied, "I'm over here dad."

PADDY APPEARS ON QUIZ

Quizmaster: "In Greek mythology, who was half man and half beast?"
Paddy: "Buffalo Bill."
Quizmaster: "What's got five fingers and keeps your hand warm?"
Paddy: "Dunno."
Quizmaster: "A glove. What's got ten fingers and keeps both your hands warm?"
Paddy: "Err.. dunno."
Quizmaster. "A pair of gloves. Who is the Queen of England?"
Paddy: "Err..would it be three gloves?"

Mummy, mummy shall I tidy my bedroom?
Not yet darling. Let the loss adjuster see how we've smashed it to pieces first.

Doctor: "Big breaths," as he picks up his stethoscope.
Girl: "Yeth, and I'm only twelth."

Chapter 8

Even More Right Rude Jokes

Did you hear about the woman who married a bisexual?
She didn't know which way to turn.

Mummy, mummy, granny's fallen on the fire.
Well, don't poke her dear and she might last all day.

VERY RUDE PARENTS

A boy has been dating this girl for quite some time and they're getting along like a house on fire. The boy notices, however, that whenever he suggests meeting her parents she keeps putting it off.
"Don't you want me to meet your parents?" asked the boy one day.
"There's no rush is there?" replied the girl.
"You're not ashamed of me, are you?" asked the boy.
The girl decides to come clean and tells the boy that the opposite would be nearer the truth as her parents are not only deaf and dumb but a bit on the rough side. The boy still persists in wanting to meet her parents and the next day the boy and girl call round.
The couple walk into the house through the open door and see the mother sitting there with a bottle stuck up her f***y and the father sitting there with his balls hanging out and a matchstick supporting his left eyebrow.
"What's going on?" asked the boy incredulously.
"I think they're having a bit of an argument," said the girl, "Because she's saying, 'Get the beers in you c***,' and he's saying, " 'Bol***ks, I'm watching the match!' "

A guy is walking in the park with his dog and the dog keeps going off on his own and the guy keeps calling it back saying, "Herpes ... Herpes ... Herpes, here boy," but the dog largely ignores it's owner.
"Why do you call the dog Herpes, it's a strange name for a dog?" asked a nearby woman.
"Because he won't heel," came the irate reply.

THE OLD SEA DOG

An old sea captain comes into port after a very long stretch at sea and the first thing he does is find himself a prostitute and they agree a price and she takes him back to her place.
The old sea wolf starts to do the business and he thinks he's doing a grand job. After about thirty minutes on the job he asks the girl, "How'm I doing? I'm not going too fast for you, am I? How fast am I going?"
"You're doing about three knots," yawned the girl, "You're not in, you're not stiff and you're not getting your money back!"

BOIL ON BUM GETS SUCKED!!

Two men are in the pub and the conversation turns to boils. Ted says, "I've got a really big boil just below my ars***** and it's driving me mad. It's really painful, I haven't sat down for weeks now and it just gets bigger and bigger."
Harry replies, "Why don't you go and see Dr Pusucker and he'll suck the boil out for you? He's really good. He did a wonderful job on the one I had on the back of my neck."
Ted takes down the address and decides to go and see him the next night.
The next night he goes to Soho and goes into this really decrepit building and goes up four flights of stairs and goes into Dr Pusucker's surgery. The place smells, the wallpaper's hanging off the walls and a rat scurries across the floor. Dr Pusucker is a really gross individual who is bald, fat, toothless, and badly in need of a shower.
"You've come to have a boil removed then, have you? Let me have a look then," said Dr Pusucker.
Ted drops his pants to reveal a massive throbbing boil just

below his ars*****.
"Wow, what a beauty," marvelled the doctor, "I'll do this one for you half price. Bend over and grab on tightly to the table in front of you." This the man does while Doctor Pusucker reaches into a grubby bag containing rusting needles, puts a magnifying monocle over one eye and then puts his teeth in. The doctor then sat on the floor beneath Ted and started to suck like mad. Ted then felt a large fart coming and try as he did to hold it back he couldn't. He farted and then followed through with the previous nights curry thus covering the doctor's face with excretia.
An angry Doctor Pusucker jumped up and exclaimed, "My good God, some people make this job disgusting at times!"

Mummy, mummy, can I get pregnant?
Of course not dear, you're only eight.
Right lads, same again.

What do you call a girl with one leg slightly longer than the other?
Eileen.

What's got hundreds of balls and f***s rabbits?
A shotgun.

Mummy, mummy, do we have to have spaghetti again tonight?
Shut up moaning or I'll pull the veins out of your other leg.

How does your girlfriend like her eggs?
Unfertilised.

How do you know when your girlfriend is starting to get fat?
When she's sunbathing and the men from Greenpeace keep trying to drag her back into the sea.

MY BACKSIDE CAN SING SONGS!

VG

A drunken tramp walks into a bar and says to the barman, "If I can sing a song out of my backside will you give me a free drink?"

"Don't be silly you old soak, no one can do that," said the barman dismissively.

"Well I can. I worked for ten years with a travelling fairground. My singing ar** was one of the main attractions!" said the drunk.

The barman thinks to himself that if the old boy's telling the truth then he could certainly pull in the customers so he decides to let him have a go.

The drunk climbs onto the bar and pulls down his trousers and pants, and the pubs clientele are dumbstruck. He then squats down and ... and ... and a massive steaming turd is dumped onto the bar. Most of the customers get up and leave the pub in disgust and the barman grabs the drunk by the throat and screams, "You said you were going to sing a song but look at what you've done, you b******!"

"Get your hands off me. Sure doesn't even Jason Donavan have to clear his throat sometimes?" shouted the tramp indignantly.

Did you hear the one about the queer sparrow?
He flew upside down for a lark.

What's the difference between Delia Smith and a cross country runner?
One is a pant in the country ...

Mummy, mummy, what's an orgasm?
That's something your father has in the bedroom in thirty seconds and I have in the bathroom afterwards.

VG

TURDS ARE INTERESTING!

A young lad gets a job working down the sewers and he spends each day working alongside old Harry who's been working on the same stretch of sewer for the last forty years.
The young lad says on his fourth day down the sewer, "You must find it really boring working down here. Nothing much ever happens, does it? All you've got to look at are turds floating past your wellies all day long."
"Well I find turds interesting," retorted old Harry, "For instance, I can tell you what person each turd came from."
"I don't believe that," sneered the youth.
"Take that light coloured runny one over there that smells of curry. That belongs to Mr Patel who runs the Indian takeaway. And see that turd over there with wood shavings in it, that belongs to Mr Chippy, the carpenter. And that one over there belongs to Mr Baker because it's got bits of dough in it," said old Harry.
"Oh really," sneered the youth still not entirely convinced, "So who does this really massive turd coming along here belong to?"
"That one belongs to the wife," said old Harry without hesitation.
"How can you be so sure that's your wife's turd?" sneered the youth.
"Because it's got my sarnies tied to it," said old Harry.

Why do girls wear Jeans in winter?
To stop them getting chapped lips.

Why are turds pointed at the end?
To stop your ar** from closing with a bang.

Mummy, mummy, why can't we give Jenny's baby a proper funeral?
Shut up and keep pulling the chain.

Why do farts smell?
For the benefit of the deaf.

I'M FROM THE COUNCIL

This women is having an affair with this man, and they're in bed together when her husband comes home early from work and starts climbing the stairs.
"Quick," whispers the wife to her lover, "Get inside the wardrobe," and this the man does.
The husband goes into the bedroom and is immediately suspicious and he opens the wardrobe to be confronted by the wife's lover. The husband says, "And what are you doing in the wardrobe?"
"Err ... I ... I'm from the local authority. I'm one of the councils moth inspectors and catchers ... There's a lot of them about you know," says the lover as he starts to swot imaginary moths with his hands.
"If you're the council moth catcher then how come you've got no bloody clothes on!" said the husband menacingly.
The lover looks down at his naked body with an amazed expression on his face and shouts, "The B*****DS!!!"

What's got a hazelnut in every bite?
Squirrel's shit.

What's the difference between kinky and perverted?
Kinky is when you use a feather to arouse your lover and perverted is when you use the whole chicken.

A load of Chelsea fans go into a pub and get p*ssed out of their skulls. One of them starts to argue with another one about who's got the biggest d**k and before you know it they've decided to have a "Biggest Willy" contest right there in the pub! They all get their weapons out and rest them on the table just as two gay guys walk into the pub.
One gay says to the other, "Oooh look, there's a buffet."

THE OLDEST HOOKER IN TOWN

An elderly couple have fallen on really hard times and they are at a loss to know where the next bit of money is coming from. They're so desperate for money that one day the old girl says, "Darling, I think I'll try going on the game for a while."
But the husband replies, "No wife of mine is going on the game. I know, we'll sell the sofa." So they sell the sofa.
Two weeks later, when the money from the sofa has been spent the husband looks at his arthritis ridden, decrepit wife with tears in his eyes and says, "Sorry love, but you're going to have to go on the game."
So the old girl puts her teeth in and borrows a boob tube, leggings and six inch platforms from her grandaughter and out she goes into the cold night air ...
She eventually returns just as dawn breaks looking half dead and bedraggled.
"How much did you earn love?" asked the old boy.
The old girl rummages through her pockets and answers, "£180. 50."
"Who was the b****** who gave you the fifty pence?" asked the old boy.
"They all did," sobbed the old girl.

FRANK SINATRA'S A MATE!

Frank Sinatra is getting ready to sing at a charity dinner and dance at Caesar's Palace when a stranger goes up to him and says, "Look Frank, you don't know me but I'm your biggest fan and I've got a date with a real stunner tonight at your show. I'll be sitting at the very front table and if you could come over and pretend that you know me my girl would be really impressed and you'd make the night for both of us. My name's Bob by the way."

Amazingly … AMAZINGLY … half-way through the concert Frank stops singing and goes over to Bob's table and says warmly, "Bob! I haven't seen you in ages! How's it going old buddy?"

Bob replies, "P*ss off Frank, can't you see I'm eating!"

DISGUSTING TWO TRAMPS TALE

Two tramps are walking along a quiet country lane....

1st tramp: "Phorr, I can smell sh*t, can't you?"

2nd tramp: "Not especially."

1st tramp: "Have you sh*t in your underpants?"

2nd tramp: "No I haven't."

The two tramps walk on a bit further....

1st tramp: "Phorrr! I can still smell sh*t. Are you sure you haven't sh*t in your pants?"

2nd tramp: "No I ain't."

1st tramp: "Well, I don't believe you. Pull down your pants!"
2nd tramp: "I ain't pulling down my pants."
After much arguing the first tramp eventually makes the second tramp pull down his pants whereupon the sh*t went all over the place. IT WAS EVERYWHERE!
1st tramp: "I thought you said you hadn't sh*t your pants!!"
2nd tramp: "I haven't. That sh*t was already in the pants when I found them."

OR.... (alternative ending)
2nd tramp: "Oh, but I thought you were talking just about today."

Daddy, daddy, what's a transvestite?
Ask your mother, he's in the kitchen.

Man to chemist: "Have you got cotton wool balls?"
Chemist: "What do you think I am, a Teddy Bear?"

What's the similarity between a modern injection and sex with an Essex man?
It's all over before you know it.

Did you hear the one about the blind gynaecologist?
He could lip read.

THE DUSTMAN'S XMAS TIP

A dustman knocks at the door for his Christmas tip whereupon it is answered by a stunning blonde who invites him in and takes him upstairs.
Once in the bedroom she takes off all his clothes and makes mad passionate love to him for an hour. The woman then goes downstairs and makes the dustman breakfast and gives him a pound coin.

The slightly confused man asks, "What's the pound coin for?" "Well," said the woman, "When I asked my husband if I should give you a twenty pound tip for Xmas he said, 'F*** him and give him a pound.' Breakfast was my idea."

TEA AND BLOW JOB

A man is staying at a hotel and the first morning there he is woken very early by a knock at the door. He gets up and answers the door wearing only his pyjama bottoms and a small ugly man with pointed ears comes into the room and puts a cup of tea on the sideboard. He then pulls the man's pyjamas down and puts the man's willy in his mouth.
"Just who the hell are you?" exclaimed the shocked man.
"I'm the Goblin teasmade," came the reply.

Did you hear about the Irish lesbian?
She likes men.

THE PERVERTED CONVICT

Two convicts are talking to each other and the first convict asks, "What are you in here for?"
"For persistently having sex with dogs?" replied the second convict.
"Bloody hell! How low can you get," said the first convict.
"Would you believe a Jack Russell," came the reply.
"Corr ... Was it male or female?" asked the first convict.
"Female of course," replied the second convict angrily, "What do you think I am, a pervert or something!"

What does a woman do with her ars***** before she has sex?
She leaves him down the pub.

What's the difference between an Ice Rink and a Chippendale? One you enter before sliding on, and one you slide on before entry.

THE CAR CRASH

Julian and Miles, a gay couple, are driving along in their Citreon 2CV car when a twenty ton articulated lorry piles into the back of them at some traffic lights.
Julian shreiks to Miles, "The stupid lorry driver. Get out Miles and go and tell him that we're going to sue him for every penny he's got."
Miles gets out of the mangled 2CV and goes up to the lorry driver's cab and says, "We're going to sue you for every penny you've got."
A huge seventeen stone, multi tatooed skinhead climbs down from his cab and growls, "Why don't you suck my c**k."
Miles gets back into the 2CV.
Julian says, "Did you tell him we're going to sue him for every penny he's got?"
Miles replies, "He says he wants to settle out of court."

Why did God give women nipples?
To make suckers out of men.

What's the similarity between bank charges and circumcisions?
They're both bloody rip-offs.

What goes Plink Plink Fizz?
Two babies falling into a vat of hydrochloric acid.

What has six legs and eats pu...
You, me and M... CENSORED

IT'S A MIRACLE

A group of disabled people go on a special trip to a little Peruvian village high up in the Andes because there have been a number of claims that the waters of the little stream above the village have miraculous healing qualities.
A man, bent over almost double with the pain of his bad back, goes into the stream and comes out upright and screams, "It worked!"
A woman then goes up to the stream and puts her head in the water. Then she shouts out, "I can hear again! It's a miracle!"
This is all too much for a man in a wheelchair and he spins his wheels furiously and gathers up tremendous speed as he hurtles towards the stream. He hurtles through the streams shallow waters at great speed and comes flying out the other side and right up the bank. When he finally comes to rest he tries to stand up but just falls over ... but he has got a new set of tyres on the wheelchair!!

What's the difference between a Big Mac and a blow job?
Err, I don't know.
How about lunch tomorrow?

What's the difference between a group of circus midgets and the British Women's Relay Team?
One's a group of cunning runts ...

VG

SHE MUST BE ROUGH!

A man goes into a brothel and says, "Give me a woman, but she's got to be a bit on the rough side because that's how I like them."
"How do you mean?" enquired the Madam.
"Well, I like my women to smoke cigars and spit on the floor occasionally. I don't like them washing too often either. I like

them hairy. I like them rough-skinned. So rough skinned that I can strike a match on their tits," said the man.
The first girl is sent in and the man tries striking a match on her tits. "She's no good," moans the man, and the next girl is sent in. The man tries striking a match on her tits and he says, "She's no good. Next!" The man tries out all ten girls employed by the Madam but none of them are acceptable to him.
"Haven't you got anyone else?" moans the man.
"You've seen all my girls. The only other woman here is Ethel, the cleaner, but she's over sixty," said the Madam.
"Bring her in," said the man, and in comes Ethel, a fourteen stone mass of butch woman. She's got a face like a bulldog chewing a wasp, more warts than a witches convention, the front two teeth are missing and she rolls her own cigarettes. The man gets Ethel to strip off and he lights a match on her tits first time so they get down to it with Ethel puffing away on a cigar as the man does the business. As the man takes a rest Ethel turns over onto her hands and knees and directs her massive rear end towards him.
"I'm sorry, but I don't like the doggy position," said the man.
"I thought you might like to open a bottle of beer," said Ethel.

Why won't a rattlesnake bite an estate agent?
Professional courtesy.

What happened to the Irish Morris dancer?
He fell through the windscreen.

WHALES HAVE BLOW JOB

Two Whales are swimming about in the sea and the navy arc on naval exercises. Consequently, there are a lot of boats about and these two whales keep banging their heads on the side of boats so the male whale says to the female whale, "I'm getting fed up with all these boats going past so why don't we have a bit of fun and swim under their boats and blow the boats over with our mighty spouts."

"Err ... oh ... alright then," said the female whale.
So they blow two boats so hard the boats capsize and all the sailors fall into the water.
"What shall we do now?" asked the female whale.
"Let's eat all the sailors, shall we?" replied the male whale enthusiastically.
"Oh no," said the female whale, "I don't mind giving a blow job, but I'm not swallowing any seamen."

How do you get rid of unwanted pubic hair?
Spit it out.

I WANT A BABY

This woman goes to the doctor's and says, "I want a baby but I don't want a relationship with a man, can you help."
"Yes, of course I can. Take your clothes off and lie down on the couch with your legs apart while I go to the store room and get a bottle of semen," replied the doctor.
This the women does while the doctor takes a sly peek at her through the crack in the storeroom door. He can't help but notice that the woman is an absolute stunner with the face of an angel and the body of a sex kitten.
After a short while the doctor comes shuffling back into the room with his trousers and pants round his ankles and says, "Sorry, but we're out of bottled, you'll have to have draught!"

What do you say to a skinhead in an old Lada who's got two Rottweilers in the back seat?
Wow! Nice car ...

What do you call a man with two raincoats in a cemetery?
Max Bygraves.

THE MAN IS KINKY

A tart takes a man back to her flat ...
The man says, "I'm a bit kinky. Do you mind?"
"You're paying," replies the tart.
"Okay then, get undressed and get into bed," instructs the man.
A short while later the tart shouts from the bedroom, "You can come in now, I'm ready."
"I've finished," replies the man.
"What d'ya mean, you're finished?" says the confused girl.
"I've just cr**ped in your handbag," replies the man.

3 WOMEN, 3 SAYINGS

How can you tell if you're making love to a nurse, teacher or airline stewardess?
A nurse will say, "This won't hurt a bit."
A teacher will say, "We're going to have to do this over and over again until we get it right."
An airline stewardess will say, "Just hold this over your mouth and nose and breathe normally."

MAN MEETS TART

Man to Tart: "How much is it?"
Tart: "For £10 you can have a quickie down a dark alleyway or for £100 we can spend the night in a nice, comfortable hotel."
Man: "Here's a £100."
Tart: "It'll be nice to spend the night in a nice hotel. Deep pile carpets, jacuzzi, clean sheets, breakfast in bed."
Man: "Who said anything about a hotel. I want it ten times in the alley!"

What's a Jewish girl's favourite wine?
Wahh! This isn't real platinum.

Why did God's chosen people wander about in the desert for forty years?
One of them had dropped some money.

What do you get if you cross a wh*re with a computer?
A f****** know it all.

What do you call two men with no arms or legs hanging on a wall?
Kurt n' Rod.

QUASIMODO HAS SEX

The Hunchback of Notre Dame wants a s**g and he asks all the local hookers but they all turn him down because he's so hideously ugly.
"There must be someone who'll s**g with me," cried the hunchback despondently, "I'll pay three times the going rate!"
"Will you?" said the Madam of the brothel as she had a ponder, "In that case I'll ask old Sally our cleaner if she'll do it. She's our cleaner now but she was one of the girls about twenty years ago."
Old Sally, a decrepit, toothless old girl, is persuaded to let the hunchback have his wicked way with her on the condition that she gets the rest of the week off on full pay and that she can put a bag over her head while Quasi does the business.
So, Quasi's sh**ging away when old Sally's bag falls off her head and she sees him close up for the first time and she throws up all over his back.
"Did you just puke over my back?" asked Quasimodo.
"I did ... sorry I couldn't help myself," said old Sally.
"Thank God for that," said a relieved Quasi, "I thought my hump had burst!"

Did you hear about the poof who was so ugly he had to go out with girls.

Why was Snow White thrown out of Fairy Tale Land?
She was caught sitting on Pinocchio's face saying, "Tell a lie, tell the truth, tell a lie, tell the truth ....."

What do you call a woman who sets all her bills alight?
Bernadette.

Lawyer to Mickey Mouse, "You can't divorce Minnie just because she has buck teeth."
Mickey replies, "I didn't say she had buck teeth, I said she was f****** Goofy!"

NO TOILET PAPER

A rabbit is walking through the jungle and he wants a sh*t so he goes behind a bush and starts to dump. Then a gorilla goes behind the same bush and asks, "Do you mind if I join you? I'm dying for a crap myself."
"No, of course not," replied the rabbit politely, so the gorilla squats down next to the rabbit and starts to sh*t. The gorilla finishes first and he looks around for something to wipe his ar** with but can't see any grass, moss, leaves or nothing. He gets really pissed off and moans to the rabbit, "I hate it when this happens. Sh*t always sticks to my fur. Does sh*t stick to your fur rabbit?"
The rabbit replies, "No," so the gorilla wiped his ar** with the rabbit.

How can you tell when a leper has used your shower?
The soap is bigger than before!

Did you hear the one about the two queer ghosts?
They put the willies up each other.

THEORETICALLY AND REALITY

A little boy asks his father, "What's the difference between theoretically and reality?"
The father thinks for a bit and then says, "I'll explain with an example. Go and ask your mum if, for a million pounds, she would sleep with any man, and then ask your sister the same question."
"Alright dad," says the little boy as he goes running off.
Two minutes later the boy returns and says, "Mum and Sis both said the same thing. Yeah, for a million quid they would sleep with any man."
"There you are then, that explains it," replied the father.
"But dad, I don't understand," said the boy.
The father continued, "Well son, theoretically we're a very wealthy family ... but in reality I live with two wh*res."

What's the difference between a white fairy tale and Puerto Rican fairy tale?
A white fairy tale starts, "Once upon a time there was ..."
A Puerto Rican fairy tale starts, "You Motherf***ers ain't gonna believe this sh*t, but..."

How can you tell that it's a New Zealander's stag night?
A sheep jumps out of the cake.

Why was the leper kicked out of the relay team?
He lost the last leg.

Why did the rooster cross the basketball court?
He heard the ref was blowing fowls.

VG

THE HIPPY SURVIVES!

An Englishman, a Scotsman and a hippy are lost in the jungle and they're captured by a tribe of savage headhunters.

According to the ancient traditions of the tribe all trespassers cannot be killed until they have been given the slim chance of survival by successfully completing three quite difficult tasks.

The Chief says, "If any of you wish to keep your heads you must achieve the following tasks ...

Firstly, you must go into the first cave here and smoke a massive joint of ganja. You must smoke it in one drag and inhale.

Then, you must go into the second cave where you will find a lion with a thorn in its paw. You must pull the thorn from the lion's paw and bring it out of the cave for me.

Lastly, you must go into the third cave and there you will find the jungle's most beautiful and totally insatiable woman, Zuhala. You must make love to her better than any man has done before and if she is satisfied then the man will be allowed to live as one of our tribe."

The Englishman goes first and goes into the first cave and smokes the ganja and promptly collapses and passes out. The tribesmen drag him away and chop his head off.

The Scotsman goes next. Into the first cave he goes and he smokes the whole joint in one and then he staggers out of the cave and into the second cave. There follows a tremendous sound of roaring, snarling and screaming. The Scot eventually crawls out of the cave with blood pouring from a mass of different wounds and his clothes torn to shreds but no thorn in his hand so the tribesmen carry him off and chop his head off.

Finally, the hippy goes into the first cave and smokes the ganja. No problem, just a normal day at Woodstock to him. He strolls into the second cave and there follows the sound of a lion

roaring and snarling loudly, followed by a brief moment of silence and then a loud purring and meowing noise.
The hippy emerges from the second cave and says casually, "Hey cats, so where is this bird with a thorn in her foot?"

Job interviewer: "Name please?"
Paddy: "Daniel O'Flaherty."
Job interviewer: "Can you spell that please?"
Paddy: "STUFF YOUR JOB!"

THE LEARNER DRIVER

Fred and Harry are having a few beers in the pub and Fred notices that Harry can hardly stay awake so he asks him if he's sleeping alright.
Fred replies, "No, I'm not as it happens. It's the wife, she keeps waking me up in the middle of the night."
"I always thought she was sex mad," laughed Harry.
"I wish it was that but it isn't. She's having an intensive course of driving lessons at the moment and she keeps dreaming in the middle of the night that she's driving a car. She grabs my dick and puts it into first gear, then second, then third, then fourth and then gives it a really good shake when she wants it in neutral. And she does this three or four times a night," moaned Fred.
"Next time she does it you want to turn her over and stick it up her bum, that'll shut her up," said Harry helpfully.
"Hmm ..." said Fred, "I might try that, thanks mate."
That night all was quiet until about 3am when the wife went, "Brmmm ... brmmmmm ... first gear (and yanks Fred's weapon into first).
Brmmmm ... brmmmm ... second gear (yanks Fred's weapon into second).
Brmm. brmmm ... third gear ... etc."
Fred turns his wife over and sticks his gear stick up her rear end and she says, "Four gallons of unleaded please."

Doctor, doctor, I love cream cakes.
There's nothing wrong with that, I'm very partial to them myself.
Really? Sexy little beasts, aren't they?

What's the difference between a Russian woman shotputter and a bowling ball?
Answer 1, You can only get three fingers in a bowling ball.
Answer 2, If you REALLY HAD TO you could eat a bowling ball.

THE QUEEN AND DI GET MUGGED! VG

One day the Queen and Princess Diana are having a drive around the Balmoral estate when they are ambushed by a man with a gun. He pulls both of them out of the Range Rover and screams at the Queen, "You're the richest woman in the world, now give me some money."
"I don't carry any money around with me," replied the Queen.
The mugger gives the Queen a very quick frisk and screams, "I don't believe this!! The richest woman in the world and no money on her!"
The mugger then turns to Princess Diana and screams, "I want your jewels, hand em over, NOW!"
"I'm afraid I don't have any with me," replied Di.
The mugger gives her a very quick frisk and screams, "I don't believe this, you're always dripping with jewellery in the photos." The extremely pissed off mugger then hears the sound of distant police sirens and he jumps into the Range Rover and drives off.
The Queen and Di start the long walk back to the castle and Di asks, "You normally carry quite a lot of cash, how come you didn't have any on you today?"
The Queen replied, "I saw the mugger approaching us out of the corner of my eye and managed to roll up all my money and conceal it in that special hiding place that only women have! How about you? You're always wearing Jewellery."
Di replied, "I saw him coming as well, so I took off all my

jewels, put them into a plastic bag and hid them in that special hiding place that only women have as well!"
The two of them walk on in silence for a while before the Queen says to Diana, "You know it's a real pity Fergie wasn't with us, we might have been able to save the Range Rover!"

Why does the Mersey run through Liverpool?
If it walked it would get mugged.

Quasimodo goes into a pub and orders a whisky.
The barman asks, "Bells okay?"
Quasi replies, "Mind your own f***ing business."

VG

THE BITTER WIDOW

A widow comes back from her husband's cremation and tips his ashes onto the table. She then says to the ashes, "You see this diamond ring. This is the diamond ring I always wanted but never got, so now I've bought it myself. You see this crocodile handbag. This is the crocodile handbag I always wanted but never got, so now I've bought it myself. You see this fur coat. This is the fur coat I always wanted but never got, so now I've bought it myself."
The woman then leant over the table and blew her husband's ashes all over the floor and said, "And this is the blow job you always wanted but never got!"

SEX IN TAXI

An Essex girl staggers out of Stringfellows blind drunk and hails a taxi cab. She gets inside the cab and says, "Take us to f****** Romford then ..."
When the taxi finally arrives at its destination the girl rummages around in her handbag and discovers that she's got no money. So she says to the taxi driver, "Sorry mate but I ain't got no dosh, right. But wot I can do, right, is to give you a

quickie in the back seat."
The cabbie agrees and climbs into the back. The girl pulls down her knickers, spreads her legs, squats over him and lowers herself onto him.
The cabbie says, "You haven't got anything smaller, have you?"

Doctor, doctor, I keep getting stabbing pains in my eye when I drink tea.
Try taking the spoon out of the cup.

Did you hear the one about the poof who fancied himself?
He never quite managed to get round to it.

"Fred's been under a lot of stress recently."

Chapter 9

Sporting Jokes

VG

IAN BOTHAM SORTS OUT THE TURTLE

Ian Botham is on tour with the England cricket team and the team go into a Chinese restaurant for a meal. Botham orders turtle soup as his first course. After quite some time one of the waiters comes up and says, "Velly solly Mr Botham but we can no do turtle soup today." The waiter went on to explain that in order to make turtle soup you had to chop off the head of the turtle before putting it in a pot of boiling water and today he only had one very stubborn turtle left in the kitchen and it wouldn't stick it's head out from it's shell.
"I know how to solve the problem," says Botham and he jumps up and goes into the kitchen and sticks one of his fingers up the turtle's backside whereupon the turtle's head immediately shoots out from under it's shell. Immediately Botham chops it's head off and tosses it into the pot.
The waiter is very impressed with all this and says, "You velly clever person ... velly clever ... How you know how to do that?"
"How do you think we manage to get a collar and tie on Gladstone Small?" replied Botham.

What did Mickey Mouse get for Christmas?
An England Football team watch.

PAT JENNINGS SAVES BABY!

A woman is trapped on the sixth floor of a block of flats by fire. She is leaning out of the window with her baby in her arms shouting, "Help me, help me, will someone save my baby?"
A crowd are gathered on the pavement below and they are urging her to throw the baby down to one of them.
"No I can't, it's too risky, you might drop her," she screamed over and over again.
Just then who should come along but Pat Jennings, the world famous retired goalkeeper, and he calls up to her, "I'm Pat Jennings the world famous goalkeeper. I'll catch your baby ... you couldn't find a safer pair of hands."
After much persuasion she throws the baby and Pat dives full length to catch the baby just before it hits the ground. With on-lookers clapping and cheering he then bounced it twice on the pavement and booted it right up the road!

DARTS AT THE NUNNERY

Eric Bristow is doing a charity gig at, of all places, a nunnery and to liven things up a bit he bets a mate a hundred pounds that he can get 180 with his next three darts. The mate readily accepts.

Eric throws the first dart and gets a double top ... He then gets a double top with the second dart ... As his mate moves forward to claim the money Eric throws the last dart half-heartedly towards the direction of the board whereupon it hits the wire and bounces right back into an eyeball of one of the nuns standing nearby.

As the nun fell to the floor Eric cried, "Hold on a minute matey ... I think I've won ... I've got one nun dead and eighty."

50 MILLION RUNNERS FOR MARATHON!

VG

The Prime Minister of India rang the Minister of Sport one day and said, "We need a Delhi marathon."

"Why sir?" came the reply.

"London's got a marathon, so has Tokyo, so has New York. Delhi needs a marathon! Get on to it right away!" ordered the PM.

Three weeks later the underling phones the PM and says, "The marathon's going great, we've had a tremendous response. We've got 50 million entrants."

"You bloody idiot! We can't have 50 million people trying to run round the streets of Delhi at the same time. Restrict the entry to only men with one testicle!" bellowed the PM.

The Minister agrees to do this and he phones the PM with another progress report some four weeks later, saying, "There are now 500,000 entrants sir, all men with only one bol***k."

"Bloody hell," said the PM, "That's still too many. Restrict it to men with no testicles at all."
The Minister agrees to do this and he rings the PM with another progress report a month later, saying, "We've now got only 500 entrants and there's not a single bol***k between the lot of them."
"Great," said the PM, "Now we need a name for the marathon. The Delhi marathon is just too predictable. We want something snappy! Something happening! Something with punch! ... I know, we'll call it The India Knackerless 500!!"

FAVOURITE SNOOKER JOKE

Tommy "The Tornado" Taylor gets back to his hotel room at two in the morning after a marathon snooker match at the Crucible. As he opens the door he is welcomed in by a snooker groupie. She's a stunning blonde and what's more she's wearing nothing but a T-shirt which says, "I LOVE THE TORNADO."
"How did you get in here?" asks Tommy.
"I did the bloke on the reception a favour," replies the girl, "Oh Tommy, Tommy! I watch all your matches. I think you're the greatest, I'm mad about you, I want you ... I want you!"
"Well, normally I wouldn't say no," replies Tommy, "but I'm shattered. I've got to get my head down, it's a big match tomorrow."
"Oh but Tommy, Tommy, I've waited so long to be alone with you, I want you. Please!" begs the girl.
The girl is incredibly gorgeous so Tommy half-heartedly says, "Oh, alright then, but it'll have to be my favourite position. That's doggy style."
"Anything you say Tommy," replies the girl.
The girl goes down on her hands and knees and lifts up her T-shirt and waits ... and waits ... and waits ... and waits ...
After a while she turns round to see Tommy, still fully clothed, standing in the far corner of the room looking at her with his hand on his chin.
"I'm ready and waiting, what's the problem?" queries the girl.
"I can't make up my mind whether to go for the tight pink or the easy brown," replied Tommy.

THE UNLOSABLE GOLF BALL

Greg and Tim are on the golf course teeing off at the first hole when Greg notices Tim's golf ball looks a bit different so he says to Tim, "What sort of ball is that?"

Tim replies, "That, Greg my son, is no ordinary golf ball. This is the unlosable golf ball. It's been specially manufactured so that it can't be lost on the fairways."

"How'd you mean?" asks Greg.

"Well, if there's snow on the ground it changes in colour from white to black and hovers six inches above the snow," says Tim.

"Really?" says Greg.

"Yes, and if it drops into water it floats to the top and swims to the side," says Tim.

"Wow, that's some ball!" says Greg.

"And if it lands in the rough it makes a bleeping noise so it can be found," says Tim.

"Wow," says Greg.

"And if it gets stuck up in a tree a pair of wings shoot out from it's sides and it flies down to the ground," says Tim.

"Wow, what a ball. Where did you get it from?" asks Greg.

"I found it," replies Tim.

BRUNO'S OPPONENT HURT

"Do you remember the guy who Frank Bruno fought in his first crack at the heavyweight championship of the world ... Well I've just heard on the news that he's been stabbed. Now what was his name? ... Tim? ... Tim With err ... Tim?"

Fallguy ... "Witherspoon!"

"No, with a knife."

Who is the most unpopular person on the football terraces of Borussia Munchengladbach?

The one who shouts out, "Give us a B."

How could you turn Brian Clough into a good coach?

Take all his teeth out and fit forty-two seats!

SUNDAY FOOTBALL IN LIVERPOOL

This young lad has just joined one of the local Sunday football teams in Liverpool and he is getting his first pre-match talk from the boss ...

Boss ... "When you get into the opponents' penalty area try to play a few one-twos with Rushie."

Lad (amazed) ... "You've got Ian Rush playing in your Sunday football team?"

Boss ... "Well, it's not the real Ian Rush but he's got a moustache and he's wafer thin and scores goals by the bucketful so we call him Rushie."

Boss (continuing) ... "Now remember if you are under pressure in the middle of the park look out for the short square ball pass to Molbers."

Lad (amazed) ... "You've got Jan Molby playing for your Sunday football team!"

Boss ... "Well, it's not the real Jan Molby but he has got a foreign accent and looks a bit overweight and he's a great long ball passer so we call him Molbers."

Boss (continuing) ... "And don't forget when we are defending from a corner I want you on our goal line by the near post ... and if you get a call from Grobblies from behind you then leave it."

Lad (amazed) ... "You've got Bruce Grobbelar playing for your Sunday football team?"

Boss ... "Y ... Yes. "

THE CHEEKY APPRENTICE

Brian Clough, so the story goes, rings down to the apprentices room and says, "Young man fetch me up a cup of tea."

The surly youth at the other end of the line replies, "Get it yourself!"

"Young man have you any idea who you're talking to?" scolds Cloughie.

The apprentice answers, "Have you any idea who you are talking to?"
"No," says Cloughie hesitatingly.
"Well bloody well get it yourself then!" shouts the voice before slamming the phone down.

Football manager to player, "I thought you did the work of three men in midfield today ... the Marx brothers!!!"

What's the difference between John Barnes playing well for England and the Loch Ness monster?
There's at least a couple of people in the country who claim to have seen the Loch Ness monster.

What's the difference between Graham Taylor and a pyromaniac?
A pyromaniac wouldn't throw his last three matches away.

What's the difference between Hitler and Alex Ferguson?
Both wasted millions but Hitler got further in Europe.

John Stalker, the ex-Chief Constable of Greater Manchester police force, has been brought out of retirement to investigate Manchester City Football Club's policy of shoot to miss.

THE DRUNK DRIVER

A policeman stops a driver for suspected drunken driving and asks him to blow into a bag.
The driver produces a card saying, "ASTHMATIC - Please don't take breath samples."
The policeman then asks to take a blood sample whereupon the driver produces a card saying, "HAEMOPHILIAC - Please don't take blood samples."
Somewhat annoyed the policeman decides it will have to be a urine test.
Once again the driver produces a card saying, "WIMBLEDON F. C. SUPPORTERS CLUB MEMBER - Please don't take the piss!"

CLOUGHIE GOES TO "THE GAMBIA"

Cloughie once took his Nott'm Forest team on a mid season break to the Gambia and on a walk through a remote African clearing he came across a young native man who appeared to be a tremendous athlete. He could run faster than a lion, hop on one foot with a coconut balanced on the other foot and kick a coconut 100 feet into the air and catch it in the back of his neck, not to mention juggling three coconuts with his feet!
Cloughie decides to bring the man back to the hotel's football pitch for a trial.
Cloughie gathers the footballers in a circle for a pre-match briefing and starts by saying, "This is Ahk-keem." He then holds up a football and very slowly and deliberately bellows, "THIS FOOTBALL ... THIS FOOOOOTBALL!" Then he points to the goal and says again in a slow, loud and exaggerated manner, "THIS GOAL ... THIS GOAL ... THIS GOOOOOAL!" Cloughie then holds up the ball again and points to it first and then to the goal and bellows, "BALL IN

GOAL ... BALL IN GOAL ... BALL IN GOOOOOAL!!!"
The African, smiling, says, "You really don't have to talk to me in that silly pigeon English manner old boy! I was educated at Harrow and speak perfect English!"
"I'M SPEAKING TO THE REST OF THE TEAM," bellowed Cloughie as he went scarlet in the face.

What first division footballer has a father who was a very famous comedian?
Imre Varadi ... son of Oliver Hardy(?).

ENGLAND'S FOOTBALLING FUTURE

The West Ham, Chelsea and England football team managers leave a Football awards ceremony in Blackpool together and decide to have a stroll along the sea front. They spot a booth where a clairvoyant is claiming to be the voice of God himself and they decide to go in for a giggle.
The West Ham manager asks God, "When will West Ham next win a trophy?"
God booms out, "In the year 2033."
The West Ham manager moans, "That's no good for me, I won't be around by then."
The Chelsea manager then asks God, "When will Chelsea next win a trophy?"
God booms out, "In the year 2076."
The Chelsea manager moans, "That's no good for me, I won't be around by then."
The England manager gets down on his knees and asks God, "When will England next win a major championship?"
God booms out, "I don't know, I won't be around by then!"

THE BOARDROOM BATTLE

During one of the many boardroom battles for control of Tottenham, Irving Scholar, Terry Venables and Alan Sugar were having a meeting to decide who should have what job for the forthcoming season.
Irving Scholar says, "I own ten million shares in the club so I'm going to be Chairman."
Terry Venables says, "I own twenty million shares in the club so I'm going to be Chief Executive."
Alan Sugar says, "I own one hundred million shares in the club ... but ... but if one of you's going to be Chairman and the other one's going to be Chief Executive, what job am I going to do?"
Terry and Irving whisper a few words to each other before Terry says, "You can be the club's sex therapist Alan."
"What's the role of a sex therapist?" asks Alan Sugar.
"When we want your f****** advice we'll ask for it!" said Venables.

YOU TRAITOR GASCOIGNE!

It's a dark, wet night in downtown Newcastle and Paul Gascoigne and Chris Waddle are driving around visiting a few old haunts. They pull up at a set of traffic lights and a group of drunken youths recognise Gazza ...
The gangs leader shouts, "HOY! YOU! GASCOIGNE! What are you doing back up in Newcastle? We don't want you back up here. You're a traitor! You left Newcastle to go to Tottenham just when we really needed you ... you deserted us. Then you deserted Tottenham to go to Lazio."
Then they spot Waddle ...
The gangs leader shouts, "AND YOU WADDLE!! You left us for Tottenham just when we needed you ... you deserted us. Then you deserted Tottenham to go to Marseille."
Stung by the criticism Gazza then, so the story goes, pulls

down his trousers and as the car pulls away from the lights he raises his backside up to car window height.
The gangs leader shouts, "AND YOU BEARDSLEY!! You left us for Liverpool ... then you left them for Everton ... and you only came back to us when you were desperate.

GAZZA'S DEBUT

Gazza, having been signed by Lazio, is about to start his very first competitive home match for his new club when, so the story goes, Dino Zoff, the Lazio manager, takes him to one side and says, "Go out there and put on a bit of a show, do a few tricks and use up your energy and I'll pull you off at halftime."
Gazza grins and says, "Why-eye-eye, that's bloody fantastic! All I ever got at Tottenham was a slice of Orange!"

THE VERY OLD CADDY

A top businessman skivies off work and goes for a round of golf. Totally unaccustomed to carting his own clubs around he demands a caddy but there are no takers despite the fact that the man is waving a £50 note about.
Just then a very old man gets up off his bench and offers to caddy for the man.
The man shakes his head and replies, "With all due respect old man I want someone who is going to be able to see where my ball's landed. The rough is very long on this course."
"But I've got the eyesight of an eagle," replied the old boy, "See that church tower over there about half a mile away? ... Well the time on it's clock reads 4. 06! ... And see that red Fiesta parked at the top of the hill? ... It's registration number is B566 VDF!"
"Wow! I'm impressed," says the man as he hands the old boy the £50 note. They set off for the first tee ...
The man slices his first shot way off into the woods to the right and he asks the old boy anxiously, "Did you see where it landed?"
"Yes," replied the old boy.

The man and the old boy walk down the fairway together ...
"Where exactly did the ball go?" asked the man as they near the woods.
"I've forgotten," replied the confused old boy.

A USEFUL XMAS PRESENT ....
A neck for Gladstone Small.

DOG LOVES CRICKET

A man and his dog are sitting in a pub when the man asks the landlord if the radio in the background can be turned up as it's covering the England V Australia test match and his dog is mad about cricket and a passionate supporter of the England team.
The landlord smiles and turns up the commentary.
The radio booms out, "Gatting bowled for a duck."
On hearing this the dog whines sadly and takes a bite out of his tail and then collapses on the floor and looks inconsolable.
Then from the radio is heard, "Bowled him! De Freitas gets a duck. Merv Hughes is on a hatrick!"
On hearing this the dog looks distraught and he puts his paws over his ears. He then chews some more of his tail off until it is just a bloody stump!
Then from the radio is heard, "Bowled him! A hatrick for Merv Hughes and Australia win by an innings and 334 runs and they retain the Ashes."
On hearing this the dog goes crazy. He runs over to the nearest wall and starts banging his head against it again and again until blood starts to trickle out of one of his ears. He then throws up all over the carpet.
"What an extraordinary dog!" exclaimed the landlord, "If he's like this when they lose what is he like when they win?"
The dog owner replied, "I don't know. I've only had him eighteen months."

Chapter 10

Yet More Right Rude Jokes

MAN MEETS GEISHA GIRL

An English businessman goes to Japan for a business deal and his hosts take him to a Geisha house whereupon he gets taken into a bedroom by a beautiful Geisha girl. Before long they are making love and the girl starts moaning, "Pushharda," so the man starts sh**ging harder.

She then says, "Pushharda," more loudly, so the man sh**s even harder. The girl then screams, "Pushharda, Pushharda," and the man sh**s harder and still harder. Finally the girl passes out and the man, feeling very chuffed with himself, gets dressed and leaves.

The next day the man is having a round of golf with his Japanese hosts when he overhits his shot on the fairway and it flies past the intended green and onto the next green which backs onto the intended green. As the ball lands near the flag the man's Japanese playing partners fall about laughing and one says, "Pushharda, pushharda."

"How'd you mean, Pushharda?" asks the Englishman.

"Pushharda mean wrong hole, wrong hole!" came the reply.

Did you hear about the gay spider?
He kept playing with his mates flies.

What's the difference between an Anteater and Arthur Daley?
One's a fly sucker ...

MOYSHE HAS HIS BARMITZVAH

It's Moyshe's thirteenth birthday and he has his Barmitzvah. After the celebrations his father takes him to the local hooker so he can reach his manhood in the family tradition.

After a lot of haggling between the hooker and the father a price of £35 is agreed and the hooker takes Moyshe by the hand and leads him into the bedroom. Moyshe's father puts his ear to the bedroom door to listen to every noise.

Moyshe undresses and his weapon is absolutely enormous. The girl lays back, legs apart and Moyshe puts in seven inches and the hooker squeals with delight. He then puts another inch in and the hooker starts begging for more.

She says, "I'll give you £5 off if you give me another inch," so Moyshe puts in another inch.

"I can't believe it's so big," she screams, "I'll give you another £15 off if you can give me another inch," so Moyshe puts another inch in.

"Please, please, I'll give you another £10 off if you can just give me another inch," begged the hooker, so Moyshe puts another inch in.

The girl then moans, "If you can give me another inch then it's free, it's free, it's free. Just give me a bit more!!"

At this point the father bursts into the room and shouts, as he undoes his flies, "Move over son, it's time to make a profit!"

Doctor, doctor, I feel like a piece of smoked ham.
Nurse, this man's already been cured.

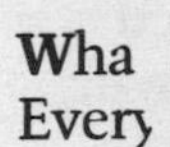

Wha s about ha ase?
Every ew faces.

What do you do if your baby swallows a biro?
Use a pencil.

FOOLING AROUND

A guy is fooling around with his new girlfriend when she asks him to put a finger inside her, and this he does. Then she asks him to put another finger in, and this he does. Then she asks him to put his whole hand in, and this the man does. Then she asks him to put a finger of his other hand in, alongside the first hand, and this the man does. Then she asks him to put three fingers of his second hand in, and this he does. Then she asks him to put the whole of his second hand in alongside the first hand, and this he does.
The girl then says, "Right, now clap your hands."
"I can't," replied the man.
"Tight, huh!" beamed the girl.

One day, sadly, Mrs T dies and goes to heaven .....
God: "Margaret, my daughter, welcome!"
Maggie: "Two things! I'm not your daughter and get out of my chair!"

What weighs ten pounds and wasn't plucked last Xmas?
Roy Orbison's guitar.

THE WORN-OUT MAN

A guy goes to the doctor complaining of being really tired all the time and the doctor asks him to describe his typical day as this sort of complaint is usually linked to a persons lifestyle. The man replies, "I normally wake at about 6am and make love to the wife and then go back to sleep. At about 8am I make love to the wife again and then shower and get dressed for work. If I have time I will sometimes make love to the wife again before I leave home for the office. I normally spend my lunchbreak nipping back home and making love to the wife. After work I get home about 7pm and I'll probably make love to my wife before we eat. Then after dinner we'll probably watch a bit of TV while we make love in front of it. About 9pm I'll probably take the dog for a walk and when I get back I'll

probably make love to the wife before going to bed and making love to the wife. Sometimes I sleep right through the night, sometimes I wake up two or three times to make love to the wife."
The man looks at the doctor and says, "Why do you think I'm so tired all the time, doc?"
The doctor replies, "To put it bluntly, I think you're sh**ging too much."
The man replies, "Oh, so you don't think it's the w**king in the office that's doing it then?"

What's the best thing about being a test tube baby?
You get a womb with a view.

THE VIRUS AND THE PARROT

A virus is chasing an ar**hole through the jungle and the ar**hole is finding it very difficult to get away when, lo and behold, it bumps into it's fairy godmother, and she says, "You may have one wish."
Quickly the ar**hole asks her to help him get away from the virus and the fairy godmother obliges by transforming the ar**hole into a parrot and putting him in a tree.
The ar**hole is sitting in the tree disguised as a parrot when the virus comes by and stops and looks up at the parrot. The virus asks, "You haven't seen an ar**hole around here have you?" and the parrot shakes his head.
"Have you been up in that tree long?" asks the virus, and the parrot shakes his head.
"You're an African Grey parrot aren't you?" asks the virus, and the parrot nods his head.
The virus starts to look more suspiciously at the parrot and it says, "You don't say much for a parrot, do you?" and the parrot just shakes his head.
"Say something then, say something then parrot," said the virus as it moved closer and closer to the parrot.
Shaking with fear the parrot opened his beak and ... and out came a massive fart!!

Doctor, doctor, I like very loud socks.
There's nothing wrong with that, Peter, I like them myself.
Great! You must come and see my collection sometime.

What's green, eats nuts and drives a chariot?
Ben Herpes.

Doctor, doctor, I've got Herpes.
No you haven't, you've got Hermes ...... You're just a carrier.

Did you hear about the sequel to Jaws that was about a loan shark?
Jews.

"Your mother? She looked a bit like Ewe."

What do you do if an Estate Agent spits at you?
Turn the grill down.

LONE RANGER IS CAPTURED

The Lone Ranger is finally captured by the Apaches and he is buried up to his neck in sand and is facing a slow and painful death when his captors decide, out of respect for their adversary, to give Lone one last wish.
Lone says, "Please, let my trusty steed Silver run free and unharmed."
The Indians free the horse. The Lone Ranger then whistles and over trots Silver and Lone whispers in the horses ear, and then the horse runs away.
An hour later Silver returns with a young blonde girl on his back. He throws the girl off and she goes over to Lone and lifts up her skirt to reveal that she is wearing no knickers. She then sits on Lone's face and wriggles.
As Lone gasps for his breath he shouts to Silver, "You silly mare! I said go and get me a posse!"

Did you hear about the Irish abortionist?
He gave up when he lost his ferret.

Doctor, doctor, was my operation a success?
Sorry sir, my name's St. Peter.

THOR RETURNS TO EARTH

Thor, the God of lightening, returns to earth after a thousand year exile and the first thing he does is head off to the brothel as he hasn't had sex for a millenium. He grabs the first available girl and hauls her off into the nearest room and sh**s her non-stop for five days. Finally, as he is getting dressed, and feeling well pleased with himself, he realises that in his haste he hasn't even introduced himself properly to the girl so he says, "I'm Thor."
"You're sore, huh ... I can hardly walk," groaned the girl.

Which one is the odd one out? Corned beef, soya bean or a vibrator?
Corned beef, because the other two are meat substitutes.

Mummy, mummy, why has daddy got his willy in the biscuit tin?
Ignore him darling, he' f***ing crackers!

Did you hear about the bellringer who got caught up in the rope?
He got tolled off by the vicar.

LITTLE BOY PLANS REVENGE

One day a little boy walks into the local brothel with a dead frog on his shoulder. He goes up to the Madam and asks for a girl.

"And what would a little boy like you want with one of our girls then?" laughed the Madam.

"I'd want to scr** her. Oh, and by the way she's got to have herpes," said the boy.

"We don't serve little boys, and we certainly don't have that kind of girl in this high class establishment. Now push off!" said the Madam.

The little boy drops two hundred pounds on the table and the Madam says, "Choose any girl you like, they've all got herpes and that's the least of their worries!" and off the boy goes with one of the girls.

The boy returns from one of

the bedrooms about half an hour later with a huge smile on his face, and he's still got the dead frog on his shoulder.
As he is about to leave the Madam asks him, "I couldn't help wondering why you want to get herpes?"
"Well," replied the boy, "When I get home I'm going to sh** the Au Pair and she'll get herpes. Then she'll give it to my dad who'll then give it to my mum, and she'll then give it to the gardener who'll then give it to cook, and she'll then give it to the milkman."
"So?" said the Madam.
"The milkman's the b*****d who trod on my frog," shouted the boy bitterly.

Mummy, mummy, is it bad to have a willy?
No dear.
So why is daddy in the bathroom trying to pull his off!

Did you hear about the man who went to bed with his sister-in-law?
He had it in for his brother.

NEVER LOOK IN TOP DRAWER

A newly married couple have just moved into their new home and that night the husband says, "Marriage is built on a certain amount of trust and see the top drawer of my locker over there, I don't want you to ever look inside it."
The wife agrees and for thirty years of wedded bliss she never looks inside the top drawer of her husbands locker. One day, however, curiousity finally gets the better of her and she has a peek inside and sees three golf balls and a heap of ten pound notes.
That night when her husband comes home from work the wife feels she must confess to what she has done and she says, "Please forgive me ... I'm so sorry darling ... I looked inside the drawer that you told me never to look in."
Her husband replies, "We've been married thirty years and you've only looked inside that draw once in all that time ... I

forgive you."
The relieved wife says, "Oh thank you darling, thank you ... Err ... err ... What were the three golf balls for?"
The husband replies, "Err ... you've been honest with me so I'll be honest with you. I put a golf ball in there every time I've had an affair with another woman."
On hearing this the wife is at first upset but after further consideration she says, "W ... w ... well three affairs in thirty years isn't too bad ... I. I think I forgive you darling," and they hug and kiss. Then the wife asks, "Err ... and what was all that money doing in there?"
The husband replies, "Everytime I get a set of six golf balls I sell them!"

What do you call a terrible fear of trainspotters?
Anoraknaphobia.

What's the similarity between an Xmas tree and a man with a vasectomy?
The balls are just for decoration.

THE DRUNK COWBOY

A drunk cowboy swaggers into a saloon and orders a whisky. He turns to the piano player and shouts, "You're crap," and takes a shot at him. The bullet flies past the piano players right ear. As the man downs the whisky he says to the barman, "Damn useless gun, I don't normally miss."
"File down the edges of the barrel," advises the barman.
This the cowboy does before ordering another whisky. He then turns to the piano player and shouts, "You're crap."
The cowboy shoots at the piano player and the bullet flies past the mans left ear.
"Damn useless gun, I don't normally miss," said the cowboy to the barman.
"Grease the end of the gun barrel," advised the barman.
The cowboy greases the end of his gun barrel, downs the

whisky and orders another. He then turns to the piano player and shouts, "You're crap," and he again shoots at him and this time the bullet flies over the piano players head.
"Damn useless gun, never usually miss," mutters the cowboy to the barman.
"Tie a sponge to the end of the gun barrel," advised the barman.
The cowboy shouts back, "First you tell me to file down the end of my gun barrel, then you tell me to grease the gun barrel and now you're telling me to tie a sponge on the end of it! Do you know what you're talking about?"
"I think I do," said the barman, "The guy who's playing the piano is Jesse James and after he's finished playing this song he's going to ram that gun up your backside!"

What did the VD scab shout out as he fell off the cliff?
I'm a goner 'ere.

Why was the Russian female shot putter arrested at Bangkok airport?
Customs officers found her with ten pounds of Crack down her knickers.

A GREEN RASH

A girl goes to her doctors and says, "I've got a rash in a very personal place."
The doctor tells her to go behind the screen and take her clothes off and this she does. The doctor has a butchers and notices green irritated areas of skin at the top of each thigh.
"What job does your boyfriend do?" asks the doctor.
"Oh a bit of this, a bit of that ... He's a gipsy," replies the girl.
"Well get dressed, go home, and tell him his earrings aren't real gold," said the doctor.

What's the difference between like and love?
Spitting and swallowing.

If the answer to the question is, "C**k Robin", what's the question?
What's up my ar**, Batman?

VG

A VERY DANGEROUS DARE

A bloke with a bit of a reputation for challenging people to dares walks into his local with a crocodile on a lead. He hits the crocodile over the head with a glass bottle and this appears to stun the animal into opening it's mouth. He then pulls out his tool and places it between the animals open jaws for ten seconds, pulling it out only a second before the crocodile snapped it's jaw shut.
"Now is there anyone here with the bottle to do a stunt like that?" shouted out the man with justifiable pride to a stunned audience.
After a short silence a little old lady in the corner stood up and said, "I don't mind having a go so long as you don't hit me too hard with the bottle!"

Did you hear the one about the queer racehorse?
He kept tossing his jockey off.

Why are bosses like nappies?
They're invariably full of sh*t and always on your ar**!

PUB LAYS ON MUSIC

Two deaf fellas go into the pub and one sits down and the other goes up to the bar and orders two pints of lager.
"That'll be five pounds please," shouts the barman.
"That's a bit expensive isn't it?" retorts the deaf guy.
"It's a bit more than usual because we've got music on tonight," came the reply.
"What sort of music? ... Rock n Roll?"
"No."
"Soul?"
"No."

"Jazz?"
"Nope ... I've got you some Country'n'Western," said the barman.
The deaf guy sits down and moans to his mate that he's had to pay five pounds for two lagers because there's music on tonight and the barman wouldn't give him the drinks at the normal price despite them both being deaf.
"What sort of music is it?" enquires the other guy.
"I dunno exactly ... It's some C*** from Preston!"

What's the difference between a woman leaving church and a woman leaving the bath?
One's got a soulful of hope and the others got a holeful of soap.

Did you hear the one about the queer candle?
It went out with a poof.

GOLF LESSONS

A golf coach has been teaching this woman to play golf for some time but she's absolutely hopeless and can't get the ball more than twenty feet down the fairway so in utter frustration he blurts out, "You're not holding the club properly ... HOLD IT LIKE YOU'RE HOLDING YOUR HUSBANDS PENIS!"
The woman then proceeds to swing at the ball and smacks it two hundred and fifty yards right down the centre of the fairway and it lands two feet from the flag!
"That's much better Mrs Green," said the coach, "Err ... you ... you can take the club out of your mouth now!"

Why do bald men have holes in their pockets?
Because they like to run their hands through their hair.

H... 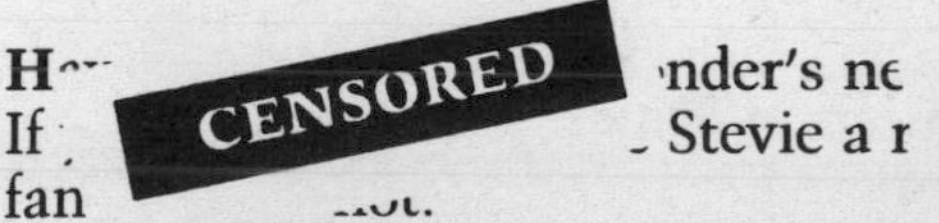 ...nder's ne... 
If ... Stevie a r... ...ther to
fan... ...ot.

MAN HAS HEAD THE SIZE OF AN ORANGE!

A man goes into a dockside pub for a drink and can't help but notice a massive seventeen stone, six foot three sailor sitting in the corner because his head is the size of an orange. Try as he does to ignore the man, he can't and after a few drinks he plucks up the courage to approach the man and says, "I er ... eerr ... I hope you don't think I'm being nosey but how ... how ..."
"How come I'm built like a brick sh*thouse but have got a head the size of an orange ... right," said the sailor.
"Err ... right," replied the man.
"It's a long story but I was shipwrecked on this island and one day this beautiful mermaid was washed ashore and she said I could have three wishes. My first wish was for a ship to appear on the horizon and one did. My second wish was for a trunk of treasure to appear on the beach and it did. The mermaid was gorgeous and my last wish was to make love to her but she said that she didn't have any reproductive organs down there. So I said, "In that case could I have a little head?"

What's thirty feet long and smells of urine?
A conga in an old people's home.

Andrew Lloyd Webber and Tim Rice have got together again to write a new musical in tribute to the life of Jeremy Beadle. It's to be called ... "Superstar? ... JESUS CHRIST!"

VG

PRIEST GIVES BIRTH!!

A top hospital surgeon has a fling with one of the fat Irish nurses on the ward and as a result she gets pregnant. Neither of them want to have their careers or marriages ruined but the nurse refuses to have an abortion on religious grounds. The months go by and because of the nurse's bulky size her condition goes unnoticed. Then she suddenly drops the baby in the hospital loos.

Neither of them want the baby, but also neither of them want it to go for adoption through the normal channels because of the publicity.

On hearing of the birth the surgeon says desperately, "Look, I've got an idea. I've just performed an emergency appendectomy on an eccentric priest and when he comes round I'll tell him the pain was due to his pregnant condition and he's had a baby and it's a miracle, a gift from God. He's nutty enough, it might just work."

When the priest comes round the baby is shuvved into his arms and the surgeon and the nurse sound very convincing. Well, the priest always wanted a child of his own so he asked few questions and took the baby boy home with him.

The boy had a happy childhood at the vicarage and when he reached the day of his fourteenth birthday his father called him into the study.

The boy said, "You wanted to have a word with me father?"

"Yes I do Toby. Please sit down because what I've got to tell you is very important. I feel you're getting to the age where you should know the truth," said the very nervous priest.

"What is it father?" asked the boy.

"I want you to know that I'm not your father," said the priest.

"What do you mean you're not my father?" replied the stunned boy.

The priest replied, "I' CENSORED other! Your father is the Archbishop of R

Mummy, mummy, it's getting hot in here. Can I come out now?
No, of course not. Do you want the fire to spread to the rest of the house?

THE FANCY DRESS CONTEST

The fancy dress contest at Butlins is under way and the compere ushers the first contestant onto the stage and asks, "Now what are you dear?"
"I'm Wonder Woman," said the old girl proudly.
"Well what a fantastic outfit, and you knitted it yourself," said the compere.
"Yes I did," gushed the old girl, "It took me nine months to knit it all. I did it especially for tonight."
"Well, what a fantastic effort Ladies and Gentlemen. Let's give her a big hand," said the compere.
The second contestant walks onto the stage and the compere asks, "And what are you, sir?"
"I'm the Pearly King of the East End of London," replied the man proudly.
"Look at all the thousands of sequins on that outfit. Can you tell us how many sequins there are?" asked the compere.
"There's 4, 435 sequins, and they've all been sewn on by hand. It took me three years to make this jacket," replied the man proudly.
"Let's give him a fantastic hand Ladies and Gentlemen," urged the compere as he turned to wave the third contestant onto the stage.
Onto the stage staggers Paddy in nothing but a pair of tatty underpants and the compere cringes and says, "Err ... what have you come as?"
Paddy replies, "I'm a Premature Ejaculation!!"
The scarlet-faced compere says, "What do you mean you're a Premature Ejaculation?"
"Oive just come in me underpants," replied Paddy.

Join the Army.
Travel the World.
Meet new and interesting people.
And kill them.

Why have elephants got big ears?
Because Noddy won't pay the ransom.

What do a walrus and tupperware have in common?
They both like a tight seal.

PRINCE CHARLES SHOPS

Prince Charles goes into his local chemist and asks for some condoms. The sales assistant replies, "Sorry Your Highness but, as you can see from the shelves in front of you, we are no longer a chemist but a spare parts shop for old cars."
"In that case," replied Charles, "Can you give me a coil for a 1961 Princess!"

A man abroad on a long business trip walks into a brothel and says, "For £200 can I have the worst blow job in town!"
The Madam replies, "Why sir, for £200 you can have the best blow job in town."
"You don't understand," said the man, "I'm feeling homesick not randy."

What's black and white and hard?
A nun lunging with a broken beer bottle.

What's the definition of a real woman?
One who kick-starts her vibrator.

THE TERRIBLE COOK

A just married husband gets home from his first day back at work after his honeymoon and finds his wife sobbing at the foot of the stairs.

"Darling, don't cry, what's wrong?" asks the husband.

The wife replies, "I've spent all day preparing a really good meal for you but it all turned out really awful. I'm useless as a wife and a cook. I'm a failure."

The husband picked his wife up in his arms and said, "Forget dinner, let's go up to bed."

The next night when the husband came home from work he again found his wife sobbing at the foot of the stairs and asked, "What's wrong darling?"

"The meal's a disaster again and I tried so hard. I wanted to be such a good wife for you but I'm useless!!" wailed the wife.

The husband picked his wife up in his arms and said, "Forget dinner, let's go to bed."

The next night when the husband came home his wife was sliding naked down the bannisters and he asked, "What are you doing, love?"
"Just keeping your dinner warm," she replied happily.

THE WEDDING ANNIVERSARY

An Italian couple, Carlo and Francesca, are having a romantic candlelight dinner to celebrate their first wedding anniversary when Carlo asks, "So, Francesca, you tella me, eh? We be married a year now, so whatta da things aboutta a me dat really annoy you? eh? eh?"
Francesca replies, "Nowwa you aska me Carlo, dere are two a da things dat you do dat driva me crazy. First, you always picka da nose, and second, you always on top!! Why is this? eh? eh?"
Carlo replies, "My Grandfather Luigi, de heada de Mafioso, he tella me two things just before he die. He say Carlo my boy, you always keepa your nose clean and you never fuckka up!!"

How do you bring a baby up in the Australian outback?
Stick your fingers down a dingo's throat.

What's Snow White's favourite drink?
Seven-up.

What did the Dalek say as he climbed off the dust-bin?
Anyone can make a mistake, luv.

1st hippy: "Hey man, turn the radio on."
2nd hippy: "Hey radio, I love you man."

OPEN-AIR TOILETS!

A man rides into a rather primitive town in the middle of nowhere and, dying for a crap, he rushes into the local saloon and asks, "Where are the toilets mate?"
He is directed to go through a door which leads him back outside the building whereupon he sees two massive piles of sh*t in front of him. Desperate for a crap he runs to the top of one of the piles and does a massive dump and gives a massive sigh of relief.

On top of the other pile an old man is also having a massive dump and the old boy looks across at the man and says, "Howdy stranger."
The man replies, "Howdy ... ... err, how did you know I was a stranger in town?"
"Because you're in the Ladies," came the reply.

Why did the Irish cook hate making chocolate chip cookies?
It took hours to peel the smarties.

What do you get if you cross a bear with a skunk?
Winnie the Phew!

A little girl says to her mother, "I know how babies are made. I looked into your bedroom last night and saw daddy put his willy into your mouth."
"That isn't how babies are made dear," replied her mother, "That's how mummy gets her jewellery!"

MASH HIM TO PULP!

A bloke built like Arnold Swarzenegger walks into a pub with his wife. The wife sits down and the husband goes to the bar to get the drinks. As the barman pours the drinks he says to the husband, "I think you ought to know that there's a little guy trying to chat your wife up."
The husband goes back to the wife and asks, "Did some bloke try to chat you up while I was away?"
"Oh, it was horrible," said the wife, "He said he wanted to lick every part of my body!"
"The dirty swine," said the husband, "Which one was it, I'll kill him."
"And then he said that he'd got a ten inch tongue and he would clean all my body orifices out with it!!" wailed the wife.
"The man's a pervert, I'll kill him, which one is he?" demanded the husband as he rolled up his sleeves.
"And then he said he would turn me upside down and fill my f***y up with Tennants until it overflowed, and then he said he'd drink the lot!" wailed the wife.
The husband then sat down and said quietly, "Best not to cause any trouble, eh love?"

"What do you mean? I thought you were going to mash him to pulp for me? Go on beat him up, it's that little creep in the corner with the moustache, go on!" urged the wife.
"Look love," said the man whispering, "I'm not f****** about with any man that can drink that much Tennants!!"

What's worse than finding a maggot in your apple?
Finding half a maggot in your apple.
What's worse than finding half a maggot in your apple?
Having large electric shocks applied to your testicles via heavy duty jump leads.

TWO DOGS SH**GING

A bloke buys two dogs and he can't stop them from sh**ging all the time no matter what he tries. He tries throwing cold water over them, he tries restricting their diets, he tries putting salt on their genitals but nothing works so in desperation he rings his vet in the middle of the night and explains the problem.
"Why don't you try bringing the phone over to the dogs and then give them a ring," suggested the vet.
"Eh? ... Do you think that would work?" said the man.
"It bloody well worked for me," said the vet before he slammed the phone down.

What gives you a hard-on and also gets your boss very excited?
A three hour 0898 telephone call.

If God had intended us to go metric why did he give Jesus twelve disciples?

Did you hear about Evil Knieval's latest daring stunt?
To drive through New Zealand in only second gear with a sheep tied to his back.

What's the definition of confusion?
Fifty blind lesbians in a fish market.

3 COUPLES HONEYMOON!

Three really good mates who have always done everything together get married simultaneously in a triple wedding ceremony and they all go on honeymoon together. The first night in the hotel the boys are having one last drink together before going up to their respective wives to consummate their marriages and one says, "I want to know at breakfast tomorrow which one of us has done the business the most number of times but I can't ask in front of the girls, so let's say that the number of slices of toast that we order for our breakfast denotes the number of times." The other two agree and they all retire to their rooms.

The next morning the three couples all breakfast at the same table and the waiter comes over to take their orders.

The first mate says, with a slight grin, "I'll have a hard boiled egg and two slices of toast, please."

The second mate says, with a large grin, "I'm feeling rather peckish this morning so I think I'll have two eggs, a rasher of bacon, mushrooms and three slices of toast."

The third mate then says, with a massive grin, "I'm ravenous this morning. I think I'll have three scrambled eggs, tomatoes, mushrooms, three rashers of bacon, baked beans, two sausages and six slices of toast ... and you'd better make two of them brown!"

What's worse, ignorance or apathy?
I don't know and I don't care.

Did you h CENSORED has brought out a new book?
Around th

What do you get if you cross an apple with a nun?
A computer that will never go down on you.

GEORGE ENJOYS AFTERLIFE

Mildred goes to see a medium and manages to make contact with her late husband George.
"What do you do up there in heaven George?" asked Mildred.
George replies, "I get up early in the morning and go for a swim, then I have a s**g, then I have a bite to eat. Then I rest for a bit before going for a swim again. Then I have a s**g again, and then I get a bite to eat, have a rest and finally go for a swim and have another s**g before retiring for the night."
"George!" replied an astounded Mildred, "You were never like that when you were alive!"
"Well, I wasn't a duck then, was I Mildred?" said George.

Mummy, mummy, why do I keep going round in circles?
Shut up or I'll nail your other foot to the floor.

A VERY UNUSUAL GIRL

Mary has been born with three vaginas, a top one, a middle one and a bottom one, all one above the other. When she's eighteen she goes off to university with her best friend Sally and they discover men. Mary has a succession of boyfriends but never seems to be able to keep them for any length of time and Sally begins to wonder if her friend will ever get into a steady relationship.
After the two leave university they lose touch, then one day ten years later they meet in the street and after they have exchanged pleasantries Sally asks, "Did you ever marry then Mary?"
She is surprised when Mary replies, "Yes, I've been married to Greg for four years now and we've got two kids."
"Congratulations," exclaims Sally, "So what does he do for a living?"
"He's a professional mouth organ player," replied Mary.

What did one lesbian say to the other?
Your face or mine.

Mummy, mummy, why does everyone keep running away from me?
Shut up, and just keep re-loading.

VG

THE DISGRACEFUL DOCTOR

Winna Bolokov, Russian women's shot putt champion, goes to see a back specialist suffering from a persistent bad back. After having made Winna do a few stretching exercises the doctor says, "Okay Winna, take all your clothes off," and this Winna does.
"Right, now lie on the floor on your back with your legs apart," said the doctor and this Winna does and she's hanging out all over the place as she's a big girl is Winna.
"Right now Winna, I want you to open your mouth as wide as possible ... that's it ... really wide ... wider still please," orders the doctor and this Winna does.
"Right now Winna, whilst keeping your mouth open as wide as possible I want you to use both your hands to pull open your lower lips as wide as possible ... that's it ... really wide ... wider still please ... Great, you've got it, just hold it there for a few seconds ... Okay, you can get dressed now Winna," said the doctor.
A slightly bemused Winna puts her clothes back on and finally she decides to speak what's on her mind and asks, "What did that business with me on the floor tell you doctor?"
"It told me that I ought to buy those two expensive pink cushions that I've seen in Habitat as they would look good on the big white leather sofa that I've got at home Winna," replied the doctor.

Mummy, mummy, is this the right way to learn to swim?
Shut up and get back in the sack.

What do you call Irish Lesbians?
Gaelics.

THE CONSIDERATE HUSBANDS

Ted is pacing up and down anxiously waiting for news about the arrival of his first child. In contrast, Brian, another expectant father, is sitting in his chair and looking very calm and unworried.
Ted says to Brian, "Aren't you nervous?"
"Nah," replies Brian, "I was for the first two but this is going to be our ninth child. It's expensive this hospital isn't it?"
"You must know all about these things," said Ted as he lowered his voice and moved closer to Brian, "Perhaps you can tell me how long I should leave it before I have sex with my wife again?"
"Are you in a public ward or private ward?" asked Brian.
"A public ward," replied Ted.
"Oh well, you'll have to wait until you get her home then!!" said Brian.

How many Kiwi's does it take to eat a sheep?
Three, one to eat, and the other two to keep a look out.

THE UNWANTED SEX-CHANGE

A man goes into hospital for a routine circumcision. However, after he wakes up from the anaesthetic he sees a large group of worried looking doctors looking down at him and fearing the worst he asks, "What's wrong?"
"Err ... there's been a slight mix up ... err ... We performed the wrong operation on you. Instead of a circumcision we gave you a sex-change operation. We removed your penis and gave you a vagina," said one of the doctors.
"What?" cried the man as he felt between his legs in disbelief, "That's terrible! You mean I'll never again experience an erection?"
"Well, you will," replied the doctor hesitantly, "but it will be someone else's."

Mummy, mummy, can I lick the bowl clean?
No, pull the chain like everyone else.

What do you call a leek in a condom?
A more than adequate replacement.

Mummy, mummy, the milkman's here. Can you pay him or shall I go out to play?

What's the difference between love and the Houses of Parliament?
Love is full of Cupid's stunts.

THE LIMP HONEYMOONER

Bill had just returned from a week of honeymooning and his best friend asked him how it went.
"The first night we did it nine times," said Bill.
"The second night we did it eight times," continued Bill.
"The third night we did it four times, the fourth night three times, the fifth night twice and the sixth night ... nothing!" continued Bill.
"Nothing?" queried his friend, "How come?"
Bill replied, "Hey, have you ever tried putting a marshmallow in a parking meter?"

"No peeping darling, happy birthday."

MAN TAKES 4 LEGGED LOVER! VG

An Eastern newspaper correspondent had just arrived in an old remote western town when he notices a curious lack of women so when he walks into the local saloon that night he asks the barman, "What do you folks do around here for entertainment?"
"Ya mean women?" asked the barman, "We ain't got none. Round here folks sc**w sheep."
"That's disgusting!" exclaimed the shocked correspondent, "I've never heard of such moral degradation."

However, after a few months without sex the correspondent's rocks were beginning to ache and the sheep were starting to look more and more attractive.
Finally, he could do without it no longer and he went out and found himself a cute sheep. He brought her back to his room, shampooed her, blow dried her coat of wool, perfumed her, tied ribbons in her hair and attached a pair of his mothers earrings to her ears. After a bottle of champagne he lured the sheep into his bedchamber and then proceeded to release all his pent up frustrations.
Afterwards he escorted his four-legged lover into the saloon for a drink. As the correspondent and his woolly other half entered the room a hush fell over the patrons, the pianist stopped playing and the anxious couple became the object of many fixed stares.
The correspondent could take it no more and he yelled out, "You goddam bunch of hypocrites! You've been sc**wing sheep for years, but when I do it and do it up right you look at me like I'm some sort of crazy pervert!"
A cowboy at the back of the crowd shouted out, "That's the sheriff's gal!!"

What's the best thing about self-abuse?
You don't have to look your best.

Did you hear about the Irishman who thought Anita Harris was an operation for haemorrhoids?

What's the difference between fear and panic?
Fear is when you find out for the first time that you can't do it a second time. Panic is when you find out for the second time that you can't do it for the first time.

STAY OFF LAGER!

A man walks into his doctor's and says, "You've got to help me doc, I'm having trouble with my sex life."
"How do you mean?" asked the doctor.
"Well, for starters when I make love to my wife it doesn't even touch the sides," moaned the man.
"I know what your trouble is, you drink lager don't you?" said the doctor.
"Yes I do," replied the man.
"Well, the problem with lager is that it makes things shrivel up," said the doctor, "What you need to do is to start drinking Guinness, it makes things big and strong. Go away and try it and come back in a month."
The man returns one month later and the doctor asks, "How's your sex life?"
"Terrific," smiles the man.
"Did you do what I said, did you drink the Guinness?" asked the doctor.
"No, I put the wife on lager," replied the man.

Mummy, mummy, I hate daddy's guts.
Well, leave them on the side of your plate then.

What's pink and wrinkled and hangs out your underpants first thing in the morning?
Your mum.

THE MUSICAL DOG

Fred walks into a pub with his dog. While Fred goes upto the bar his dog climbs onto the piano stool and proceeds to play the piano perfectly. The pub's clientele are amazed at this and the barman says, "That's some dog you've got there."
"He certainly is," said Fred proudly, "He can play any musical instrument."
On hearing this a man took a guitar off the wall and the dog played it perfectly.

The amazed barman says, "Hey, we could make some money here. Why not bring the dog back to the pub in a couple of days time and I'll advertise about a special evening whereby if anyone can bring in an instrument that the dog can't play then they win £100. If the entry fee is £20 we should make a tidy profit."

Fred agrees and two days later he and the dog return to the pub. One man gives the dog a flute but he plays it well. Another man brings in a cello but again the dog plays it well. A harp, an oboe and clarinet all follow but all are played competently.

At the end of the evening the barman rather rashly says, "Okay, if someone cares to give the dog one final challenge it's winner takes all."

Just at that moment a Scotsman walks into the pub and throws his bagpipes onto the floor. The dog runs upto the bagpipes and bites it. Then he shoves it a bit with his paw. Then he starts to bark at it, then run away and come darting back. Then he drags the bagpipes across the floor a bit and starts to wrestle with it.

"I've won the bet," beamed the Scot as he started to stuff his winnings up under his kilt.

"Not so fast," said Fred, "When the dog realises he can't f*** it he'll play it!"

OLD LADY JOINS THE QUEUE

An old lady is walking along a side street in Soho at the same time that the Old Bill are raiding a brothel. The police have lined up all the tarts in the street and the old lady sees the queue and asks the tart at the end of the line, "Excuse me dear, but what are you all queueing for?"

"We're queueing for honeysuckle favoured lollipops!" replied the tart sarcastically.

On hearing this the old girl joined the end of the queue.

A policeman goes down the queue questioning the tarts and when he comes to the old girl he says, "You're a bit old for this game aren't you?"

The old girl replied defiantly, "I may not have any teeth but I can still suck!"

SANTA VISITS HOSPITAL

It's Xmas eve and Santa has just come down the chimney into the amputations ward of the local hospital. The patients have all left a letter for Santa at the foot of their beds requesting what they want for Xmas. Santa goes up to the first bed and reads that the man wants an arm, so he reaches into his bag and pulls out an arm and leaves it in his stocking.

Santa goes up to the second bed and reads that the man wants a leg, so Santa reaches into his bag and pulls out a leg and leaves it in the man's stocking.

Santa continues going along the beds dishing out various limbs as requested until he gets to the very last bed in the ward and sees that the bed belongs to just a head, being kept alive by a multitude of pipes and tubes. The head's letter requests two arms, two legs and a torso so Santa delves into his bag only to discover that the bag is now devoid of any more spare parts. "SH*T!!!" curses Santa. Being right out of presents Santa tries to think real hard about what he can give the head. He then takes the pull-string out of his sack and puts it into the head's stocking together with a short note which reads, "Thread through throat. ENJOY! Go conkering!!"

What's the largest drawback in the jungle?
An elephant's foreskin.

Mummy, mummy, what's a nymphomaniac?
Shut up, and help me get granny off the doorknob.

Chapter 11

A few more Crackers

What goes Boo-Hoo, Boo-Hoo, Boo-Hoo, SPLATTTTT?
A child crying his eyes out.

What do you call a WPC who shaves her pubes?
C**tstubble.

What's black and white and quivers?
A nun with a vibrator.

PASSION IN THE PARK

A young man goes to the Hammersmith Palais but he's having no luck at all and can't pull anything. It's getting near the end of the night and he's just about to leave when he sees this girl in a wheelchair making eyes at him. He goes over to her and starts chatting to her. At the end of the night she asks him if he'd mind pushing her home as her sister had left her on her own and he agrees.

The man and the girl are halfway home when the girl says, "Let's take the short cut through the park," and the man agrees.

When they're in the middle of the park the girl starts crying and says, "Will you make love to me, I've never been made love to before. The boys just see the wheelchair and aren't interested."

"Of course I will," replied the man, "but,..err..how?"

"Why don't you lift me out of my wheelchair and hook my

thick aran jumper over one of those spiked railings over there and then you'll be free to have your wicked way with me," suggested the girl helpfully.

The man agrees and hooks her jumper over the railings so her legs are off the ground and he then gives her a good seeing to.

He then takes her home whereupon he meets the girls father on the doorstep.

The father has a torch in his hand and he says to his daughter, "I was just coming to look for you."

The man says, "You'd nothing to worry about sir. I've taken good care of her."

"I bet you have," sneered the father.

The man, feeling guilty and starting to blush, says, "I can assure you sir that nothing improper happened."

"I suppose I ought to be grateful," sneered the father as he looked at his daughter's torn jumper and said, "All the other blokes just left her dangling there."

If you find salt in salt cellars.
If you find beer in beer cellars.
If you find wine in wine cellars.
Where do you find knives?
In Monica Seles.

Heard about the new film release which has been a big success in Iraq?

It's called, "Honey, I skudded the Yids."

THE TORTOISE AND THE HARE

A tortoise and a hare were talking one day when the tortoise suggested a race. The hare accepted at once, in the knowledge that hares were many times faster than tortoises.

The tortoise then said, "And why don't we have some money on it?"

The hare noted the tortoise's confidence and also remembered the story of what had once happened to a cousin of his in a

similar race against a tortoise and he asked suspiciously,
"You've got no ears have you?"
"Nope."
"And you've got no eyebrows have you?" continued the hare.
"Nope."
"And your skin ... it's all scaly," continued the hare, "Are you sure you're not Nicki Lauda?"

A bloke goes into the Post Office and says, "Cnan ny knave a knirst knass knamp knease."
"Sounds to me like you need some TUNES!!!" said the counter assistant cheerily.
"Why?" replied the man, "Knill knat knure a cleft Knallette knen?"

What's grey and comes in pints?
Elephants.

ADOLF HITLER RETURNS!

A journalist is having a quiet drink in a Berlin bar when he sees two old men chatting at a table and he thinks they look vaguely familar. He gets closer and closer to them and then goes up to one of them and says, "Forgive me for interrupting you, but aren't you Joseph Goebbels, the former Nazi Head of Propaganda?"
"Das ist correct," replied Goebbels, "but keep your voice down!!"
"And isn't your companion Adolf Hitler," continued the astonished man.
"Yah, dis ist true. I am Adolf Hitler. Your Führer!" said Adolf.
"So what are you two boys doing back in Berlin? I thought you were both growing coffee in South America," asked the journalist.
"Adolf and I are planning to resurrect the third reich very

shortly," replied Goebbels.
"And this time," added Hitler shaking his head, "NO MORE MISTER NICE GUY!!!"
"Yah," nodded Goebbels, "This time we are going to do things properly. We are going to round up 30 million Jews, and we are going to round up the two opening batsmen from the English National cricket team!"
"You're going to round up the two opening batsmen from the English National cricket team?" repeated the journalist.
"There," said Adolf as he turned to Goebbels, "I told you no one would give a damn about the Jews!"

How do you tell the sex of a chromosome?
Pull down it's genes.

Who are the Australian Nobility?
Those who can trace their ancestry back to their fathers.

Did you hear about the man who entered his dog at Crufts?
He got six months.

What word has 24 letters, begins with 'N', ends with 'N', has an 'N' in the middle and has to do with constipation?
NNNNNNNNNNNNNNNNNNNNNNNN.

What's pink and has seven dents in it?
Snow White's hymen.

What do you call a Vietnamese family with two dogs?
Livestock farmers.

Why are sheep able to eat quickly in Sellafield?
Because two heads are better than one.

COLONEL SMITHERS, DSO, VC, OBE "THIS IS YOUR LIFE"

Colonel Smithers, DSO, VC, OBE, the famous legless and armless wartime hero is being honoured on the TV program, "This is your life." One by one an impressive array of fellow wartime hero's and dignatories pay tribute to the Colonel's bravery and achievements ...

Aspel ... "Before the show ends I must ask you Colonel, because the viewers at home will be wanting to know, how exactly did you come to lose both your arms and both your legs?"

Colonel ... "Well Michael, I was lost alone in the Burmese jungle when a Jap appeared from nowhere. As I took aim with my pistol he cut my arm off with his samarai sword. As I tried to pick up the gun with my other hand he cut my other arm off with his samurai sword. As I lay on the ground, being British, I defiantly tried to kick out at him with my legs, so he cut both my legs off with his samurai sword. And you know what Michael? ...The rotten b*****d left me lying there to slowly bleed to death!"

Aspel ... "That's right. And you haven't seen him for over fifty years so we've flown him 6,000 miles from his home town of Osaki so that he could be with you tonight ..."

Why have Irishmen got T.G.I.F. on their shoes?
Toes go in first.

Did you hear about the stowaway caught on deck by the gay Captain?
He was told he would have to work his passage.

How can you tell the widc  ral?
He's the one wearing the t

IF I DON'T SCORE TONIGHT I'LL TOP MYSELF!!

Richard was thirty-five and still a virgin! Every Friday for the last eighteen years he had gone down the local disco with his mates and whilst they always pulled left, right and centre he always returned home to his dingy bedsit alone ...
One Friday, as Richard was getting ready to go to the disco he made a promise to himself, "If I don't get my end away tonight I'm going to top myself!"
That night at the disco Richard, as usual, was having no luck at all. With an impending suicide looming nearer and nearer and with only ten minutes remaining before the disco ended Richard spotted the ugliest, fattest girl he had ever seen. Taking a deep breath he went over and asked the girl if she would like a drink.
"Quit the crap, let's go back to your place and scr**!" she immediately replied.
VG
As they started to make love back at Richard's bedsit Richard stopped and looked down at the girl and said, "Do you mind if I turn the light off?"
The girl started to cry and sobbed, "You want the light off because I'm really, really fat and really, really ugly and 'orrible don't you?"
"No, of course not," comforted Richard, "It's just that I keep scorching my backside on the lightbulb!"

Bill: "Flob-a-lob-a-loba-loba-lob."
Ben: "Oh, flob-a-lob-loba-loba-lob."
BR Interviewer: "Congratulations boys, you can start as platform announcers on Monday."

Did you hear about the blind skunk?
He fell in love with a fart.

What do you call a condom with sand in it?
An organ grinder.

FAMILY FALL FOR SKUNK!

A family of four fly to Arizona for a camping holiday and have a great time. Whilst there they start feeding a wild skunk and all the family fall for it ...

The wife says, "Why don't we try to smuggle the skunk back through Customs and have it as a pet back home?"

"Yeah, why not? You could put it down your knickers when we go through Customs dear," replies the husband.

"Yeah, but what about the smell?" asks the wife.

"If it dies, it dies," replies the husband.

At the World Epileptic Disco Dancing Championships yesterday the eventual winner expressed some surprise at being awarded the trophy.

He said, "I only got up to go to the toilet!"

What was Terry Waite's specialist subject on Mastermind?

Lebanese radiators, 1985-91.

VICAR SEES TRULY AWFUL SIGHT

A vicar is out for a walk when he gets caught short so he pops into a pub and goes into the gents. In the toilets he is deeply shocked to see three men all with their trousers down around their ankles all interlocked with each other "conga" style. The vicar stumbles out of the loos and over to the landlord. Having told the landlord what he has just seen the landlord asks, "Was the man in the middle a small guy with a moustache and glasses Reverend?"

"Yes he was," mumbled the shocked vicar.

"Yeah, the lucky b*****d always wins at dominoes as well!" sneered the landlord.

A woman wakes up with a terrible hangover. She's in a strange bed with an elephant lying next to her!!...

Woman: "Phorr, I must have been tight last night!"

Elephant: "Well actually, no."

MUMMY
K

SCHOOL

Chapter 12

The Top Thirty Funniest Jokes in the Whole World

The Top 30

1ST PLACE
THE APPRENTICE MORTICIAN

These two old guys, Harry and Ted, are in the workers rest room of the local mortuary when one of the young apprentice morticians comes running in and says very excitedly, "I think you ought to come and have a look at the woman in room three, drawer twenty one."
"Oh yeah," replies Harry, "and why is that then?"
"I know this sounds really strange but she's got a whelk up her f***y," said the young lad excitedly.
"Look, we'll come and have a look after we've finished our coffee break," said Harry, "but I don't think we'll find a whelk up her f***y. I don't think you know what the bloody hell you're talking about young man!"
Having finished their coffees Harry and Ted go into room three with the young lad and pull out drawer twenty one. Harry takes off the white sheet covering the woman's naked body and asks the young lad and old Ted to hold and part a leg each while he investigates with his torch.
"There it is," cried the young lad excitedly, "There's the whelk. I told you she had a whelk up her f***y, but you wouldn't believe me."
"That's not a whelk, you pratt," growled old Harry, "That's a woman's clit****."
"Well, it tastes like a whelk," said the young lad.

2ND PLACE
TOP OF THE CLASS

A Puerto Rican kid comes home from school and says to his mother, "We had a history test at school today mum. The history teacher said that I came top. Is that because I'm black?"
"No son, that's because you're clever," said his mother reassuringly.
The next day the boy comes home from school and says, "We had a maths test at school today and the maths teacher said that I came top. Is that because I'm black?"
"No son, that's because you're clever," replied his mother reassuringly.
The next day the boy comes home from school and says, "We had PE today mum."
"That was nice for you darling," replied his mother.
"Mum," says the boy, a little worried, "After PE we all had a shower and I couldn't help noticing that my willy was twice as big as all the other boys willies. Is that because I'm black?"
"No son," replied his mother, "That's because they're all seven and you're fourteen."

The Top 30

3RD PLACE
JOHN PLAYS FISHY FINGERS

Little Johnny is sent home from school early and his mother rings the school to find out why.
"He's been very naughty," says his teacher, "He's been caught putting his hand up little Mary's skirt playing Fishy Fingers."
The mother gives little Johnny a good telling off and sends him to bed early.
A few days later little Johnny comes home from school early again and this time the mother gets a call from the Headmaster who says, "Johnny's been caught playing Fishy Fingers with little Mary again and her mother is furious. I'm afraid to say that if it happens again I shall have to expel your son."
The mother is, naturally, very worried and she decides to frighten the little boy.
"Johnny you mustn't ever put your fingers up there again because little girls grow teeth up there as they get older and the teeth will bite your fingers off," says the mother.
The little boy is really frightened by this tale and never plays Fishy Fingers again.
Twenty years later Johnny is a fully qualified dentist and he's just got married, and he and his bride have just retired to the bridal suite. Immediately they both strip off and fool around for a while ... and a while ... and a while ...
Eventually the bride becomes impatient and says, "Well, aren't

you going to put your willy in?"
"You must be joking," gasps Johnny, "You've got teeth up there, my mother told me. You might bite my thingy off!"
The bride rolls about laughing at this, but no matter how hard she tries to convince him otherwise Johnny keeps saying, "I'm not putting it up there, you've got teeth up there, you might bite my thingy off."
"Look," says the girl in desperation, "Shine a torch up there and see if you can see any teeth," and this Johnny does with great caution.
"There now, you can see I haven't got any teeth up there, have I?" giggled the bride.
"I'm not surprised," gasps Johnny, "Have you seen the state of your gums!!!!"

4....4....4....4

BIG GIRL VISITS DOCTOR

Olga Bolorov, Russian female shot putt champion, goes to her doctor suffering from a persistent sore throat. The doctor takes down a few preliminary details and then looks down her throat. He then says, "Olga, I'd like you take all your clothes off," and this Olga does.
"Right, now Olga I'd like you to go down on your hands and knees," said the doctor. This, a slightly bemused Olga does and everything is hanging out all over the place because she's a big girl is Olga.
"Right now Olga," continued the doctor, "I'd like you to go over to that corner of the room on your hands and knees," and this Olga does.

The Top 30

"Right, now go over on your hands and knees to the window, so I can see you properly in the strong light," continued the doctor, and this Olga did as the doctor put his hand on his chin and weighed things up.
"Right then Olga, can you now just go over on your hands and knees to the far corner of the room by the door please," continued the doctor, and this Olga does.
"Okay Olga," says the doctor, "You can put your clothes back on now," and this Olga does.
Having dressed Olga asks, "What's the verdict then doc?"
Without hesitation the doctor replies, "You've got a sore throat Olga!!"

"Well, I knew that before I came here!" exclaims a disgruntled Olga, "What was the purpose of me going about on my hands and knees without any clothes on?"
"Well Olga," replies the doctor, "I'm getting delivery of a big white leather sofa tomorrow and I wanted to try to decide where the best place to put it was!"

The Top 30

5....5....5....5

A POTATO MIGHT HELP!

Two mates, Fred and Joe, join the local swimming club because they've heard that that is where the best of the local talent hangs out. Before long Fred, the stronger built of the two, is pulling left, right and centre, but poor Joe is having no luck at all. One day Joe moans to Fred, "I can't believe the amount of women you're scoring with. I'm really p***ed off, I haven't had so much as a nibble since I joined this club. Can you offer any advice?"
Fred looks his rather puny mate up and down and has a ponder before saying, "Why don't you try putting a small potato down your swimming trunks? It might make a difference."
Joe agrees to give Fred's suggestion a try and they part company.
Two weeks later Fred decides to give Joe a ring and says, "Joe old buddy, how's your love life you old ram!"
Joe replies rather dejectedly, "Still no luck I'm afraid."
Fred responds, "Perhaps you're coming out with the wrong lines or something ... Look, let's go down the swimming club tonight and I'll watch you in action with the birds."
Joe and Fred agree to meet by the pool that night and when Fred gets there he sees that Joe has already had a dip and has sidled up to a cluster of nookie by the waters edge.
Fred waves Joe over and over Joe comes. Fred whispers to Joe, "Try putting the potato down the front of your trunks."

The Top 30

6....6....6....6
AN OLD MAN'S DELIGHT

A man has looked after his elderly father for a number of years but he's getting more and more of a handful so the son tells him one day, "Sorry dad, but the time has come when I've got to put you in a home. I'm sorry but I can't cope anymore."
The old coffindodger doesn't want to go and kicks up a right fuss but ends up in the home anyway. On his first day there the old boy rings his son and says cheerily, "It ain't so bad in here after all son. A really pretty young nurse gave me a bath this afternoon and you'll never guess what son?... I had my first hard on in twenty years ... And you'll never guess what son? The nurse saw it, was really pleased for me and gave me a blow job. It was bloody fantastic!"
"You lucky old git," says the son.
"I wish you'd got me in here sooner son," chuckles the old boy.
The phone call over, the old boy goes for a walk around the grounds. While walking he falls over and struggles and struggles to get upright again. As he's bent over double trying to stand up a male nurse accosts him from behind and interferes with him.
Eventually, the poor old boy regains his composure and he goes back to the payphone and rings his son and sobs, "Son, you've got to get me out of this place."
The son replies, "I just don't understand you dad! Only about half an hour ago you loved the place and now you're dying to leave. You loved the blow job didn't you? What's the problem?"
"The problem is," sobs the old boy, "At my age I only get one hard on every twenty years but I fall over about four times a day!"

The Top 30

7 . . . . 7 . . . . 7 7

MAN WINS £2 MILLION

A man wins £2 million on the pools but he's got no one to enjoy spending the money with. He hasn't got any family and he hasn't got any friends except a woman penpal who lives out in the wilds of Northern Canada. The man decides to write to the penpal he has never met. He writes, "I've won £2 million on the pools, why don't you come over and help me spend the money? We could have the time of our lives. We could go deep sea fishing , surfing, skiing, flying ... we could do the lot!"
The penpal writes back, "I'd love to come, but I think I ought to tell you that I've only got one leg. Does that matter?"
The pools winner writes back, "It doesn't matter, come over."
The penpal writes back, "I'd love to come over but I think I ought to tell you that I've also only got one arm. Does that matter?"
The pools winner is starting to wonder what's he letting himself in for but she's the only friend he's got so he writes back, "It doesn't matter, come over."
The penpal writes back, "I'd love to come over but I think I ought to tell you that I lost an eye in a car crash and I wear a patch. Does that matter?"
"It doesn't matter, come over," was the reply.
The penpal writes back, "I'm really looking forward to coming over but I think I ought to let you know that I suffer from a slight abnormality in that my breasts protrude from the back of my body rather than from the front. Does that matter?"

The Top 30

The man shakes his head in utter disbelief and curses before writing back, "It doesn't matter, come over."

The penpal writes back, "I've bought a complete new set of holiday clothes and I've found someone to rent the house to while I'm away and I'm really looking forward to coming over. There is one thing I feel I ought to tell you before I come over and that is that I've got a second head growing out of my backside. Does that matter?"

"It doesn't matter, come over," came the reply.

The penpal writes back, "I'll be arriving at 9.15 on the twenty second of March at Gatwick, terminal three. Looking forward to meeting you at last. Thanks for coming to the airport to pick me up."

The pools winner writes back, "See you soon. Before you leave send me a photo so I'll know which one you are at the airport."

The Top 30

8....8....8....8
VERY EXPENSIVE SHOES

An ageing, rich playboy has got a date lined up with a stunning bimbo and he wants to let her know he's worth a bit so he decides to buy himself an expensive pair of shoes.

He goes into a West End shoe shop and asks, "What have you got in a size nine that's a bit tasty?"

"We've got a very nice pair of snakeskin shoes sir, although they're a bit pricey," said the assistant.

"How much?" asked the man.

"They cost £199 sir," said the assistant.

"Got anything else that's a bit more exclusive?" asked the man.

"We've got a lovely pair of crocodile shoes for £550 sir. They're very exclusive sir, normally only worn by pop stars and heads of state sir," said the assistant.

"Are they the most expensive pair of shoes you sell?" asked the man.

"Err ... no sir. We have these sir," said the assistant bringing out a pair of very soft black shoes, "These shoes are made totally from human skin sir and they retail for £1400 sir. We've only ever sold one pair and that was to the Sultan of Brunei sir."

The man tries the shoes on and they feel just great and he asks, "Have you got them in any other colour?"

"We've got them in white for £3. 99," replied the assistant.

The Top 30

9....9....9....9
TIDDLES DIES AND GOES UP TO HEAVEN

Little Lucy went out into the garden and saw her pet cat lying on the ground with it's eyes shut and it's legs in the air. She fetched her dad to look at Tiddles and on seeing the cat he said, as gently as he could, "I'm afraid Tiddles is dead Lucy."

"So why are his legs sticking up in the air like that daddy?" asked Lucy as she fought back the tears.

At a loss for something to say her father replied, "Tiddles legs are pointing straight up in the air so that it will be easier for Jesus to float down from heaven above and grab a leg and lift Tiddles up to heaven."

Little Lucy seemed to take her cats death quite well. However, two days later when her father came home from work Lucy had tears in her eyes and she said, "Mummy almost died this morning."

Fearing something terrible had happened the father shook the girl and shouted, "How do you mean Lucy? Tell daddy! Tell daddy!"

"Well," mumbled Lucy, "soon after you left for work this morning I saw mummy lying on the floor with her eyes shut and her legs in the air and she was saying, "Oh Jesus! I'm coming, I'm coming!" and if it hadn't been for the milkman holding her down she would definitely have gone daddy."

The Top 30

10 . . .10 . . .10 . . .10

YOU'VE GOT ZACHARY SYNDROME

A worried young woman goes to her doctor's and says, "You've got to help me doctor, I'm almost twenty seven and I've never had a boyfriend. I think there's something wrong with me. Please help me."
The doctor takes down a few details and then says, "Could you please remove all your clothes Miss Brown," and this the girl does. The doctor then says, "Now, could you please bend over and touch your toes," and this the girl does. The doctor then bends down and studies the girls rear end very closely indeed.
"What is it doctor? Please tell me, I knew there was something wrong with me, what is it?" pleaded the girl.
"I think you're suffering from Zachary syndrome," said the doctor.
"What's Zachary syndrome? I knew something was wrong with me. What's Zachary syndrome? Please tell me," pleaded the girl.
"Before I say anything I'd like a second opinion," replied the doctor, "So can you please get dressed and go into the corridor, turn left and take the second door on the left, and go and see my Chinese colleague, Dr Chan." This the girl does.
The girl says, as she walks into Dr Chan's room, "I'm almost twenty seven and I've never had a boyfriend, I think there must be something wrong with me, please help me."
Dr. Chan says, "You take clothes off," and this the girl does.
Dr. Chan then says, "You bend over. You touch toes," and this

The Top 30

the girl does. The doctor then studies the girls rear end very closely indeed.
"What is it doctor? What's wrong with me? Please tell me?" pleaded the girl.

"Hmm ... you got Zachary Syndrome," said Dr. Chan.
"That's what the first doctor said. Please tell me. What is it? What is Zachary Syndrome?" pleaded the girl.
The Chinese doctor replied, "Face look Zachary like backside!"

The Top 30

11 . . . 11 . . . 11 . . .11

MAKING MEDICAL HISTORY

A man goes to the doctor's with a swelling on his forehead and the doctor says, "This is a very unusual swelling so I'm going to take a small sample from it and send it away to a laboratory to be analysed. Come back in two weeks and I'll have the results for you."

The man returns two weeks later and it is clearly noticeable that the swelling is bigger.

"What is it doc?" asks the man.

"I've got your results back. Congratulations Mr Coleman!" said the smiling doctor as he patted the man on the back, "You're making medical history. You've got a penis growing out of your forehead."

"You're pulling my leg," laughed the man.

"No I'm not. Within four weeks it'll have grown into a full size penis the same size as the one you've got downstairs," said the doctor.

The man gasps, "Can't it be removed doc?"
"Too risky I'm afraid," said the doctor, "You see the new penis is connected to the brain and it's removal could result in brain damage or even death."
"Are you trying to tell me doc," said the man becoming increasingly agitated, "That every day when I get up and look in the bathroom mirror for a shave I'm going to see a life size willy looking back at me."
"Well, err ... hmm ... not quite," said the doctor hesitantly.
"Look," demanded the man, "Give it to me straight. When I get up in the morning and look in the bathroom cabinet mirror WILL I SEE A PENIS LOOKING BACK AT ME OR NOT?"
The doctor replied, "No you won't see a penis looking back at you when you look in the mirror ... err ... You won't be able to see the mirror because you'll have a bol***k dangling over each eyelid!"

12...12...12...12
CARLO'S PATHETIC BRODDER

Two Italian brothers marry two sisters and they have a joint wedding ceremony and also go to the same honeymoon hotel that night.
After the first night Carlo, the elder brother, asks Luigi, "Eh, Luigi, how many times did you f**ka yo wife last night?"
"Eh, brodder, I f**ka her two times," replied Luigi.
"Only two times, you sissy! You shame a da family! I f**ka ma

wife 23 times!!!" said Carlo as he slapped his brother across the face.
"Your a kidding, how could you?" said Luigi.
"Donna forget you a Italian. Tonight you try a da harder," said Carlo.
The next day Carlo eagerly asks his brother, "Eh, Luigi, how many times you f**ka da wife last night?"
"Eh brodder, last night I try really hard, I f**ka her four a times," replied Luigi.
"Four a times! You're pathetic! I f**ka ma wife thirty five times. Donna let Pappa find out. Tonight you try real hard, eh?, eh?" shouted Carlo.
The next day a very similar conversation takes place and Luigi says, "Eh, Carlo, I did my best. Ma wife cannot walk this morning. I f**ka her six times and we're both dead."
"You're no brodder of mine! Call yourself Italian! I am ashamed," shouted Carlo as he slapped Luigi across the face.
"Carlo, I begga you, you tella me how you do it so many times, pleasa, pleasa," pleaded Luigi.
Carlo puts his hands on his hips and thrusts his pelvis forward and says, "Dats a one." He thrusts his pelvis forward again and says, "Dats a two, ... dats a three ... dats a four ..."

The Top 30

13...13...13...13

JOHN MAJOR'S PUNISHMENT

John Major, John Smith and Paddy Ashdown all die in a plane crash and they float up to heaven and are taken to see St. Peter. St. Peter takes them down a long corridor and they get to a wooden door. It opens and inside are a wooden table, wooden chair, wooden floor, wooden bed and a glass of water and a piece of stale bread.

St. Peter turns to Paddy Ashdown and says, "For all the sins that you have committed during your lifetime, Paddy Ashdown, this is your punishment for the rest of eternity." Paddy is pushed into the room and the door is locked.

St. Peter then walks along to the next door which is made of stone. The door opens and inside the room there is a stone table, stone chair, stone floor, stone bed and a glass of water and crust of bread. St. Peter turns to John Smith and says, "For all the sins that you have committed during your lifetime, John Smith, this is your punishment for the rest of eternity." John Smith is then pushed into the room and the door is locked.

St. Peter and John Major then walk on to the next door and it swings open and they both go in. In the corner of the room a log fire burns, the room is covered with deep pile carpets and famous works of art hang on the walls. The table is full of food and wine. In the centre of the room is a massive four poster bed and lying on the bed is Cindy Crawford, and she's stark naked. A large grin breaks out over John Majors face.

St. Peter says, "For all the sins you have committed during your lifetime, Cindy Crawford, this is your punishment for the rest of eternity."

The Top 30

14...14...14...14
DUMP ON MY CHEST

This girl's a bit kinky because she likes her boyfriends to crap on her chest and rub it in. She gets this new boyfriend and explains her fetish to him and he agrees to oblige. He does a massive dump on her chest and rubs it in and the girl's writhing in ecstasy at this.

The relationship continues for some time and the boy always comes round to her flat on the same three days in each week and always does a massive dump on her chest, without fail, whereupon the girl always goes wild with pleasure. One day, however, the bus was late for the journey taking the boy to visit the girl and he couldn't hold out any longer so he dashed into the public toilets and had a crap there.

When he eventually arrived at his girlfriends flat she was already sprawled out on the carpet completely naked and she was patting her chest and saying frantically, "Dump on me, dump on me." The boy tried as hard as he could but nothing would come out and there was a distinct air of anti-climax as the girl got herself dressed.

The boy apologised saying, "Look Cheryl, I'm really sorry ... It's never happened before ... I ... I just couldn't hold on any longer so I had to use the public loos. I'll make it up to you, I promise."

The next time the boy is on his way round to see the girl the bus is again late and he can't wait any longer so he again has a crap in the public loos. When he gets to the girl's flat he is again unable to dump on the girl's chest and she, rather annoyed, sends him home early.

The next time the boy goes to see his girl he again has to have

a crap before he gets there and he has to say for the third consecutive time, "I'm sorry but I had to use the public loos again."
"Why don't you tell the truth," said the girl sadly with tears in her eyes, "You're seeing someone else aren't you?"

15 . . . 15 . . . 15 . . .15
A WOMAN CONFESSES

A woman goes into the confession box and says, "Please forgive me Father as I have sinned."
"Tell me my child, how have you sinned?" asked the priest.
"I called a man a F***ING B***ARD," said the ashamed woman.
"How dare you commit such a heinous act, not once but a second time in this very house of our Lord," said the priest angrily.
"I'm sorry Father," said the woman as she started to sob.
"And why, my child, did you call this man such a terrible, terrible thing?" asked the priest.
"Because he started to fondle my breasts Father," said the woman.
"What you mean like this my child," said the priest as his hands reached through the hatch and fondled her breasts.
"And then he started kissing me all over," said the woman.
"What you mean like this, my child," said the priest as he climbed through the hatch and started kissing her all over.
"And then he touched me between the legs," said the woman.
"What you mean like this, my child," said the priest as he put

his hand up her skirt.
"And then he took all my clothes off," said the woman.
"What you mean like this, my child?" said the priest as he took off all the girl's clothes and then his own.
"And then he went the whole way with me," said the woman.
"What you mean like this, my child," said the priest as he started to do the business.
"And then he told me he'd got VD!" said the girl.
"The F***ING B*****D," screamed the priest.

16...16...16...16

GOODBYE WEDDING TACKLE

A man went to the doctor's complaining of a constant headache and a constant ringing sound in his ears. After a very thorough examination the doctor said, "You have got an infection of the testicles. They are swollen and rubbing together and this is the reason for your headaches and the constant ringing noise in your ears. I'm very sorry to have to tell you that the only solution to the complaint is to have both your testicles removed."
The man is deeply shocked at this and leaves the surgery vowing never to agree to such a remedy. However, the headaches and the constant ringing noise in his ears continue to drive him round the bend and he seeks a second and third opinion from two other specialists. Sadly, they both say exactly the same thing so the man reluctantly decides to have his manhood removed.
After the operation the man does indeed no longer suffer from

headaches nor the constant ringing noise in his ears but he is still obviously feeling a bit low and decides to cheer himself up by buying a complete set of new clothes from a renowned local tailor.

The man entered the tailor's shop and told the tailor what he was after. The tailor looked him up and down and said, "Ah yes, you'll be wanting a 34 inch waist, a 33 inside leg, a 15 inch collar and a 44 inch chest."

"My word that's amazing! How did you know that?" said the man.

"Well, I've been in the trade for over 35 years, and I can also tell you that you take size 10 shoes, 9 inch hat size and medium size underpants," said the tailor.

"Well, that's right ... apart from the underpants. I wear small size underpants," replied the man.

"No, no definitely not," said the tailor, "A small size underpant on you could be very serious. Why they could make you sterile, and you could suffer from headaches and a really annoying ringing sound in your ears!"

17 . . . 17 . . . 17 . . . 17

THE BEST WAY TO DIET

A really fat man goes to his doctor's and claims that he's tried everything to lose weight but to no avail.

The doctor, realising that the man's obesity could be life threatening says, "Given your family history of heart conditions I really must demand that you take one of two possible courses of action. You can either have your jaws wired together and take in nutrients through a straw, or you can try a revolutionary new method for losing weight from Japan which is called Rectal feeding."

"Well I ain't ever having my jaws wired together, so what's this Rectal feeding business then?" replies the man.

"Well," says the doctor, "In a nutshell, you stuff food up your backside instead of into your mouth. The walls of the rectum are four times thicker than that of the stomach and therefore a much smaller percentage of your foods calories are actually absorbed into the bloodstream. Clever huh? You will absorb enough nutrients to sustain good health whilst at the same time you'll lose weight rapidly."

Three weeks later the man returns for the follow up appointment and he's lost a lot of weight. He's down from 22 stone to just under 14 stone. The doctor shows him into the surgery and the man takes a seat.

"Wow, you've lost a lot of weight, you must be pleased," says the doctor, as he notices that the man seems to be bouncing up and down in his chair a bit.

"Yep doc, I feel like a new man," beams the man.

"Are you sure you feel okay?" asks the doctor as he continues to notice that the man was bouncing ever so slightly up and down in his chair.

"Yep, I feel great," replies the man as he continues to shift and bounce in his chair.

"Please forgive me but I can't help noticing that you seem to be continually bouncing up and down a bit in your chair. Why is that?" asked the doctor.

"Just chewing gum," replies the man.

The Top 30

18...18...18...18

THE RISE OF VAN LESBIAN

A show business agent goes into a night club and sees a very impressive act. The guy can sing great, the guy can dance great and he's a great comedian so the agent dashes backstage after he's finished his turn and says, "I'm Leo Eckstein, I'm the agent for most of the top stars around here. You were great, I can make you a star. What's your name?"
"Penis Van Lesbian," said the man.
"Well I'd like to sign you up but you'll have to change your name," said the agent.
"I couldn't change my name sir. Van Lesbian has been the family name for the last four hundred years. It's a name that is revered throughout Holland," said the man.
"You'll never get anywhere with a name like that. Look kid I really want to sign you up but only on the condition that you agree to change your name," said the agent.
"There's been a famous Dutch painter in our family, and a famous General, and a cabinet politician. They were all Van Lesbians. I'm not changing my name," insisted Penis Van Lesbian.
The agent then storms off shouting, "You'll be a beggar all your life."
Many years later the agent is walking along Broadway and he sees the red carpet out and a mass of photographers for what is obviously a very important opening night. A large Rolls-Royce pulls up outside and who should get out but Penis Van Lesbian.
"Remember me," shouts the agent, "I don't believe it ... you ... you made it to the top without changing your name."
Penis Van Lesbian replies, "Well I did change it a little bit ... I'm Dick Van Dyke now!"

The Top 30

19 . . . 19 . . . 19 . . . 19

SANJIT PLAYS DARTS

Sanjit returns home to his father's house in Bombay after a three month visit to England spent working in his Uncle Rajiv's curry house.

His father asks, "Tell me Sanjit, my son. Were you getting to see much English way of life on England visit?"

Sanjit moans, "Huh, all I see on England visit is the place they are calling Uncle Rajiv's Curry house. I am working whole flippin time wasn't I. Sanjit serve dishes say Rajiv. Sanjit clean always toilets say Rajiv. Only once I am becoming outside curry house during all staying time."

"And where are you going when you are outside of curry house?" asked Sanjit's father.

"I follow some men into a place they call pub," said Sanjit.

"And what is it they are doing in place called pub?" asked the father.

"They are having pieces of wire father. These pieces of wire have feathers one end and point sharp other end and they are throwing wire at circle on wall," explained Sanjit.

"Tell me more of this thing they are doing in place called pub," said the father.

"If piece of wire is landing just inside outer circle they are shouting, 'Double Top,' and man you play buy you drink ...
If piece of wire is landing just inside inner circle they are shouting, 'Treble nineteen,' and stomping foot on ground and man you play buy you drink and man behind bar buy you drink. And if piece of wire land in very centre circle everybody in place they call pub shout, 'Bullseye!' and everybody buy you drink,"

explained Sanjit.
"And what are they calling this game they play in place they call pub?" asked his father.
"Bloody jammy git," replied Sanjit cheerily.

20...20...20...20
THE DOCTOR'S ADVICE

A young man goes to see his doctor and somewhat embarrassed he confides, "Doctor, I don't know if you'll be able to help me or not but I'm very worried that I might be gay."
"And what makes you think that?" replied the doctor.
"Well, you see my father is gay," said the young man.
The doctor laughed aloud and said, "Just because your father is gay doesn't mean that you must be!"
"Well it's not just that ... you see my grandfather was also gay," continued the young man.
"Just because your father and grandfather were gay doesn't mean to say that you'll be gay," retorted the doctor, "Why I bet you've got a brother who can't keep his hands off women."
"Well actually," continued the young man, "my elder brother Peter and my twin younger brothers, Kevin and Paul, are all gay."
On hearing this the doctor starts to lose his patience and exclaims, "Good God man! Doesn't anyone in your family make love to women?"
The young man replied, "My sister does."

The Top 30

21 . . . 21 . . . 21 . . . 21

MAN'S LAST NIGHT ALIVE

A women goes to see the doctor about her husband who has been under the weather.

The doctor says, "We've got back all the results and I'm very sorry to have to tell you that your husband's illness is terminal."

With tears in her eyes the woman asks, "How long has he got? A year? ... Six months? ... A week?"

"I really am very sorry but if you want the truth I must tell you that he will almost certainly be dead by tomorrow morning," replies the doctor.

The woman collapses and starts to cry hysterically. In a state of shock the woman then stumbles home and bravely tries to think of ways to make her husband's last night alive a special one. She puts on her sexiest underwear and performs as never before in bed that night.

At about four in the morning after six hours of rampant sex the husband says, "Darling ... its never been quite as wonderful as this before do you mind if we do it again, I know it's the seventh time but ... "

"Of course not," replies the wife as she fought to hide the tears.

The husband couldn't rest because of the newfound enthusiasm his wife exuded and the passion continued ... and continued ...

After a brief rest after the tenth session the husband turned one more time to his wife and tapping her on the shoulder he whispered, "Darling do you mind if we ... "

His wife snapped, "Oh, it's bloody well alright for you ... You don't have to get up in the morning!"

The Top 30

22 . . . 22 . . . 22 . . . 22

BED-WETTER VISITS DOCTOR

A woman has a serious bed wetting problem so she goes to see a specialist. After taking down a few written details the doctor asks the woman to take off all her clothes and this she does.

"Right now, Mrs Adams, you see that full length wall mirror over there, I'd like you to do a handstand up against it with your belly button facing the mirror," said the doctor, and this the rather confused woman did.

"Well done," said the doctor, "Now legs apart ... well done." To the woman's surprise the doctor then got down on his knees and rested his chin on the woman's crotch and started sticking his chin in and out. The doctor then stood up and told the woman to get dressed and this she did.

The woman then asked the doctor, "What's the verdict then?"

"The problem as I see it Mrs Adams," said the doctor, "Is that you are drinking too many fluids late at night."

"Is that all you can tell me?" said the rather upset woman, "All that business about me taking my clothes off, what did that tell you?"

"It told me, without any doubt, that the lads down the squash club are right," replied the doctor, "I would suit a beard."

The Top 30

23 . . . 23 . . . 23 . . . 23

THE PHONE-IN WEIRDO

The Top 30

24...24...24...24

HE'S NOT A NUTTER

A doctor moves to a new job where one of his duties is to make annual tours of the local mental hospitals to make patient assessments. One day he speaks to this patient who can converse on any subject with great common sense and intelligence and the doctor says ...

Doctor ... "There's no way you should be in here, I'll get you out of here by tomorrow."

Patient ... "That's great news."

Doctor ... "You've been in here five years, a long time. What's the first thing you'll do when you get outside?"

Patient ... "I'm going to make myself a catapult."

The doctor is very disappointed to hear this rather strange reply and decides that he can't release the man after all.

The following year the doctor meets the same patient and they again have a long conversation, with the patient again displaying considerable intellect and common sense and the doctor says ...

Doctor ... "There's no way you should be in here, I'll have you out of here by tomorrow."

Patient ... "That's great news. I've been stuck in here for six years now."

Doctor ... "What's the first thing you're going to do when you get out?"

Patient ... "I'm going to make myself a catapult."

The doctor is again very disappointed by this answer and decides not to release the man.

The following year when the doctor is touring the same mental

The Top 30

hospital he comes across the same patient and again they have a long and interesting conversation. The doctor is particularly impressed with his awareness, intelligence and common sense and says ...

Doctor ... "There's no way you should be in here, I'll have you out of here by tomorrow."

Patient ... "That's great."

Doctor ... "Err ... What's the first thing you're going to do when you get out?"

Patient ... "Well, I've been giving this matter some thought and I thought the first thing I'd better do is get myself a girlfriend."

Doctor (relieved) ... "That's probably what I'd do if I was you."

Patient ... "I'd get myself a flat of my own and invite her back there."

Doctor ... "Go on."

Patient ... "I'd make a nice meal for the two of us, and light a couple of candles."

Doctor ... "Go on."

Patient ... "I'd give her loads of wine to drink, and then perhaps we'd dance to some slow romantic music, like say Lionel Richie or Diana Ross. Which one would you choose?"

Doctor ... "I'd go for Lionel Richie. It works every time! My wife told me she loved me for the first time after we'd just danced to 'Truly'."

Patient ... "So I'd put on Lionel Richie then we'd dance a bit, then drink a bit, then dance some more, then drink some more. By then she'd hopefully be in the mood and I'd get her to lie on my bed. Then I'd turn the stereo down real low and blow out the candles, and put the cat out for the night. While I gently caressed her hair with one hand I'd gently ease down her knickers with the other, get the elastic out of them and make catapult and smash all the windows in this bloody nuthouse."

25 . . . 25 . . . 25 . . . 25

LOVE ON THE ROOF

A guy calls into the local brothel and says, "I'd like a session with one of your girls but I'm a bit kinky ... does that matter?"
"How do you mean kinky?" enquired the Madam.
"Well I can only get turned on if I do it in a place I've never done it in before and the only place left is the roof," said the man.
"I'll go and get you Fifi, she'll agree to anything but it's going to cost you an extra £50," replied the Madam.
Anyway, Fifi and the man get up onto the roof, rip all their clothes off and proceed to go at it full steam ahead. What with the man's frenzied thrusting the couples intwined bodies start to inch nearer and nearer to the edge of the roof and eventually the couple fall off the edge and fall down four stories onto the concrete below. Both are stone dead and their bodies are still perfectly entwined in the missionary position.
A short while later a little old man comes walking past and sees the couple lying there and he decides to knock on the brothel door.
The Madam opens the door and the little old man says, "I don't want to give you any business but I thought I'd let you know that your sign's fallen down!"

The Top 30

26...26...26...26

TWO IRISHMEN BECOME PALS

A well-oiled man walks into a pub and says to the barman, "Oy'll have a poynt of Guinness so I will ... be Jeysus."
As he then proceeds to down the pint the well-sloshed man next to him says, "Excuse me but would I be royt in tinking dat you would be from over de water loik meeself?"
The first man replies, "I am surely ... bey Jeysus you don't get that many from the auld coyntry around here. Would you join me for a drink?"
The second man replies that he would and they soon sink a couple of pints each ... The conversation continues ...
1st Man ... "What part of Ireland do you come from?"
2nd Man ... "Oy'm from Dublin."
1st Man ... "I do not believe it ... Oy'm from Dublin meeself." The two men shake hands and have another drink together on the strength of that.
The conversation continues ...
1st Man ... "And what part of Dublin would you be from?"
2nd Man ... "Oy'm from round the back of de trinity college there so I am."
1st Man (very excited) ... "Oy do not believe it ... Oy'm from that very part of the town meeself!"
And on the strength of this they agree to have another drink together.
The conversation continues ...
1st Man ... "You wouldn't by any chance know that wild priest Father O'Flaherty?"
2nd Man (very excited) ... "Know him ... know him ... be Jeysus

The Top 30

that man christened me ... Oy've confessed to him many a time I can tell you."

And on the strength of this the two men embrace and decide to have another drink together.

The conversation continues ...

2nd Man ... "You wouldn't by any chance have gone to St. Michaels school would you?"

1st Man (very excited) ... "I do not believe dis!! ... I did surely ... until I got expelled at fourteen."

And on the strength of that they decide to have another drink together.

The conversation continues ...

1st Man ... "You wouldn't by any chance remember me auld teacher?... Now what was he called?... Brady?..."

2nd Man (very excited) ... "Whacker Brady ... Be Jeysus oye do. He retired early because of me!! Ha ... Ha."

And on the strength of this they decide to have another drink together. After another pint or two they finally stagger from the pub together with their arms wrapped round each other.

As the last bell approaches the landlord comes down from the room above and asks the bargirl if there had been much business that night ...

Bargirl ... "No, its been pretty dead all night really."

Landlord ... "Did you get any of the regulars in?"

Bargirl ... "No, none of them ... apart from the Murphy brothers again."

The Top 30

27 . . . 27 . . . 27 . . . 27

THE HYPNOTIST'S REVENGE

John, Jim and Eddie are out on a pub crawl and well p*ssed when they pass the local theatre and read that a hypnotist is performing that very night so they decide to go in and watch for a laugh.

The show gets under way and the three mates are sitting in the front row. Throughout the whole performance the three mates heckle the hypnotist with shouts of, "It's a fix," and, "She's a stool pigeon."

The hypnotist finally loses his patience with the three of them and he jumps down off the stage and confronts them. He clicks his fingers in front of each man's eyes and says to them,

"When each of you gets home you will do whatever your wife tells you to do."

The three men just laugh and carry on heckling until they are thrown out of the theatre. The three men continue their pub crawl for a while and then decide to return to their respective homes.

As John goes through the front door of his house a gush of wind catches the door and it shuts behind him with a tremendous crash.

His wife yells out angrily, "Why don't you just smash every window in the house?"

Before John realises what he's doing he's gone round with a hammer and smashed every window in his house.

A very confused John then thinks, "Oh my God! What the hypnotist said has come true, I'd better go round and warn Jim."

The Top 30

John runs over to Jim's house. When he gets there there are fire engines everywhere and he sees Jim and asks him what had happened.
Jim replies, "When I got home I fell asleep in front of the fire and my cigarette dropped out of my mouth and onto the carpet. The wife yelled at me, 'Why don't you just burn down the whole bloody house?' so I did!"
John says, "We've got to warn Eddie!" and the two of them run over to Eddies house where they find Eddie wandering around in a very confused state. He's naked and appears to be holding a lump of meat in one hand.
John asks, "What happened Eddie?"
Eddie mumbles, "I climbed into bed alongside the wife. Shc told me to cut it out ... So I did!"

28...28...28...28

THE POWER OF LOGIC

Sean meets Patrick in the street and asks him, "How come you haven't been down the Fox and Hounds on Thursdays for thc darts match recently?"
Patrick replies proudly, "I've been too busy bettering myself. On Thursdays I go to evening classes to learn all about logic."
"And what good would that be to you when you're digging holes all day long Patrick?" asked Sean.
"It's powerful stuff, so it is," replied Patrick, "Herc, let me show you what I mean. Do you keep fish?"
"Yes," nodded Sean.
"Then you must have a pond?" said Patrick.

"Yes," nodded Sean.
"If you have a pond then you must have a garden," said Patrick.
"Yes," nodded Sean.
"If you have a garden then you must have a house," said Patrick.
"Yes," nodded Sean.
"If you have a house then you must have a wife," said Patrick.
"Yes," nodded Sean.
"And if you have a wife you're not a w**ker," concluded Patrick proudly.
"I see what you mean Pat. It's powerful stuff dis logic, so it is," remarked the impressed Sean.
The men part company and a few days later Sean meets Dermot in the street. Dermot asks, "Where's your mate Patrick on Thursday nights now? I haven't seen him down the Fox and Hounds for a long while."
Sean replies, "Patrick has decided to better himself. On Thursdays he goes to evening classes in logic."
"Sure what use is logic to a man?" sneered Dermot, "And what is it about anyroad?"
"It's powerful stuff Dermot," said Sean, "Shall I give you an example?"
"Right you are, go on then," replied Dermot.
"Do you keep fish?" asked Sean.
"No," replied Dermot.
"Well, you're a w**ker then!" said Sean.

The Top 30

29 . . . 29 . . . 29 . . . 29

THE DISAPPEARING TURD

A school headmaster is returning home late one night from a parents' evening when he becomes desperate for a crap, very desperate! It's a dark, drizzly night and he's driving down a very quiet semi-rural lane so he decides to take a chance. He parks the car and climbs over a fence and whips down his trousers, squats and craps. As he quickly pulls up his trousers he looks down to look to inspect what he's just done and to his surprise he can't see his turd. The man climbs back over the fence, gets into his car and drives off.

As he is driving along, the matter of his disappearing turd begins to play on his mind. So much in fact that when he gets home he says to his wife, "Where's the torch?" With torch in hand he then drives back to the same fence as before and climbs over it determined to find his turd.

The man had been looking for some while when another torch suddenly shone right into his face. The voice said menancingly, "Are you the same bloke who was here about 40 minutes ago?" The headmaster replied, "Err ... y. yes."

"Hey, I know who you are! You're the headmaster at my Ian's school, aren't you?" said the voice.

The very embarrassed headmaster replied, "Err ... y. yes."

"So why," said the voice menacingly, "did you crap all over my boys pet tortoise?"

The Top 30

30 . . . 30 . . . 30 . . . 30

FANTASTIC SWIMMING FEATS

The British Olympic swimming team manager is pacing up and down the Olympic swimming pool hall when he gets the terrible news confirmed by radio that the coach carrying all the British team members to the pool has crashed. Realising that none of his team will get to the pool in time but any entrant gets at least one point for coming last the team manager picks up a loud speaker and says to the crowd, "Is there a British person in the crowd who would like to swim for their country in the 100 metres freestyle?"

As luck would have it there were some Brits in the crowd ... A coach load of amputees on a special Olympics holiday and one of them comes running down the steps saying, "Let me swim for my country. I won't let you down."

The team manager sees that the man has no arms and says, "I'm sorry but you haven't got any arms. You won't be able to swim 100 metres of freestyle."

The man replies, "Yes I can. I can swim using just my legs. My legs are extra strong."

After much pleading the man is allowed to compete and to everyone's amazement he wins!

A short while later the team manager appeals to the crowd again saying, "Is there a British man prepared to compete in the 100 metres breaststroke for his country?"

A man with no legs rolls down the steps shouting, "I can do it. Let me swim for my country."

The team manager replies, "I'm sorry but you've got no legs.

The Top 30

How could you possibly swim 100 metres of breaststroke?"
The man replies, "I can swim breaststroke with just my arms and I'm good."
After much pleading the man is allowed to compete and to everyone's amazement he win's.
A short while later the team manager appeals to the crowd saying, "Is there a British man who would like to compete in the 100 metres butterfly for their country?"
A woman comes down the steps and she's carrying a carrier bag. A voice from inside the carrier bag shouts, "I can do it. Let me at them! I'll get gold for Britain! I can do it! Let me at them!"

The team manager looks inside the bag and is stunned by what he sees. He then says, "But you're just a head! You've got no arms or legs or torso. You couldn't swim 100 metres butterfly. How could you propel yourself through the water?"

The Top 30

"I can do it," says the head, "I propel myself through the water with my extra strong ear muscles. I'm a brilliant swimmer, I'll get gold for my country just you wait and see!"

After much arguing and despite deep reservations on the part of the team manager the head gets his chance. The swimmers all line up at the edge of the pool, the starting pistol is raised and fired. The head is thrown in and immediately sinks like a stone to the bottom of the pool. The pool's attendants and spectators look and wait ... and wait ... and wait ... but the head just lies there blowing the occasion air bubble. The head goes purple and it's eyes start to roll so someone dives in and brings it out of the water.

"I thought you said you could swim okay?" muttered the team manager.

"I'm normally bloody brilliant I am," gasped the head, "but ... but I got terrible cramp in both ears!"

Chapter 13

Favourite Jewish Jokes

Why do Jewish women use gold diaphrams?
Because their husbands like coming into money.

Why did the Jewish lady refuse a colostomy?
She couldn't find a pair of shoes to match the bag.

HYMIE! FIND YOURSELF A WIFE AND I'LL BUY YOU A MERCEDES!

Moyshe turns to his thirty year old son Hymie and said, "It's about time you went out and found yourself a woman and got married. I want the family business to be handed down from generation to generation. Get a woman and I'll buy you a Mercedes."

One month later Hymie said to his father, "I've met a really nice girl dad."

"What's her name?" asked the father.

"Coleen Finnegan," replied Hymie.

"She's Irish?" said the father, "Lovely people the Irish but Hymie, HYMIE! Do you think I've spent the last thirty years building up M.Cohen Crimplene Dresses Worldwide for it to be infiltrated by paddy stock! Go out and meet someone else!"

A month later Hymie says,"I've met a nice girl dad."

"What's her surname son?" asked Moyshe.

"Fellini," replied Hymie.

"She's Italian?" said the father, "Lovely people the Italians but Hymie, HYMIE!! Do you think I've slaved for the last thirty years to build up M.Cohen Crimplene Dresses Worldwide only

to see it infiltrated by a bunch of greasy wops!! Go out and meet someone more suitable and I'll buy you a new Mercedes."
Two months later Hymie said to his father, "I've met a really special woman dad. We're getting married next week!"
"Hymie, this is all very sudden," replied the father before asking anxiously, "What's her surname?"
"Goldberg," replied Hymie.
"Congratulations my boy!" exclaimed the father as he threw his arms around Hymie. He continued, as he picked up the phone, "Let me ring her right away and invite her round for Sunday lunch..Er what's her first name?"
"Whoopi," replied Hymie.

What's a Jewish mothers dilemma?
Having a gay son who's dating a lawyer.

What did the Jewish bloke say to the absolutely stunning blonde?
Corr!! I wouldn't mind lending you one.

VG

I WANT TO BE JUST LIKE THE RED BARON!

A Jewish couple try for a child for ten years without success then suddenly and unexpectedly the wife falls pregnant. The couple are over the moon when little Moyshe is born and as he grows up the kid is spoilt something rotten. His parents shower him with love and affection and cater to his every whim.....
One day, with Moyshe's tenth birthday approaching fast, the father asks, "What do you want for your birthday son?"
Now the night before Moyshe had watched a film that was all about the famous German flying ace The Red Baron so he replies, "I want to go up in an open top bi-plane and do cart-wheels, flip overs, fly upside down and do nosedives, just like the Red Baron used to do."
The father is petrified at the very thought and he replies, "I can't arrange that son. I'll buy you that thirty gear racer you've

always wanted, eh?"
Little Moyshe wails, "I WANT TO FLY JUST LIKE THE RED BARON," and his little left foot stomped up and down angrily.
Moyshe wails for two days non-stop so, as usual, his father eventually gives in and they go to see one of the country's top aeronautical display pilots....
The pilot says, "For £500 I'll take you up and give you the most thrilling experience of your lives. I'll do a figure of eight, back rolls, side rolls, nosedives, the full and complete works."
"£500 for a little ride. On my life! No way!" replied the father, "Come on Moyshe, let's go home. I'll get you a bike instead."
Little Moyshe stomped his foot on the ground and screamed, "I DON'T WANT A BIKE! I WANT TO FLY LIKE THE RED BARON! YOU PROMISED DAD!"
"Look," said the pilot, anxious to get the business, "This really is the thrill of a lifetime, I promise you. Look, if you both go up in the plane and both manage not to make a single noise for the whole duration of the flight then I won't charge the £500! You can have the ride for free!"
The father decides to accept the pilot's offer and up the three of

them go in the three seater bi-plane....
The pilot gives them the full treatment including some of the riskiest stunts he's ever done...but there's no noise from the two of them...
He does a loop-de-loop around some electricity pylon cables carrying 60,000 mega-watts but still no noise....
He does a complete circuit of the M25 motorway flying under all the bridges but still there are no screams or yelps...
The ride is so terrifying that even the pilot starts to scream...
The pilot lands the plane and as it taxies down the runway the pilots shouts to the father behind him, "I just can't believe that you didn't make a single noise!"
The father replied, "I almost did when my boy fell out!"

Why did the Jew cross the road?
To franchise the other side.

Did you hear about the Jewish kamikaze pilot?
He dive-bombed his brothers scrapyard.

What's the difference between a Jewish girl and Blancmange?
A blancmange will move about a bit when you eat it.

What's the difference between a Jewish girl and trash?
Trash gets taken out once a week.

VG

RABBI TAKES A CONFESSION

Rabbi Levy is visiting Father O'Connor's church when he says, "I've always wondered what a confession is like, could I sit in on one or two?"
The priest replies, "Of course you can," and the two of them go into the priest's confessional booth.
A woman comes into the other booth and says through the

hatch, "Please forgive me Father for I have sinned. I have committed adultery twice since my last visit."
The priest replies, "You have committed a terrible sin my child. Say two hail Mary's, two our Father's and put £10 in the collection box." This the woman does and she leaves.
Another woman enters the confessional booth and says, "Please forgive me Father for I have sinned. I have committed adultery twice since my last visit."
The priest replies, "You have committed a terrible sin my child. Say two hail Mary's, two our Father's and put £10 in the collection box." This the woman does and she leaves.
At this moment a man comes running over to the booth and says, "Father O'Connor can you come quickly, it's Mrs Dowey, she's dying and she wants the last rites. I don't think she'll last longer than fifteen minutes or so."
The priest turns to his friend the Rabbi and says, "Could you carry on the confession for me, I'll be back soon. Don't worry, it's a piece of cake."
The Rabbi agrees and shortly after a woman comes into the booth and says, "Forgive me Father for I have sinned. I have committed adultery since my last visit."
"And how many times did you commit adultery?" asks the Rabbi.
"Just once of course," sobbed the woman.
"Only once...." deliberated the Rabbi as the woman continued to sob, "Well say two hail Mary's, say two our Father's, put £10 in the collection box and we'll owe you a f***!"

What was the last thing Moses said to God when at the top of Mount Sinai?
Now let me get this right...You say that we are to be the choosen race and yet you want us to cut the tops of our WHAT'S OFF!!!

Did you hear about the Jewish tailor on Mastermind?
His specialist subject was crimplene dresses, £3.99 to £4.99.

Why are the Jews an optimistic race?
Because they don't know how big it's going to get but they still cut a bit off!

D.I.Y. CIRCUMCISION

Moyshe wants to get little Hymie circumcised so he rings around for some prices........
"£300," said the first Mohel.
"Too much," replied Moyshe as he quickly put the phone down.
"£250," said another Mohel.
"Too much," replied Moyshe as he slammed down the phone.
"£180," said a third Mohel.
"You want £180 for one little cut and five minutes work!" said Moyshe as he started to lose his patience.
"Bloody rip-off merchants," thought Moyshe as he shouted down the phone, "TOO MUCH!!"
Moyshe decides to do the simple task himself and with his wife looking on he gets a knife from the kitchen and puts little Hymie on the table. With the deed done a bloodied Moyshe anxiously turned to his wife and asked for her opinion of his handiwork.
"Too much," came her reply.

Have you heard about the Jewish Santa?
He comes down the chimney laden with toys and offers upto 30% discounts on high-street prices.

What's a Jewish dilemma?
Half-price ham.

Why did the Jewish smash and grab thief get caught?
He went back to get the brick.

HYMIE VISITS THE TAX MAN

Hymie has been ordered to appear at his local tax office for a chat with his tax inspector and he asks his good friend Moyshe what should he wear.

Moyshe replies, "Wear your best clothes Hymie. If you look smart he will think you are an honest man and not a cheap con-merchant."

Hymie nods and later that day sets off for the tax office. On the way he meets Max and Max says, "If you're going to see the tax man you should dress in poor mans clothes. Look like a real down and out and he'll feel sorry for you and he'll go easy on you."

This throws Hymie into a quandary so he decides to ask his Rabbi...

The Rabbi says, "My daughter asked me a similar question the day before she got married. She asked me if she should wear a virginous long woollen nightie on her wedding night or a skimpy baby doll nightie. My answer to you is the same as my answer was to her....It doesn't matter what you wear, either way you're going to get f***ed!"